A KINDER, GENTLER RACISM?

AMERICAN POLITICAL INSTITUTIONS AND PUBLIC POLICY

A KINDER, GENTLER RACISM?

The Reagan-Bush Civil Rights Legacy

Steven A. Shull

M.E. Sharpe
Armonk, New York
London, England

Library of Congress Cataloging-in-Publication Data

Shull, Steven A.
A Kinder, Gentler Racism? : the Reagan-Bush civil rights legacy /
Steven A. Shull
p. cm.—(American political institutions and public policy)
Includes bibliographical references (p.) and index
ISBN 1-56324-239-7 (c)
ISBN 1-56324-240-0 (p)

1. Afro Americans—Civil rights.
2. Civil rights—Government policy—United States.
3. Reagan, Ronald—Views on civil rights.
4. Bush, George—1924-—Views on civil rights.
5. United States—Politics and government—1981–1989.
6. United States—Politics and government—1989-.
I. Title.
II. Series.
E185.615.S5 1993
323.1'196073—dc20
93-2785
CIP

⑧

Printed in the United States of America
The paper used in this publication meets the minimum
requirements of American National Standard for
Information Sciences—Permanence of Paper for
Printed Library Materials, ANSIZ 39.48-1984.

BM (c) 10   9   8   7   6   5   4   3   2   1
BM (p) 10   9   8   7   6   5   4   3   2   1

To my wife, Janice, and children, Amanda and Ted.
I also dedicate this book to my parents, Arthur and Mildred Shull.

Contents

Tables and Figures

Tables

Figures

Foreword

One of the tests to which we subject our presidents concerns their capacity to lead, their ability to achieve their political and policy goals. This is the test of whether presidents make a difference to their institution, their government, and their country.

Professor Steven A. Shull applies this test to Presidents Ronald Reagan and George Bush. His focus is on their civil rights policies, not only in theory and rhetoric, but also in practice. Shull examines this area of public policy as a measure of presidential leadership and substantive policy change. His objective is to document how two conservative presidents confronted and confounded a policy they opposed: the primacy of the national government in ensuring social and economic equity, particularly among minorities and women.

Using a stimulus-response model set within the context of the public policy process, Shull examines three discrete issues of civil rights policy: school desegregation, equal employment, and fair housing. Although he documents presidential involvement at each stage of the policy making and policy implementation processes, he shows that presidential influence is greatest in setting the agenda, refining the debate, and recasting specific policy goals. The more people that are involved at subsequent points in the processes and the longer the time frame, particularly if it extends toward the end of a president's term and beyond, the more apt presidential influence is to decline.

Shull's principal contribution in this study is to demonstrate that presidents can and do make a difference and to indicate how that difference can be achieved. Second, he notes the limits of presidential power by his comprehensive description of policy processes and of the roles others play inside and outside government that affect the final outcome. Third, in his discussion of an important and controversial policy area, he indicates that nothing is immutable. Presidents can change the public debate and affect public policy, but these changes are not cast in stone. As Reagan and Bush could revamp civil rights policy and restructure the national government's role in that policy, so too can subsequent presidents revamp and restructure it anew, which is precisely what we would expect the Clinton administration to do.

Shull's study is an important book for anyone who wishes to understand the exercise of power by presidents in the formulation and implementation of policy process. He helps us to appreciate the discretion and constraints presidents have and the policy impact they can achieve if successful.

Stephen J. Wayne
Georgetown University

Preface

A Kinder, Gentler Racism? The Reagan-Bush Civil Rights Legacy posits that Ronald Reagan returned civil rights to a place of prominence on the national agenda but did so by attempting to cut back on federal protections. He made many statements and initiated many actions that had long-lasting policy results. Did George Bush simply maintain that legacy, or did he pursue the "kinder and gentler" policies of most of his predecessors? The evidence suggests the former. Despite early high support from minorities, Bush continued—perhaps expanded—the Reagan retrenchment from previous federal protections. Leadership from these two ideological conservatives led to substantial changes in civil rights policy. This book compares Reagan and Bush with other recent presidents (including, where appropriate, Bill Clinton); its primary theme is that presidential influence leads to policy change.

The book is organized according to a stimulus-response model not unlike the process of making public policy itself. Chapter 1 lays out the conceptual framework while chapter 2 provides a historical overview of civil rights policy in the United States. This study covers the full range of statements and actions (stimuli), and results (responses). Presidents make *statements* through public communications that may be symbolic or substantive (chapter 3). They take *actions* legislatively and administratively and seek other avenues to assert their policy preferences in the area of civil rights (chapters 4–5). How do others react to these presidential statements and actions (chapters 6–7), and what are the *results* or consequences (chapters 8–9)? My ultimate aim is to assess the impact of statements, actions, and results.

A Kinder, Gentler Racism? is an up-to-date treatment of how modern presidents making policy interact with others inside and outside government. The book incorporates empirical data—in a fashion ap-

propriate for advanced undergraduate and graduate students—and interviews, anecdotes, and examples to show how presidents can influence policy change in this crucial and discretionary policy area. Four
detailed case studies of presidential influence help ascertain policy
impact: Reagan's and Bush's vetoes of major legislation in 1988 and
1990 constitute the cases of legislative actions (chapter 4). Their nominations to the Civil Rights Commission and the Justice Department
illustrate important executive actions (chapter 5).

Using case studies can help develop theory and build knowledge.
The cases illustrate whether the policy resulted in conflict and stalemate or cooperation and success. Considerable attention near the book's
end is given to policy impact. Using case analysis and a stimulus-
response model in tandem help us understand the president's role in
civil rights policy change.

This book is envisioned as a supplemental text for presidency and
public policy courses and for advanced American government courses,
particularly those taught by faculty incorporating a public policy perspective.

I received assistance from numerous sources for this project. First, I
would like to thank Greenwood Press for allowing me to use portions
of my 1989 monograph, *The President and Civil Rights Policy*. Graduate students Sheng Chen, Stephen Meinhold, Kerry Ordes, and Colleen
Walligora helped in data collection and read parts of the manuscript.
Former graduate student Albert Ringelstein collected the data for chapter 3 and commented on its contents. Several friends and colleagues,
including Christine Day, Randall Ripley, Mark Stern, Joseph Stewart,
Jr., and my wife, Janice Shull, gave me useful comments on draft
chapters. The College of Liberal Arts at the University of New Orleans provided research funds for software and reference books. The
university's Office for Research awarded me a coveted research pro-
fessorship that allowed me valuable released time and travel funds.
The Department of Political Science assisted in printing and photocop-
ying the manuscript. Finally, the professionals associated with M.E.
Sharpe, Inc., provided me with invaluable assistance. Political scien-
tists and series editors Kenneth Meier and Stephen Wayne both made
helpful comments about the book. Michael Weber, the company's political science editor, supported this project from the beginning and
guided its progress.

Part I

The Nature of Civil Rights: Presidential Influence and Policy Change

1

Introduction

Ronald Reagan returned civil rights to a place of prominence on the national agenda. But Reagan's was a different kind of prominence. He was opposed to busing, affirmative action, and aggressive enforcement of civil rights laws. He eased enforcement through personnel decisions, executive orders, budget cuts, program changes, and reorganizations. When called upon to defend his civil rights record, Reagan simply noted that his actions in civil rights were consistent with his general objective of reducing the scope and intrusiveness of government in all policy areas.

Two prominent actions taken by Reagan appear as case studies (chapters 4–5). The first was his veto of the Civil Rights Restoration bill in March 1988. The veto of this popular bill was overridden by both houses of Congress just five days later. Reagan's ideology had gotten in the way of his pragmatism, and he relinquished the initiative to Congress. In an administrative appointment, he was more successful. His controversial nomination of Clarence Pendleton to the U.S. Civil Rights Commission (CRC) in 1981 was charged with politicizing the agency. Yet it greatly helped him achieve his policy goals, among which was an agency less aggressively promoting civil rights than before. Reagan paid for these actions; subsequently, Congress monitored his actions more closely.

Although he did not always initiate, Reagan was frequently the stimulus for many responses from those inside and outside of government. I disagree with a recent account of Reagan's influence, which argues that the impact of his statements and actions was quite limited (Detlefsen 1991). Reagan left a substantial civil rights legacy, but it was quite different from that of his predecessors. He recast civil rights to a degree not seen since Lyndon Johnson.

Did George Bush simply maintain that legacy, or did he pursue the "kinder, gentler" policies of most of his predecessors? The evidence suggests the former. Two such actions constitute important cases later in the book and are summarized very briefly here. On October 22, 1990, Bush vetoed Senate Bill 2104, claiming that he supported civil rights but not quotas. To avoid another veto override the next year, Bush had to compromise (some said cave in) in the face of inevitable passage of the bill by large margins. The second case relates to the nomination of an African American early in his administration. The defeat of this nominee to head the Civil Rights Division (CRD) in the Department of Justice brought civil rights supporters together and was an early sign of trouble. Like the Reagan cases, these decisions had long-lasting effects in relinquishing leadership on civil rights policy to Congress and other actors.

Bush quickly fell out of favor with civil rights proponents. When his administration began, civil rights groups and the general public hoped for more support for civil rights than had been forthcoming under Reagan. Bush's public support from African Americans was higher than that for any other modern Republican president. Shortly, however, his opposition to civil rights legislation and his conservative appointments diminished these hopes. Subsequently, public support for his handling of civil rights was lower than for other issues, and support from African Americans dropped into the single digits. A coalition of civil rights groups called the administration's civil rights record "deplorable."

Bush was seemingly caught between pressure from the right and from the more moderate elements of the Republican party. Conservative columnists criticized the president for having no "public philosophy" or "moral compass." Even a Republican official saw "the Bush Legacy as four years of lost opportunity because Bush never outlined a clear philosophy about the federal government's role in combating discrimination." (Washington Post National Weekly Edition, August 24–30, 1992, 9).

This book will show that George Bush actually went beyond Ronald Reagan in his efforts to cut back the federal role in civil rights. He was more, not less, rhetorical than Reagan and took more assertive actions (including legislative, budget, and administrative decisions). Leadership from these two ideological conservatives led to substantial changes in civil rights policy. Reagan and Bush are compared with their predecessors as well as with each other. This book's primary theme is that presidential influence leads to policy change. Both Presidents Reagan and Bush left a substantial civil rights legacy.

Why Study Civil Rights?

Good theoretical reasons exist for studying presidential influence in civil rights and policy change. Foreign, economic, and domestic policy may be too general to identify patterns of behavior. Further, the literature suggests that policies are often interrelated (LeLoup and Shull 1979; Sigelman 1979). Social welfare would be a good policy area for analysis, for example, but it seems closely tied in with economic policy. On the other hand, civil rights policy is not likely to be tied to economic issues, the business cycle, or the election cycle. Presidents make it and implement it with much greater discretion.

This book focuses on civil rights, particularly on equality for groups. What do we mean by civil rights? At first blush, it might seem easy to define. It can be distinguished from civil liberties, which are constitutional protections against government. *Liberties* involve participation in the political system and apply to all of us naturally and *individually* (Black 1990, 246). *Rights*, on the other hand, refer more to protection for particular *groups*, especially minorities and women. Rather than being inalienable, they are bestowed by government. Rights also have constitutional roots.

Civil rights issues have never been far beneath the surface of American history. Perhaps because of their highly emotional content, they have varied in salience over time. Certainly in the modern era, civil rights emerged as a prominent public policy concern (Converse 1964; Walker 1977; Marshall 1990; Carmines and Stimson 1989). Occasionally, it has been the most salient domestic policy area. It was particularly visible in the last two generations, evolving rapidly during the period following World War II. Yet, salience increased in the 1960s and 1980s and decreased in the 1950s and 1970s (see *Gallup Opinion Index*). The temper of the 1990s and Bush's temperament initially seemed likely to reduce its prominence on the government's agenda. However, civil rights controversies among those both inside and outside government remained highly salient. For example, perhaps the thorniest problem early in the Clinton presidency concerned gays in the military.

Civil rights policies are not as critical to life as most foreign policies, particularly national security, but they are more changeable. Because actors on civil rights policy often cooperate, some might think that such policies usually are bipartisan. Yet partisanship over civil rights is growing. A possible explanation for this phenomenon is that the Republican and Democratic parties are further apart on this policy area than on any other (Carmines and Stimson 1989). This increasing partisanship and diffused support generally for civil rights could lead to increased conflict between the parties in the future.

The 1988 Civil Rights Restoration Act had general bipartisan support, but legislation on affirmative action and comparable worth (or other issues subject to the charge of reverse discrimination) seems to be dividing the parties further. Indeed, legislation in 1990–91 was more partisan because of such divisions. Bush seemingly did not have the ideological rigidity of his predecessor but got into even greater trouble with Congress over that legislation and on civil rights generally than did Reagan. Such conflict prevents either leadership or policy change and could ultimately threaten the ability of government to govern.

Civil rights attitudes remain important in shaping mass belief systems (Carmines and Stimson 1980, 10). Race in particular has contributed to heightened issue consistency and a greater structure of political beliefs today than American politics experienced in earlier years. Race is now increasingly important in differentiating political candidates and parties (Edsall and Edsall 1991). The deep effect of civil rights policy on the mass public in the post-Vietnam era has a corresponding influence on relations among political institutions. During Reagan's last year and during Bush's four years, Congress renewed its efforts to provide leadership in civil rights. Apart from mass opinions, civil rights is also salient to elite policy makers. Decisions by those within and outside government provide the parameters within which future presidents must interact in the realm of civil rights.

The Book's Themes

The ultimate question addressed in this book is whether and how presidents influence civil rights policy making. Is the president the central actor in a discretionary area of public policy? Do presidential statements and actions translate into desired results? All evidence suggests that the Johnson administration made a difference in civil rights. Did the Reagan administration usher in a new era in presidential policy making in civil rights, with the president leading a conservative charge? Ronald Reagan and George Bush reversed the direction that civil rights policy had taken during the previous generation. Such a dramatic policy change revealed the president as the major catalyst for policy innovation.

These concepts—presidential influence and policy change—are the book's twin themes. First, I develop the meaning of the themes. Influence (or leadership) refers to the president's effect or control on each actor and at each stage of civil rights policy making. The primary question is whether presidents matter: Can presidents influence civil rights directly, and what factors limit their influence? Although presidents occupy the center of the policy-making arena, they must interact effectively with significant others to see their preferred civil rights policies prevail. When they do so, presidents can often obtain their preferred policy result.

Why Presidential Influence?

Nature of Leadership

Defining leadership is not easy. Richard Neustadt (1980) sees leadership largely in terms of bargaining and persuasion to attain desired ends. He equates leadership with power, but the term also relates to purposes or goals and influence. Bert Rockman sees leadership as "the capacity to impart and sustain direction" (1984, 6), while leadership to David Loye requires intervention to achieve desired ends (1977, 3). Robert Tucker views leadership as "the ability to analyze causation and the capacity to articulate a vision based on that analysis and inspire others to it" (cited in Rockman 1984, 208).

James Burns views leadership as inducing "followers to act for certain goals that represent the values and motivations—the wants and needs, the aspirations and expectations—'of both leaders and followers'" (1978, 19). Burns's definition is less dependent upon manipulation than Neustadt's. Critics accuse Neustadt of stressing means rather than ends toward which power is directed (Sperlich 1975; Burns 1978, 389; Cronin 1980, 131). Although leaders of democracies may be held responsible for the consequences of the directions they set, leaders and followers may not always share a common interest. The question of when and whether leaders lead or largely follow is surprisingly difficult to answer (Jones 1988, vii).

Another conceptual ambiguity with the term *leadership* is whether the individuals matter more or less than the institutions. Some scholars (Neustadt 1980; Kernell 1986; Kellerman 1984) see personal traits as decisive, while others, particularly Rockman (1984, 179), Campbell (1986), and Burns (1978), see institutional and contextual factors as more important determinants of leadership potential. Apart from the individual versus institutional argument, writers also disagree over whether presidential leadership consists primarily of opportunities or of constraints. Such resources and limitations occur both in presidents' formal or constitutional powers (e.g., to submit legislative programs) and in their informal or acquired powers (e.g., to lobby Congress for such programs).

Sources of Leadership

Presidential leadership in civil rights comes from many sources, and the strategies chosen will very likely depend on the political environment. This study posits that individuals do make a difference. Despite Rockman's emphasis on constraints rather than opportunities, even he admits that the "president remains the most visible single source of establishing coherent direction" (1984, 29). Some presidents simply attempt much more than others. I presume that the major bases of presidential leadership are ideological commitment and assertiveness.

Presidential party is also important. Democratic presidents have come to be seen as more favorable toward government action and also more assertive than are Republicans. Second, while it may be hard to separate the man from the party, differences among individual presidents are dramatic, particularly among Republicans. Presidents need not take an individual leadership role, but we will see whether assertive and/or ideologically committed presidents like Lyndon Johnson can make a difference in civil rights policy making.

As conservative Republicans, Reagan and Bush should have been ambivalent and relatively passive on civil rights, but they were not. Reagan's ideology might have predicted greater activism to reverse the direction of government programs in civil rights. His statements and actions seemingly had such an effect. George Bush was initially more of a pragmatist. As an ideological moderate, what advantage would Bush see in perpetuating the Reagan legacy? Nevertheless, he did so, and my purpose is to uncover the extent to which his statements and actions mirrored those of his predecessor and what results ensued.

Apart from individual president and political party, other factors affect presidential influence and leadership capability. Style, personality, and skills of the president are three attributes that have attracted scholarly attention. Assertiveness is a main component of style, and I have suggested that assertive presidents will provide greater stimuli (statements and actions). Personality relates to assertiveness, at least the active-passive dimension of the dominant thesis based on personality (Barber 1992). Other studies focus on the personal skills needed to succeed, such as selling and management abilities (Whicker and Moore 1988; Kernell 1986; Neustadt 1980). Empirical evidence on the effects of all these attributes is extremely limited, however, and thus they are used only peripherally in this analysis.

Why Policy Change?

The previous discussion of presidential influence suggests a second theme of this book—policy change. Change has been the dominant characteristic of civil rights policy throughout American history: change in the roles of the president and other actors, change in the subissues and participants in civil rights, and change in the relative importance of civil rights generally on the public policy agenda. Several dimensions of change are considered in this book, particularly the roles of presidents in the policy making process. How do their roles vary according to stimuli and responses, and how does temporal change in civil rights itself affect these relationships?

The two themes of this book—influence and change—are necessarily related. Presumably the former leads to the latter, although policy change can alter presidential leadership. Civil rights has experienced enormous substantive change during the past generation, both in groups targeted and in issue areas of government policy. However, major change in public policy at any given time is rare, and, even when accomplished, change may not be significant or intended. Considerable debate exists over whether leaders really accomplish much policy change, even presidents on a relatively salient and discretionary area of public policy such as civil rights.

Meaning of Change

Change in several manifestations is perhaps the most important characteristic of U.S. civil rights policy. This study considers several types of change. First, there are changes across and within presidential terms and by presidential party. Wide variations in stimulus-response by individual presidents and political parties are posited. Another type of change deals with the magnitude of statements and actions by various actors in civil rights policy making: Are they nonincremental (i.e., seeking large-scale policy change)? How does the relative influence of actors vary over time? A third type of change in actor relations refers not so much to change across time but to change across stages of the policy-making process. This study assesses these changing roles across differing policy stimuli and responses and the changing nature of substantive issues.

Overview of Three Issue Areas

Civil rights has a peculiar status in U.S. history; its course is dramatic, and its implications are rich. The modern era of civil rights began with the U.S. Supreme Court's 1954 decision that state-supported segregation of public schools violated the equal protection clause of the Fourteenth Amendment (*Brown v. Board of Education*). School desegregation is only one important issue area; others include equal employment and fair housing.[1] The following preliminary comparison of three subissues reveals significant similarities and differences. They continued to dominate civil rights in the Reagan and Bush administrations. Major events in these content areas will be summarized in chapter 2.

School Desegregation. The focus here is on public elementary and secondary schools. Higher education is probably a unique civil rights subissue that is more likely to overlap the employment category with such concerns as affirmative action and quotas. Still, higher education receives some attention. The primary impetus for a federal role in this issue area was, of course, the famous Supreme Court decision *Brown v. Board of Education*. This decision ended the long-standing legalization of "separate but equal" schools. Chief Justice Earl Warren argued that separate schools could not possibly be equal. No one knows whether the Court would have taken such a bold stand had the southern states provided more equal facilities, but general agreement exists that schools were not equal (Rodgers and Bullock 1972, 70–72; Kluger 1976, 134).

Although this decision disturbed the South, not until the 1964 Civil Rights Act (PL 88–352) were major enforcement provisions enacted and upheld by the Court. The Justice Department was authorized to sue noncomplying districts (Title IV) and to join suits filed by private plaintiffs (Title IX). Another key provision of the act denied federal funds to segregated institutions (Title VI). During the remainder of the 1960s, the Department of Health, Education and Welfare (HEW) frequently set strict guidelines, and the courts began to require schools to desegregate. The courts limited the freedom of choice plans pushed by southern school districts, and some major changes occurred in the late 1960s (see Bullock and Lamb 1984).

The primary school desegregation concern of the 1970s was busing, a concern that has persisted to the present. Opponents called it "forced" because it involved efforts to equalize the racial composition of neighborhood schools. Congress, initially through the instigation of southern legislators and later with growing support from northerners also under orders to desegregate, made many symbolic efforts to limit the federal role. It succeeded in restricting HEW funds for busing but failed by a single vote in several instances to restrict courts from issuing busing orders (*Congress and the Nation*, 5:1981, 659, 800). Congress also frequently made federal funds available to local schools, thereby easing the desegregation process.

Public sentiment against busing grew throughout the 1970s and federal efforts at enforcement through busing dwindled in response. Interest groups took opposing sides on the issue. Except for Johnson and Carter, Republican presidents were less committed to desegregation, opposing the remedy of busing. The prior activism of the Departments of Justice and HEW declined greatly under Reagan, the president most opposed to busing and to requiring private schools to desegregate (Lamb 1985, 85). Until Reagan, Congress initiated virtually no new civil rights legislation since the 1960s, while the courts were usually more aggressive than Congress in upholding the law. However, even the courts began to "limit change to that necessary to comply with constitutional requirements" (Bullock 1984b, 60). The more conservative judiciary responded to the changed political climate.

Equal Employment. While school desegregation is a subissue focusing mainly on blacks, equal employment has much broader ramifications that are not always easily identifiable by target group.2 Also, unlike the issue of school desegregation, in which the courts took the lead, employment is an issue area in which presidents lead and initiate policy. The first provisions for equal employment were a series of executive orders dating from 1941 (see chapter 5). These four orders, the only basis for federal law until 1964, prohibited job discrimination in the federal government and in federally funded projects. It was not until the Civil Rights Act of 1964 that major legislation ensued. The former created the Equal Employment Opportunity Commission (EEOC) to prohibit job discrimination by private employers (Title VII), while the latter expanded the agency's authority. Major legislation on fair employment passed in 1991 over Bush's initial opposition.

Unlike the government agencies dealing with school desegregation, the varied agencies involved in equal employment practices have been weak, ranging from the Fair Employment Practices Commission, to the EEOC, to the Office of Federal Contract Compliance Programs (OFCCP). Harrell Rodgers (1984, 95–96) shows how these agencies have had to rely heavily on voluntary compliance and generally have not had the resources to fulfill their vague mandates. Frequent debates over whether monitoring implementation of the 1964 law lay with EEOC or with courts have been only partially resolved.

EEOC's jurisdiction grew considerably during the 1970s, as it obtained the power to sue for workers suffering from job inequalities in the federal, state, and local governments. Several agency guidelines and administrative reorganizations also expanded the federal role over job discrimination in both the federal government and with private contractors. A series of important Supreme Court decisions buttressed these administrative rules, which drew a fine line between quotas and voluntary affirmative action plans, the latter being the accepted course of action. The Court also allowed the federal government to allot a portion of contracts to minority businesses.

Apart from the legal and bureaucratic tangles, interest groups played a less aggressive role in equal employment opportunities than in school desegregation. Not only did labor unions fight against admitting women and blacks as members, but any "extraordinary" efforts to impose hiring quotas or affirmative action cut deeply into the union tradition of seniority—last hired, first fired. Some consequences of union opposition included lower minority pay, advancement, seniority, and job retention during layoffs. While I shall explore the results of equal employment efforts more fully toward the end of this book, the struggle for equal opportunity has obviously been more difficult in this subissue.

Fair Housing. Of these civil rights subissues, fair housing has been the hardest to enforce, perhaps because of its sensitivity or because it covers transactions between individuals *(Congress and the Nation,* 2:1969, 350). It was the only issue area *not* covered specifically in the 1964 Civil Rights Act, and, while Congress later passed legislation on public housing, laws regulating private housing have proven much more difficult to enact. I mention legislation because, unlike school desegregation, in which the courts and interest groups took the lead, Congress, even though it acted late, was the most significant actor in fair and equal employment, in which the executive has dominated, Con- housing.

An early civil rights law (1866) granted property rights to all citizens, and the Fourteenth Amendment to the Constitution prohibited states from violating these rights. Still, housing was the last civil rights subissue to receive congressional attention. Perhaps this explains its slow progress and lack of implementation (Lamb 1984, 148; Amaker 1988, ch. 5; Orfield 1980). Federal policies have themselves encouraged housing segregation and racial exclusiveness, including development of public housing and the interstate highway system (which encouraged the growth of suburbs); the laws have not required an end to discrimination. Sanctions and enforcement provisions have been very limited. One reason may be that minority politicians have seen efforts to expand the suburbs as a dilution of their power base (Lamb 1984, 149). The lack of minority support is another reason for the perpetuation of segregation through state and local zoning laws.

Those outside government have strongly opposed desegregating housing. Whites fear for their property values, while realtors have long engaged in such practices as racial steering, blockbusting, and redlining.[3] Racial and ethnic groups have preferred some homogeneity in housing patterns, and much segregation that occurs may be due to preferences and economics *(Washington Post National Weekly Edition,* December 2, 1985, 32). Whatever the reason, the United States has a long history of housing discrimination and segregation.

Federal intervention has had limited effect. Kennedy's executive order (11063) in 1962 banning discrimination in federally assisted housing covered only 18 percent of new housing. He opposed a stronger recommendation made by the Civil Rights Commission (*Congress and the Nation*, 2:1969, 401). The 1968 Fair Housing Act (PL 90–284) was much more comprehensive. It prohibited discrimination in the sale and rental of housing, including single-family residences. However, it contained significant loopholes, exempting smaller owner-occupied dwellings and privately owned homes sold or rented without involving realtors. All in all, critics have termed the act a "vague and weak" arsenal in obtaining fair housing (Lamb 1984, 177). Nor have federal agencies played major enforcement roles (Lazin 1973). Perhaps all these reasons account for Bullock's contention that fair housing is the least successfully implemented civil rights policy (1984a, 188). Legislation in 1988 attempted to remedy these problems.

Comparison and Assessment

These three issue areas of civil rights are interrelated. Housing is closely related to employment patterns and, particularly, to education (Orfield and Ashkinaze 1991). Unemployed people tend to be poorly educated and housed. *De facto* if no longer *de jure* segregation perpetuates poverty, inequality, and racism. All three subissues show that it is easier to enact federal laws affecting public facilities than federal laws affecting private facilities. The role of the Reagan and Bush administrations in each of these issue areas and the consequences of their actions are examined throughout the remainder of this book.

Interest groups were much more active and supportive on school desegregation than on fair housing. Presidents played a greater early role in employment, while the courts took the initiative in school desegregation. If Congress took any leadership role, it was in fair housing. Similarities in and differences among the subissues are also revealed in the target groups served. School desegregation has been almost entirely a race issue, although it is less a black concern today than it was in the 1960s. Fair housing began as largely race related but has broadened to include discrimination against the disabled and those with young children. Equal employment has the broadest coverage, including practically every group subject to work-related discrimination. These vast similarities and differences among policy subissues should allow useful comparisons in later chapters.

The Book's Approaches

Why the Stimulus-Response Model?

This book is organized according to a stimulus-response model. Under this model, statements and actions (stimuli) incite a variety of results (responses). Statements and actions are covered in chapters 3–5, while responses are covered in chapters 6–7. All these components produce policy outcomes (chapters 8–9). Readers will note the similarity of the stimulus-response model to the policy-making process, a device widely incorporated in the literature.

I assert that the roles, emphases, and behavior of actors vary across stages of the policy process. As should be readily apparent, fluidity is an important part of policy making, which the sequential (or process) approach to public policy highlights. This process approach is advantageous in examining actor interactions to see whether policy preferences are similar. In addition, the approach avoids rigidly assigning specific functions to particular actors. By emphasizing such interactions, the sequential approach also lends itself to meaningful comparisons across substantive policy areas (Anderson et al. 1984, 9). Because policy often is chronological and not static, many writers have used the sequential approach to highlight its fluid, cyclical nature.[4]

However, the sequential approach tends to oversimplify the enormously complex policy-making process (Sabatier and Jenkins-Smith 1993). Policy sometimes emerges without a clear beginning or end and frequently is not as orderly or rational as a literal interpretation of the sequential approach may imply (Kingdon 1984, 215–16). Critics of the process approach contend that it encourages the assumption of a rational process "with each part logically tied to each succeeding part" (Lindblom 1980, 4). Lindblom further argues that actors, strategies, and issues vary little across the policy stages (1980, 3; see also Heclo 1975).

Acceptance of some of these criticisms as valid need not require rejection of the sequential scheme of policy making. The process is "messy," but it is not random (Kingdon 1984, 215–17). We cannot draw neat lines between the point where one stage ends and another begins, and it probably matters little that we cannot (Jones 1984, 91). The process of policy making should be thought of as fluid, as depicted in Figure 1.1, with primarily one-way relationships but with places where reciprocal (feedback) relationships can also occur. Indeed, each

Figure·1.1. **Stages in the Policy-Making Process**

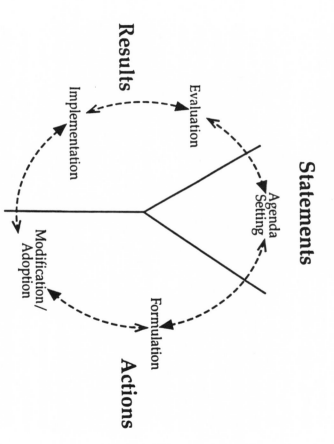

Results

Statements

Evaluation

Implementation

Agenda
Setting

Modification/
Adoption

Formulation

Actions

Note: Solid arrows depict the normally cyclical process of policy making from agenda setting through evaluation. The lines are dotted because the stages are not fixed or always sequential. The counterclockwise arrows reflect potential feedback in policy decisions.

stage can occur at different times. For example, another problem frequently reaches the agenda before an existing agenda item is formulated. Still, the sequential approach to policy making (encompassing agenda setting, formulation, modification-adoption, implementation, and evaluation) has considerable utility when boundary and other conceptual difficulties are taken into account (see Anderson 1990, 263).

The civil rights policy arena, with the president placed at its center, is dynamic and includes a variety of conditions and influences that complete the policy cycle. Policy is established not just from one decision but almost always from a series of decisions or patterns of action (Anderson 1990). Numerous *inputs* influence the decisions made. After *decision making* on a particular policy or program, it can have widely differing effects. *Ouputs* refer to programs themselves, while *outcomes* refer to the impact or result of those programs on actors, governments, and society (Ranney 1968a; Easton 1965, 351–52). Some will probably perceive outcomes as conferring benefits, but others will see them as being detrimental. If groups feel strongly about the way they are affected, they make their views known (*feedback*). This feedback leads to later inputs by these participants, completing the policy-making cycle.

These policy terms generate considerable definitional problems and disagreement over the relative importance of particular components. Nevertheless, the rough diagram in Figure 1.2 clarifies the policy arena surrounding the president. The policy process is quite compatible with the stimulus-response model, with statements and actions analogous to stimuli and results similar to responses. Both the policy process and stimulus-response approaches emphasize dynamism and interrelationships among policy-making activities.

The stimulus-response and policy process approaches strive toward greater generalization, comparison, and empirical investigation. They stress both the process and substance of public policy in examining the president's interactions with others in the stages and areas of policy. Policy research can help us understand the political system. It need not be mission oriented, nor need it advocate that a particular policy be initiated or implemented, though it may do so. A policy approach can provide an integrative, unifying focus for research. One may summarize political scientist Austin Ranney's (1968b, 12) arguments for conducting policy-oriented research as further justification of its usefulness: to evaluate programs and advise policy makers, to advocate new programs and reform old ones, and to better understand the political system. Describing and explaining public policy making is necessary for those seeking to understand politics.

Why Case Studies?

Case studies have been criticized in political science literature as insufficient for theory building. They are often considered too discrete for generalization and cumulative knowledge. Theories depend upon patterned behavior (more than one instance), so scholars and students are encouraged to seek regularity rather than singularity (Thomas 1983). Critics say case studies may provide interesting detail but usually do not push much beyond description toward explanation, let alone prediction (Edwards 1981).

Statements   **Actions**   **Results**

Inputs   Decision making   Outputs   Outcomes

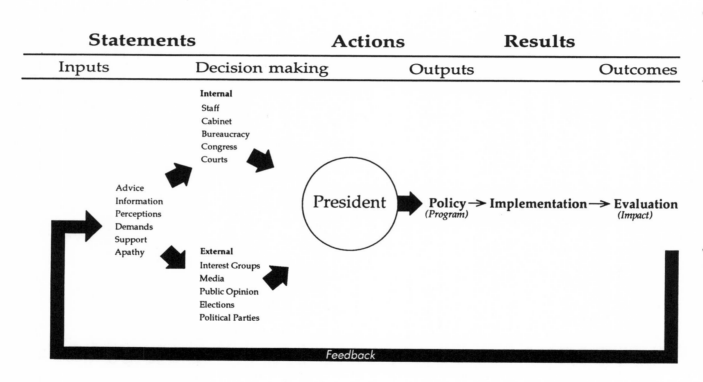

Internal
Staff
Cabinet
Bureaucracy
Congress
Courts

Advice
Information
Perceptions
Demands
Support
Apathy

External
Interest Groups
Media
Public Opinion
Elections
Political Parties

President

Policy → **Implementation** → **Evaluation**
(Program)   *(Impact)*

Feedback

Figure 1.2. Components of the Presidential Policy Arena

Because in this book I seek to describe and explain regular patterns and to achieve systematic knowledge, one might think that little credence would be given to the case study approach. Yet Bruce Russett (1970) argues that case studies can lead to more cumulative knowledge. Joe Feagin et al. (1991) also point to numerous advantages of case studies. Certainly cases have helped provide or develop theoretical frameworks.[5] Selected cases are used to illustrate concepts in the analysis, particularly policy process, the relationships among institutions in the political environment, presidential influence, and policy change. The dominant patterns are discussed following the cases, and the consequences (outcomes) of each case are considered in chapter 8. Thus, case analysis can help attain generalizations, cumulative knowledge, and further our understanding of policy making.

Stimulus-Response Model of the Policy Process

I assert that the outcomes of civil rights policy making are largely a function of actor relations and the nature of issues. These conditions are highly variable and greatly determine the leadership potential of the president. Presidents operate within an environment but with some chance to alter all these "givens." Presidents take on or inherit a set of continuing policies that serve as a starting point for their administrations. Although presidents may be able to set the stage (advocate an agenda and formulate proposals), whether these proposals become law (let alone are implemented) is largely under the discretion of other actors. Those inside and outside of government also respond to and evaluate such policies. Presidents often are followers, but they can also be leaders in civil rights policy making.[6] Although presidential statements, actions, and results are subject to constraints, they are also subject to manipulation.

Expectations about Presidential Influence

Randall Ripley and Grace Franklin (1975) have identified three critical components of policy making: statements, actions, and results. These three components guide the research and establish the sequential nature of the policy-making process. This book investigates the context in which presidents Reagan and Bush used statements and actions to obtain their desired results in civil rights. Achieving results consistent with their statements and actions should indicate presidential influence. Presidents may now be unwilling actors who must show some rhetorical support for civil rights, but their actions may not always correspond with their public statements. This gap between statements and actions suggests that civil rights may contain a symbolic dimension, an idea developed more fully in chapters 3 and 4. In general, however, modern presidents use policy statements to "go public" on their policy preferences. Obviously, presidents hope that their statements and actions will lead to the results they desire.

Several expectations about the involvement of presidents in civil rights seem plausible. First, presidents should increase their influence through the use of policy statements and actions. Thus, presidential attention early in policy making should help exert their influence later. In short, presidents who actively articulate an agenda and formulate legislative initiatives may minimize modification and also should attain substantial adoption of their preferences. Moreover, implementation should correspond more closely with their goals. Thus, presidents are more likely to obtain their policy preferences (results) by being assertive in their statements and actions early rather than late.[7]

Although changes in civil rights policies may seem dramatic, the process is not altered easily or in large ways. Policy tends to change slowly, since government as a conservative entity often resists change. Policy makers will defer hard decisions if possible, perhaps because uncertainty is inevitable, but still feared by politicians and because the electorate also prefers stability and continuity to change and innovation. Even though policy change is a slow (incremental) process in the United States, political leadership can affect it. I expect to be able to observe measurable results from the statements and actions of actors in civil rights policy making. The president, in particular, can influence the process of policy making. If leadership and change can be shown using both quantitative and qualitative evidence across time, this study will contribute to knowledge of both the presidency and civil rights policy.

Linking Statements, Actions, and Results to the Policy Process

We have already seen the relationship among statements, actions, and results to the stimulus-response model and to stages of the policy making process. This next section lays out these relationships in greater detail, showing the variables and preliminary expectations by process stages from agenda setting through evaluation. Figure 1.1 shows these steps in the policy-making process more clearly. Although each stage is listed separately, overlap among them occurs.

Agenda Setting

An issue usually reaches the public (government) agenda as a result of conflict over the allocation of resources (goods and services) (Kingdon 1984). According to Robert Eyestone, an "issue arises when a public with a problem seeks or demands government action and there is public disagreement over the best solution to the problem" (1978, 3). Thus, conflict and its resolution generally influence what reaches the public agenda. In Charles Lindblom's words, "Agendas are determined by interaction among persons struggling with each other over the terms of their cooperation" (1980, 4). Although controversial issues are most likely to appear on the public agenda, so also are issues that affect a large number of persons (Elder and Cobb 1983, 152–53).[8]

Although this study does not necessarily equate public communications with the public agenda, research suggests presidents can use rhetoric to set their own, if not always the broader, government agenda (Shull 1983, ch. 2; Light 1982). Much of what appears on a later government agenda can probably be traced to presidential communications. Public statements are particularly important in giving presidents the opportunity to set the stage for policy innovations, which usually come from the White House (Light 1982; Redford 1969; Kingdon 1984; Shull 1983). Chapter 3 discusses presidential statements setting forth civil rights agendas.

One political scientist has emphasized that "presidents are symbolic and political as well as programmatic leaders" (Fishel 1985, 8). Symbols are an important leadership tool for reassuring or persuading the public (Elder and Cobb 1983, 13–15). Perhaps because of its emotional content, civil rights seems to be a policy area ripe for symbolic leadership by presidents (Kessel 1984, 113; Elder and Cobb 1983, 2–4). Symbolism, then, is a potential source of presidential leadership in civil rights. The president's agenda is less symbolic when statements and actions are consistent.

Formulation

Agenda setting merges with formulation as policy initiatives are formally proposed. Initiation or formulation consists of *acquisitive* actions, more concrete than merely *rhetorical* statements because means are developed for problem solving (see Ripley and Franklin 1975, 11, for a discussion of these terms). The term *initiation* suggests innovation (Polsby 1984, 12), which seldom occurs in formulating policy; decision makers offer few totally new or innovative ideas. Thus, regardless of what is sought or said, usually only modest (small or incremental) change occurs. Even actions that seemingly encompass considerable change are seldom innovative, and no decision at all may be a conscious policy action.

Policy formulation includes information gathering, screening and weighing of alternatives, and the development of a preferred choice. This choice may be reflected in general goals or in more specific programs. Scholars frequently equate policy formulation with *decision making*, although that activity broadly defined occurs in each stage of the policy process. Often formulation must proceed without clear problem definition. Nevertheless, alternative methods and a planned course of action constitute government's proposed solution to the problem.

Chapters 4–5 discuss various presidential actions to influence those inside and outside government. Presidents formulate policy through legislative proposals, budget requests, and numerous administrative and judicial actions (such as executive orders, nominations, and taking positions on court cases). As happens with agenda setting, the lines between formulation and later stages blur. For example, requesting legislation may be formulation, but issuing executive orders may constitute policy adoption or even implementation (see Gleiber and Shull 1992). Nevertheless, presidents formulate policies with an eye to modification and to those compromises necessary to secure their adoption. Thus, presumably, they take consistent actions to obtain desired results.

Modification-Adoption

Modification involves preliminary assessment of the formulated proposals. Like the other policy stages considered here, modification has several components. It includes the selling of proposals through coalition building and the mobilization of group support, frequently involving the expenditure of considerable resources. Also included is the dissemination of information about the justification and intent of the proposed policy. During this process, policy makers will receive feedback from their constituents. Because proposals normally must pass through many decision stages, there are multiple points of access and opportunities for influence by those both inside and outside government. As with other policy stages, modification usually reflects little policy change, largely because actors have considered political feasibility in their agenda setting and formulation decisions.

Adoption requires accommodation among many participants and final government approval. Because prior agreement or acquiescence need not lead to agreement on actual policy, a multitude of demands must be satisfied. Governmental acceptance of the proposed solution constitutes legitimation by elected representatives and appointed judges. Although the president can adopt some issues on his own (for example, through executive orders), Congress must authorize and appropriate funds for most policy items. The courts also have wide latitude in interpreting civil rights policies.

Chapters 6–7 discuss the variety of actor responses possible. We will see that actors outside government generally responded negatively to the civil rights initiatives of the Reagan and Bush administrations. Probably no presidents ever received more negative press coverage over their civil rights policies. While important, these actors were not powerful enough in themselves to change presidential action. Policies reducing government's role persisted, as the data will show. Responses from Congress include support of presidential budgets, positions on bills, and nominees to courts and relevant agencies. Judicial responses include the extent to which judges support presidential positions on specific suits and on general civil rights policy.

Implementation

Implementation refers to the execution or carrying out of public policy. Frequently it leads to substantive or procedural modification of formulated proposals because goals, intentions, and directives are not always clear. Although policy formulation gets more attention, the way programs are implemented (or administered) often is a more important reflection of policy preferences. Responsibility for implementation is firmly entrenched in the cabinet and the permanent bureaucracy. Partly because of its complexity, policy implementation is an activity that is less subject to presidential influence than either policy formulation or adoption.

Presidents frequently complain of bureaucratic intransigence (Seidman and Gilmour 1986). This perception seems true because the president must delegate the enforcement and coordination of programs to executive actors who do not always share his views, timetable, or outlook (Neustadt 1980). Policy implementation is an important function, but one should not assume that the president always (or even usually) gets his way. Few programs are self-executing. The rest of the executive branch can show support or nonsupport of the president in a variety of ways. Chapter 6 considers several budgetary and programmatic responses to presidential statements and actions.

Responses to presidential statements and actions vary greatly by participant. Actors outside government generally have had lower profiles, but their responses intensified during the Reagan and Bush years (see chapter 7). Among those inside government, the courts have been most supportive of civil rights but, like Congress, became more conservative by the late 1970s. This institutional conservatism of late is in contrast to the gradual increase in mass public support for civil rights, at least as broadly defined. Even the bureaucracy has played a diminished role in policy implementation, either deliberately or due to generally decreased attention to civil rights by institutions within and outside government.

Evaluation

Evaluation refers to assessments of the effectiveness and consequences of actions and policies. Impact is the "ultimate" result of presidential statements and actions. However, empirical evidence on the impact of governmental programs is difficult to obtain, since it is usually attempted after the fact. Nevertheless, evaluation (including feedback from interested and affected groups) often leads to adjustments and refinements in public policy, which reflect later policy formulations.

We should consider policy evaluation only loosely as a stage of policy making. Evaluation is an omnipresent, continuous process that occurs informally, if not always formally. Ideally, it involves an objective calculation of the costs and benefits of government programs. Evaluation focuses upon whether program goals have been met. Such information is often difficult to obtain, particularly when the original goals have not been explicitly stated, thereby providing no standards against which to judge. Often the assessment of costs and benefits is by the relatively easy-to-acquire dollar measures, but many impacts are not subject to fiscal comparability. In addition, fiscal measures are frequently imperfect indicators of policy preferences or performance (Shull 1989b).

Because of its importance, I devote two chapters to policy evaluation. Chapter 8 assesses the consequences of the case studies and judges the effects or results of Reagan-Bush policies across the three issue areas of civil rights. The conclusion (chapter 9) assesses the presidential role (impact) at various stages of the policy process and by subissues within it. Is the president primarily a responder rather than a leader? Is presidential intervention crucial, as argued in this book, for lasting change in civil rights policy to occur?

Summary

This chapter fleshed out the analytical framework. I argued that civil rights policy making exists in a highly volatile political environment. Civil rights is a discretionary policy and, thus, should be subject to presidential influence and policy change. Case studies in civil rights policy making help us compare and understand both presidential influence and policy change. A stimulus-response model also helps track the dynamism and interrelationships that occur in civil rights.

A stimulus-response model emphasizes interactions as part of an interdependent system in producing public policy. It stresses the *policy-relevant* (and manipulable) functions of presidential relations that have received too little attention. This policy process approach assists in associating and interpreting disparate information, thereby offering a more secure basis for policy decisions. A carefully woven policy thread can also provide an understanding of where civil rights policy is (and should be) heading in the 1990s following growing dissatisfaction with its direction since the late 1960s and early 1970s. The increased consensus that existed for several decades now seems to be breaking down, and that reduced consensus allowed Reagan and Bush considerable latitude.

As the issues in civil rights have changed, so have the roles of the participants. Presidents, in particular, have opportunities for influence. Looking at civil rights suggests that policy content should be returned to its once-revered place in the public policy literature. In this study, variation in presidential activity in civil rights should reveal considerable discretion as well as explanatory power. Dramatic changes in salience in civil rights over the past two generations suggests variance across the policy-making process as well as within issue areas of civil rights.

The policy-making process and changes in the content of civil rights create an atmosphere for presidential influence. Presidents can affect civil rights from agenda setting through implementation and evaluation. Although previous literature suggests that the president's influence generally wanes as the policy process unfolds, I assert that presidents can influence even the implementation of civil rights (Halpern 1985; Shull 1989b). Presidents like Johnson and Reagan should make a difference, not only in setting the agenda but throughout the process of making civil rights policy. Indeed, the president may be the only actor involved in each stage of policy making. If this expectation proves to be true, Reagan and Bush could indeed leave a substantial civil rights legacy to their successors. Much of the expected policy change is likely to be attributable to presidential influence.

Notes

1. Voting receives less emphasis in this book because it is considered a more universally accepted right. In addition, important research already exists on voting rights. See particularly Amaker 1988; Binion 1979; Bullock 1981; Engstrom 1986; Thernstrom 1987; Parker 1990; Davidson 1984; Garrow 1978; Scher and Button 1984.

2. This book focuses on the following target groups: blacks, women, Hispanics/Native Americans, age, and other (including disabled and institutionalized persons).

3. Racial steering is the practice of realtors' showing minorities properties only in minority or in "changing" neighborhoods; blockbusting refers to encouraging whites to sell properties quickly (and often cheaply) because minorities have moved in; redlining refers to various practices making loans more difficult for minorities to obtain (Lamb 1984: 150–51).

4. Sources using the sequential (process) approach include Jones 1984; Anderson 1990; Anderson et al. 1984; Ripley 1985; Shull 1989a; Polsby 1969, 66–68; Gleiber and Shull 1992; MacRae and Wilde 1979.

5. One important collection of case studies that lead to more general theory is Irving Janis's Groupthink (1982), which analyzes faulty decision making resulting from the psychological tendency toward like-mindedness. Another important and more directly related work (Bullock and Lamb 1984) encompasses cases but also lays a theoretical framework of ten factors that should influence the implementation of civil rights. Barber's Presidential Character (1992) advances a "predictive" model of presidential personality based upon biographies (case stud-

ies). LeLoup and Shull (1993) use sixteen case studies within an analytical framework of congressional-presidential policy making.

6. Levine and Wexler (1981) reveal the many participants in civil rights policy making in a careful case study of the history of the Education for All Handicapped Children Act. This case shows how interest groups, the state and federal courts, and Congress were all more instrumental in getting this policy approved than was the president. In fact, they conclude that the president was an obstacle who had to be worked around. Nonetheless, even as an obstacle, the president was a critical focus for the proponents. This example illustrates the president's contrasting leader-follower role (see also Scotch 1984).

7. Whether the president can exert leadership is related to many phenomena. Various environmental conditions suggest that actor perceptions are important. The personality of the president, the extent to which he seeks innovative change, the nature of the economy and the times in general, the timing of presidential proposals, the quality of his liaison staff, his previous experience, the extent to which he becomes involved personally, the degree of congressional assertiveness, the partisan and leadership composition of Congress, and the general strength of the political party system may all be important in assessing actor interactions in the policy-making process. Obviously this study cannot measure the effects of all these conditions.

8. An exception occurs when a small elite succeeds in placing an item on the public agenda in opposition to presidential preferences. Moreover, some issues are purposely left off the public agenda and, therefore, are nondecisions.

2

Civil Rights in American History

Concern for civil rights by policy makers has varied throughout American history. Although questions about civil rights, particularly racial equality, have arisen since the introduction of slavery into the colonies, almost no pro-equality governmental policies were promulgated until much later. The Declaration of Independence asserted equality for "all men" but seemed to exclude all but white and propertied men. The Founders postponed the slavery question with Article 1, Section 9, and, notably, the Constitution said nothing about equality. The concept appeared eighty years later in the Fourteenth Amendment phrase "equal protection of the laws." Today concern with equality—racial and otherwise—pervades American politics, although sometimes it is beneath the surface. While rarely the most important issue to Americans, many aspects of contemporary politics, including modern differences between the two political parties, are based in racial and civil rights issues (Carmines and Stimson 1989, 14). Civil rights policy is, in fact, extremely important in American politics.

Since World War II, civil rights issues have been particularly salient for presidents and other actors. In some policy areas, such as economic and national security matters, the participation of modern presidents is no longer discretionary. Domestic policy areas, however, like civil rights, usually allow presidents greater latitude. Indeed, the American president is the most prominent catalyst for public policies. Presidents can influence the entire policy process, from setting priorities through assessing results (evaluation). Presidential interactions with those inside and outside government are important, but what presidents choose to do is largely up to them. Presidents can play a crucial role in shaping civil rights because major and lasting policy changes may depend on their influence. This is the main theme of this book.

Presidents have not usually initiated civil rights policy, however; their role has been primarily reactive. Agents other than the president have in the past been the source of demands for governmental action in civil rights; and, when these demands were strong enough, presidents were forced to respond. Some presidents have led, most often to advance the cause of civil rights (as with Lyndon Johnson) but sometimes to restrict the government's role (as with Ronald Reagan). Whether advancing or restricting government action, presidents since World War II have increasingly been leaders in civil rights policy. Committed presidents lead, and without that leadership little else happens. Ronald Reagan and George Bush took advantage of myriad statements and actions to pursue their policy preferences, using their influence to change civil rights policy.

The civil rights policy area exists in a highly charged atmosphere that has altered significantly over the years. This changing climate reveals the dynamism of civil rights policy making. Over the last forty years influence shifted as political conditions changed and as new issues moved to the forefront of the political agenda. The institutional setting became fragmented. Interest groups, mass protest, and judicial politics became more important in civil rights than in most policy areas. An agenda was thrust upon government, and in response presidents came to lead in civil rights policy making.

The Changing Policy Agenda

Slavery began in the American colonies in the early 1600s. Together with the related issue of states' rights, it was the most divisive issue in the United States' first century. From the 1820s to the late 1840s, critics focused on the slave trade instead of on the institution of slavery as practiced in many states. The enormous expansion of U.S. territory contributed to sectional rivalries over slavery that culminated in the Civil War.

The war ended slavery, but segregation by law in the South and usually by custom in the North marked the next hundred years. The Supreme Court encouraged such segregation by abolishing several Reconstruction laws. In 1896, in *Plessy v. Ferguson*, it validated the separate but equal doctrine. Racial inequality persisted, and government offered little leadership. As often as not, presidents equivocated, and the limited agenda and leadership came initially from Congress and then from the courts.

The modern era began with the *Brown v. Board of Education* decision in 1954 that overturned *Plessy*. The civil rights movement then placed civil rights squarely on the national agenda and challenged most remaining forms of racial discrimination. No one could doubt the considerable progress in political equality, but economic equality lagged, and therein lies a large remaining controversy in American public policy.

Although often submerged throughout American history, civil rights issues have never been far from the surface. American society exhibits many forms of racism, from the earlier extremes of slavery and lynching to today's more subtle school and housing discrimination. In the modern era, civil rights as a public policy concern has expanded beyond race. What most saw until the 1950s as primarily a black problem has come over the past four decades to include concerns about full rights for Native Americans, Hispanics, other racial and ethnic groups, women, individuals with disabilities, institutionalized and incarcerated persons, gays, and the aged. Like blacks, these groups fought for equality, yet little change occurred until they mobilized politically. Native Americans did not receive the vote until 1924—it was actually imposed on them—and they remain among the most economically disadvantaged groups.

Apart from groups perceiving themselves affected by civil rights policy, issue areas also have changed. Civil rights today increasingly involves foreign policy (e.g., human rights) and economic issues. Major subissues include education, employment, housing, voting, and public accommodations.[1] Because of the gap between political and economic equality, some civil rights advocates consider legislative and judicial victories hollow. Blacks in particular want more than ballots; they wish to share in economic prosperity as well. Jesse Jackson and civil rights groups have shifted their emphasis from political to economic rights. Some women's groups demand comparable worth (equal pay for jobs requiring equivalent skills, training, or education). The Reagan administration vigorously opposed comparable worth, perhaps the major civil rights issue of the 1980s. During that decade government actions compensating certain groups for past discrimination became increasingly controversial. George Bush also opposed such actions, helping make quotas the "hot button" word on civil rights in the early 1990s.

The expansion in policy scope led to major disagreements about the goals of civil rights policy (Sniderman and Hagan 1985). Is equal opportunity enough, or are affirmative actions necessary? Should we merely remove barriers to equal opportunity, or should we also seek equal results through compensatory action? If we accept the latter, then what are the appropriate remedies to obtain desired social ends? If guidelines and affirmative action are acceptable, are comparable worth and quotas also legitimate? If so, what about reverse discrimination and resentment? Demands for economic equality have come head-to-head against strong American norms favoring individual initiative but opposing reallocating wealth. While expansion of civil rights policy areas has broadened the public base of support, it may also have diluted the focus and diminished public sympathy.

Civil rights and especially race remain cleavage issues in American politics. Civil rights affects the mass public deeply and relates to the U.S. cultural order. Racial attitudes in particular have contributed to a growing structure of political beliefs. In fact, Carmines and Stimson (1980, 17) argue that American ideology is largely a racial dimension. The maturing of civil rights as a policy area has altered policy-making roles. Although I necessarily introduce other key participants, the primary focus remains on the president.

Civil Rights Issues to 1950

Slavery and Inequality

The public comments of early American presidents help convey public attitudes and perceptions of civil rights.[2] Early presidents sought little in the way of civil rights legislation. In 1820, James Monroe advocated an act making slave trading illegal and subject to capital punishment, while John Quincy Adams sought legislation requiring slave ships within U.S. jurisdiction to act humanely (Richardson 1899, 2:62, 401).[3] As the only former president to serve subsequently in the House of Representatives, Adams continued to challenge the institution of slavery in that body.

Several early presidents, including Andrew Jackson and Millard Fillmore, apparently said nothing about slavery in their public statements. In contrast, others strongly opposed the slave trade, frequently criticizing other nations for allowing its continuance.[4] Presidents favoring expansion of the nation had to contend with the question of slavery in the new territories. Most were equivocal in their positions and supported *popular sovereignty*, leaving the decision to the prospective state itself.[5]

The courts perpetuated states rights policies. Perhaps the most infamous Supreme Court case ever was *Dred Scott v. Sanford* (1857). A black man left a slave state with his owner and went to a free state, where he claimed freedom. The Court said slaves were not citizens of any state and therefore could not sue. Slaves were property, and people cannot be denied their property without due process of law. The decision also nullified the Missouri Compromise that had outlawed slavery in territories north of 36°30'. The decision outraged many in the North. Sectional rivalries heated up and hastened the Civil War.

Until that time, presidents and Congress had offered little leadership on the slavery issue. Although he was not an abolitionist, the political environment made it possible for Abraham Lincoln to make the radical departure. In the Emancipation Proclamation, he stated:

On the first day of January, . . . 1863, all persons held as slaves within any State or designated part of a State the people whereof shall then be in rebellion against the United States, shall be then, thenceforward, and forever free. . . . And upon this act, sincerely believed to be an act of justice, warranted by the Constitution upon military necessity, I invoke the considerate judgment of mankind and the gracious favor of Almighty God. (Bardolph 1970:20)

Reconstruction

The period immediately after the Civil War witnessed much civil rights activity by the Radical Republican Congress. The 1866 Civil Rights Act gave all U.S. citizens equal rights to inherit, purchase, lease, sell, hold, or convey real or personal property. Congress also secured three amendments to the Constitution: the Thirteenth in 1865 outlawed slavery; the Fourteenth in 1868 gave citizenship to all persons born or naturalized in the United States and guaranteed them the equal protection of the laws; the Fifteenth in 1870 gave them (black men) the right to vote.

Lincoln's successors were more equivocal about racial equality. The southerner Andrew Johnson said that the individual states had the right to decide who would have the franchise (Bardolph 1970, 29; Richardson 1899, 6:564–65). Johnson vetoed a bill, which Congress overrode on April 9, 1866, that placed blacks on the same legal footing as whites. In contrast, the northerner Ulysses Grant in his second Inaugural Address in 1873 pushed for allowing blacks to vote (Bardolph 1970; Richardson 1899, 7:221). If Johnson and Grant offered contrasting views, Rutherford Hayes evaded the issue.

Between 1866 and 1875 Congress enacted five major civil rights acts to enforce the three amendments. Blacks acquired major roles in most southern state governments. The Republican party and newly enfranchised blacks embraced one another. But within a decade Reconstruction came to an end. The compromise of 1877 removed the last federal troops from the South. Radical governments collapsed, and conservative Democrats regained control of southern state governments. Black voting rights were rescinded by Jim Crow laws.

The Supreme Court helped push race off the national agenda and ensure a subordinate status for blacks. The *Slaughter-House Cases* (1872) and the *Civil Rights Cases* (1883) deferred to the states, taking the position that the Reconstruction amendments did not apply to private accommodations and that the federal government had no jurisdiction over what were termed social rights. The *Plessy v. Ferguson* case proclaimed the separate but equal doctrine. Two years later, the Court upheld the legality of literacy tests in exercising the right to vote. During the last two decades of the 1800s racial separation became entrenched in every aspect of southern life. Federal civil rights policies ended for the time being.

The Reawakening of Civil Rights

Before the Civil War, abolitionists were loosely organized to oppose slavery and help free slaves via the underground railroad. Once slavery was outlawed, no organized opposition to racial inequality emerged until the next century. The National Association for the Advancement of Colored People (NAACP) (1909) and the Urban League (1911) began with largely white leadership and conservative approaches to further the cause of blacks. The vote for women was long in coming, perhaps because paternalism and protection characterized discrimination against women more than for blacks. The Supreme Court ruled in 1875 that the Fourteenth and Fifteenth Amendments did not apply to women. Women received the vote in 1920 as former suffrage leagues reorganized into the modern-day League of Women Voters.

There was little concern about civil rights in the early twentieth century. Theodore Roosevelt sought southern support for his policies at the expense of progress toward racial equality (Bardolph 1970, 199–200). Many of his successors followed suit. Woodrow Wilson's conservative southern heritage gave little encouragement to blacks and thus he made no efforts. Warren Harding stated:

The black man should seek to be, and he should be encouraged to be, the best possible black man and not the best possible imitation of a white man.... One must urge the people of the South to take advantage of their superior understanding of this problem and assume an attitude toward it that will deserve the confidence of the colored people. (Bardolph 1970, 183)

By the 1930s, Herbert Hoover and Franklin Roosevelt took conciliatory actions but did not push for legislation of any kind. One hundred fifty civil rights bills were introduced in Congress between 1937 and 1946, but Roosevelt was unwilling to take legislative positions or to do anything to encourage their passage (Carmines and Stimson 1989, 31).

Congress, divided and decentralized, was a bastion of conservatism on civil rights. Southern domination of key congressional committees gave the region considerable clout on race issues. Thus the New Deal coalition was badly split on the policy area. Although this coalition managed to push civil rights onto the agenda in the late 1930s no legislation emerged from Congress (Sinclair 1985). The House passed an antilynching bill in the late 1930s and several poll tax measures between 1942 and 1949, but none survived the Senate. No civil rights legislation even reached the floor during the 81st and 82d Congresses (1949–52), largely because conservatives in the Senate successfully used the filibuster.

President Harry Truman was the first modern president to be a leader in civil rights issues, pushing for an extensive federal role to ensure equality (Congress and the Nation, 1:1965, 1597). His action was particularly courageous in light of defections by southern Democrats during his 1948 reelection campaign. The Democratic party took a clear stand favoring racial equality for the first time in its history. In 1948, Truman sent Congress the first comprehensive civil rights legislation since Reconstruction and followed up with requests in subsequent years. He continually pushed Congress and issued executive orders to reverse the long acceptance of discrimination (Vaughn 1976).

The Modern Era of Civil Rights

Evolving Presidential Leadership

The political environment for civil rights changed radically after the 1954 *Brown* decision. By the early 1960s, the civil rights movement, a broadly based protest movement, together with the Supreme Court and the media, had brought the plight of African Americans dramatically to the public's attention. Women mobilized through the National Organization for Women (NOW), created in 1967, and several other national women's organizations. Native Americans, Hispanics, the disabled, and the elderly mobilized and sought legal protection. Presidents could no longer ignore civil rights. None did, but civil rights was not of equal concern to modern presidents.

Dwight Eisenhower provided little direction on civil rights, once stating that "you can't change men's hearts with laws" (Rodgers and Bullock 1972, 203). Although Eisenhower requested creation of the Civil Rights Commission in 1957 and abolition of literacy tests and the poll tax, he only reluctantly signed weak civil rights laws in 1957 and 1960. He proposed no civil rights legislation at all during his first three years in office, and not until 1959 did he recommend school desegregation legislation. Showing little commitment to civil rights, Eisenhower opposed a measure near the end of his tenure banning discrimination in schools built with federal funds. "Benign neutrality" probably best characterizes his civil rights views (Miroff 1976). Even favorable biographers fault his reluctance to exert leadership (Ambrose 1984; Greenstein 1982).

John Kennedy's campaign for president had led leaders of the civil rights movement to expect more from him than he was willing to offer. He believed that potential political costs and the need for legislative support for his other domestic programs prevented earlier and stronger advocacy. In refusing to push for legislation, he stated that "he would take on civil rights at the right time on the right issue; when I feel that there is a necessity for congressional action, *with a chance of getting that congressional action,* then I will recommend it" (Sorenson 1965, 535). Civil rights did not receive a high priority during 1961 and 1962 (Shank 1980, 45). Only in the last few months before his death did he seek action. The perception that Kennedy was a strong advocate of civil rights is perhaps too generous (Brauer 1977; Miroff 1976). Unlike Eisenhower, Kennedy was unable to persuade Congress to allow the attorney general to initiate suits for noncompliance with school desegregation. Each of these two presidents issued three executive orders concerning civil rights.

Lyndon Johnson sought to overcome his parochial record as senator from Texas by becoming a civil rights advocate (Goldman 1969, 515). He emerged as civil rights' strongest champion, much more active legislatively in civil rights than were his predecessors. He took positions on practically every civil rights vote in Congress, and he was the first president to request open housing legislation. He sought not only political but economic equality. The major Civil Rights Act of 1964 (HR 7152) and the Voting Rights Act of 1965 (S 1564) passed with his strong endorsement. Congress supported Johnson in all his positions in 1964 and 1965 but not in 1966 and 1968, when he sought to file desegregation suits, initiate employment legislation, and withhold HEW funds for noncomplying school districts.[6] Congress and the president did cooperate, however, in passing three major civil rights laws.

The late 1960s to mid-1970s witnessed a clear break in presidential advocacy of civil rights. Presidents Richard Nixon and Gerald Ford took office in a different environment. The focus of policy making had passed from the courts and Congress and was moving to the bureaucracy. Enforcement became more critical than the passage of new legislation. Nixon and Ford paid less attention and gave less support to civil rights in their public statements (Formisano 1991, 60). They particularly questioned busing as a valid means to attain racial balance. Nixon pushed the so-called Philadelphia plan to increase minority participation in federal construction projects but in 1972 sought a one-year moratorium on busing orders. Both presidents hedged on affirmative action in employment. Although both supported ratification of the Equal Rights Amendment (ERA), critics claimed they retreated from the civil rights goals of the 1960s and the efforts of the previous administrations (Kessel 1975, 52; Panetta and Gall 1971; Schell 1975, 40–44).

Nixon issued two executive orders on civil rights, and Ford issued none (see chapter 5 for a detailed discussion of executive orders). Both presidents strongly opposed busing. Busing controversies ensued. The Supreme Court had said "in the field of public education, the doctrine of 'separate but equal' has no place" (Bullock 1984, 56). Eleven southern states fought the decision vigorously. Because of substantial congressional and public opposition, the Court had ordered schools to desegregate with "all deliberate speed." There was more deliberation than speed, however, as organized groups such as the NAACP Legal Defense Fund opposed mostly grass-roots antibusing organizations. Very little progress toward school integration was made until the 1964 Civil Rights Act, which passed despite the objections of powerful southerners in Congress. The courts were much more supportive of busing than either Congress or subsequent Republican presidents (Bullock 1984b, 81).

Neither offered much legislation. Nixon reluctantly supported the requirement that schools must desegregate to receive federal aid. Still, as early as 1971 he opposed (as did Congress) using federal funds for busing. Title VII of the Educational Amendments Act (PL 92–318) contained antibusing provisions. Nixon sought unsuccessfully to obtain aid for local schools attempting to desegregate. The Emergency School Aid Act, which gave funding authority to HEW, was extended in 1974 but contained an amendment prohibiting forced busing under certain circumstances.[7]

Ford made few legislative requests (his antibusing proposal failed) and did not take positions on any civil rights votes while in office even though Congress continued to take conservative stands on busing. Although Ford's early rhetoric was aligned more with the forces favoring equality than were Nixon's, critics have noted the similar positions of these two presidents. Apart from busing, which both opposed, neither president seemed interested in civil rights.

One of the few vetoes of a civil rights measure occurred in 1980 when President Jimmy Carter blocked an appropriations bill that would have stripped the Justice Department of authority to order busing for school desegregation (Congress and the Nation, 5:1981, 676). Despite consistent support for civil rights, including the ERA, critics say

Table 2.1

Major Events in Civil Rights Policy Relating to Race, 1954–1980

1954:   *Brown v. Board of Education of Topeka* holds that segregated schools are inherently unequal and violate the Fourteenth Amendment's equal protection clause.

1955:   Martin Luther King, Jr., leads a bus boycott in Montgomery, Alabama.

1957:   President Dwight Eisenhower sends federal troops to enforce desegregation of a Little Rock, Arkansas, high school.

1957:   Southern Christian Leadership Conference (SCLC) is founded.

1957:   Congress passes first civil rights law since Reconstruction (PL 85–315) creating the Independent Civil Rights Commission and Civil Rights Division in the Department of Justice.

1960:   Another limited-impact civil rights law is passed (PL 86–449); black college students begin lunch counter sit-ins in Greensboro, North Carolina.

1961:   Freedom rides; President John Kennedy dispatches federal marshals to protect demonstrators.

1961:   Kennedy issues Executive Order 10925 forbidding discrimination in all federally financed construction.

1962:   Kennedy's Executive Order 11063 requires federal agencies to eliminate housing discrimination.

1962:   James Meredith attempts to enroll at the University of Mississippi; Kennedy sends troops to maintain order.

1963:   Civil rights demonstrators numbering 250,000 march on Washington.

1963:   Mass demonstrations in Birmingham, Alabama, protest segregated public accommodations and job discrimination.

1963:   Black students attempt to enroll at the University of Alabama.

1964:   The Civil Rights Act (PL 88–352) forbids discrimination in public accommodations, provides that federal grants and contracts may be withheld from violators, forbids discrimination by employers, empowers the Justice Department to sue violators, and creates the Equal Employment Opportunity Commission (EEOC).

1964:   The Twenty-fourth Amendment ends the poll tax in federal elections.

1964:   Three civil rights workers are murdered in Mississippi.

1964:   Martin Luther King, Jr., receives Nobel Peace Prize.

1965:   The Voting Rights Act (PL 89–110) sends federal registrars to southern states and counties to protect blacks' right to vote and empowers registrars to impound ballots.

1965:   Executive Order 11246 requires companies with federal contracts to take affirmative action to ensure equal opportunity.

1965:   Riots break out in Los Angeles's Watts district and in Selma, Alabama.

1966:   *Harper v. Virginia* holds that the Fourteenth Amendment forbids making a tax a condition of voting in any election.

1966:   The Black Panther party is founded.

1967:   Cleveland becomes the first major city to elect a black mayor, Carl Stokes.

1967:   Rioting occurs in Newark, Detroit, Milwaukee, and other major urban areas.

1968:   *Jones v. Mayer* finds all discrimination in the sale or rental of housing to be illegal.

1968:   The Fair Housing Act (PL 90–284) prohibits discrimination in the sale or rental of housing.

1968:   *Green v. County School Board* establishes that school boards must formulate workable desegregation plans.

1968:   Martin Luther King, Jr., and Bobby Kennedy are assassinated.

1968:   Riots sweep through many cities following King's assassination.

1968: Kerner Commission identifies racism as the cause of the riots.
1970: The Voting Rights Act is extended until 1975.
1971: *Swann v. Charlotte-Mecklenburg County Schools* approves busing as a means of combating state-enforced segregation.
1972: President Richard Nixon calls for moratorium on court-ordered busing.
1972: Title VIII includes antibusing provisions to the Educational Amendments Act (PL 92–318).
1972: Nixon provides discretionary funds to noncomplying school districts.
1972: Civil Rights Act authorizes EEOC to sue on behalf of workers suffering from discrimination.
1973: *Keyes v. Denver School District #1* ruling opens the way for court-ordered busing in the North.
1973: Los Angeles elects a black mayor, Tom Bradley.
1974: Congress extends School Aid Act through 1976 and places school education funding in the Department of Health, Education, and Welfare.
1976: *Hills v. Gautreaux* holds that public housing must not be concentrated in primarily minority areas.
1977: Congress begins using its appropriations powers to prohibit federal authorities from requiring busing.
1978: Administrative reorganization gives EEOC jurisdiction over job discrimination within the federal government.
1978: *Regents v. Bakke* strikes down racial basis for medical school admissions.
1979: *Dayton Board of Education v. Brinkman* upholds school busing as a remedy for school segregation in the North.
1979: *United Steelworkers v. Weber* approves voluntary affirmative action plans.
1980: *Fullilove v. Klutznick* approves earmarking a share of federal contracts for minority businesses.
1980: President Carter vetoes appropriations bill because it prohibits the Justice Department from bringing legal action to require busing.

Carter's words spoke louder than his actions (Shattuck 1978). Granted, Carter was hampered by inept legislative relations, both personally and through his liaison staff (Christenson 1982; Davis 1983). Congress continued to vote conservatively on busing issues. For example, in 1980 both houses barred the Department of Justice from bringing or joining suits that would require busing, resulting in the above veto. Neither Carter nor Congress could point to much legislative achievement in civil rights. Perhaps for that reason, he turned extensively to executive orders. He also appointed many women and minorities to important government positions and reorganized federal personnel policies (see LeLoup and Shull 1993, 157–60).

Civil rights has been an evolving policy area, passing through identifiable stages in the modern era. Table 2.1 summarizes the important events from Eisenhower through Carter. The 1950s can be identified as the judicial decade, in which the impetus for civil rights came primarily from the courts, which acted first and alone. Judicial actions stirred executive and legislative branches into activity, with pushes from the civil rights movement as well. The 1960s was the legislative era, when much (although obviously not all) of the civil rights activity emanated from Congress. The Johnson era was an anomaly, as the president shared leadership in civil rights. The next stage, for convenience described as the 1970s, was the administrative era. During this period executive enforcement of statutory law, presidential directives, and court decisions were the central thrusts.

Reagan and Bush Change the Focus

In the 1980 election, Ronald Reagan received the lowest percentage of the black vote of any Republican presidential candidate in history. In the White House, his civil rights policy seemed to be returning to the era of benign neglect of the early 1970s. Like Richard Nixon, Reagan sought to end or ignore many government civil rights programs (Amaker 1988; Detlefsen 1991; Orfield and Ashkinase 1991). But in actuality Reagan was a civil rights activist who forced a redefinition of that term. Instead of extending civil rights, he sought to reduce government's role. He called the 1988 Civil Rights Restoration Act a "federal power grab" and vetoed it (see chapter 4). Frequently he felt compelled to defend his civil rights record. Reagan's actions and statements brought civil rights once again to the forefront of the national political agenda. Nevertheless, he has been called the "chief apostle of conservatism on race" (Carmines and Stimson 1989, 54).

In the 1988 campaign, the racist innuendoes of the Republican's Willie Horton television commercial seemed an inauspicious beginning for the Bush administration. Still, George Bush had called for a "kinder and gentler America," which some saw as promising greater support for civil rights. The administration's four years did not settle the question of Bush's level of commitment. Although he had endorsed the legislation in the 1988 campaign, Bush was slow to bestow his blessing on a bill prohibiting discrimination against the disabled (including AIDS sufferers). Civil rights advocates criticized several of his appointments (see chapter 5). Yet, during 1989 the administration backed, and a Senate committee approved, the Americans with Disabilities Act, which passed in 1990. Much greater controversy arose over legislation the same year to tighten the remedies against job discrimination. Political events in 1991 forced Bush to support legislation similar to that he had vetoed the previous year. After this controversy, attention to civil rights waned. Bush's foreign policy interests and emerging events in Europe, Asia, Latin America, and, particularly, the Middle East, moved the administration to focus on international concerns.

With the shift in presidential approach to civil rights under Reagan and Bush, Congress became more assertive and ideological. Congress can offer leadership, but it frequently responds to actions of presidents, bureaucrats, the courts, and those outside government. During the crucial 1960s, it shared leadership with presidents—prodding Kennedy and acceding to Johnson—but it did not back down from its own preferences. Despite some grumbling about subsequent conservative Republican presidents, the Democratic Congresses did not push ahead on civil rights. Only under Reagan's direct challenge to civil rights near the end of his administration did Congress fill the void in leadership. It also more closely scrutinized Reagan appointees. Early in Bush's administration, Congress was willing to let others set the agenda. But controversy over legislation and Bush's conservative nominees (see chapters 4, 6) induced Congress to continue its leadership role. Major events in civil rights under Reagan and Bush appear in Table 2.2.

Since Johnson, no president has been as active legislatively in civil rights, but Reagan was assertive in different ways. His administration initiated a presidential decade. George Bush led moderately, but the rest of the 1990s could signal a return to the judicial decade of the 1950s—in a conservative direction. At the beginning of the 1990s, Congress challenged both the executive and the judiciary with legislation overturning conservative decisions on civil rights. It is clear that civil rights has a prominent place on the national agenda.

Competition for Leadership

Agents outside and inside government have and will continue to have significant roles in civil rights policy making. Agents outside government with an influence on civil rights policy making include interest groups, public opinion, political parties, the media, and elections. Actors within the government are the president, Congress, the courts, and the bureaucracy.

Those outside Government

Interest groups have traditionally played a significant role in civil rights policy. From the abolitionists in the 1850s to the present-day Leadership Conference on Civil Rights, interest groups exert pressure

Table 2.2

Major Events in Civil Rights Policy Relating to Race, 1981–1992

1981:   Federal jurisdiction over private contractors' personnel practices is rewritten to exclude all but very large companies.

1981:   Ronald Reagan's Executive Order 12320 increases federal government support to historically black colleges and universities.

1982:   The Voting Rights Act is extended for 25 years.

1983:   Chicago elects a black mayor, Harold Washington.

1983:   Philadelphia elects a black mayor, Wilson Goode.

1983:   Martin Luther King's birthday is declared a national holiday.

1984:   *Memphis Fire Department v. Stotts* holds that whites may not be laid off to be replaced by blacks with less seniority.

1984:   *Grove City College v. Bell* restricts the reach of four antidiscrimination statutes to specific programs or activities within larger organizations receiving federal aid.

1986:   *Wygant v. Jackson Board of Education* protects white public employees against most racially motivated layoffs but also endorses affirmative action generally, including plans that cost whites entry-level jobs.

1986:   Senate Judiciary Committee rejects (for only the second time in forty-nine years) a Reagan nominee for the federal bench due to his positions on civil rights.

1987:   *Johnson v. Transportation Agency* approves greatly expanded use of affirmative action in promotions.

1987:   *United States v. Paradise* upholds the constitutionality of temporary promotion quotas.

1988:   The Civil Rights Restoration Act (PL 100–259) overrides a presidential veto to overturn Supreme Court's *Grove City* decision.

1988:   The Fair Housing Act (PL 90–284) extends the antidiscrimination provisions of 1968 act to handicapped individuals and to families with children.

1989:   *Richmond v. Croson* declares any government program favoring one race over another (through minority set-asides) to be "highly suspect."

1989:   New York City elects a black mayor, David Dinkins.

1989:   Virginia elects a black governor, Douglas Wilder.

1989:   Congress rejects George Bush's nominee William Lucas for head of the Civil Rights Division.

1989:   *Wards Cove v. Atonio* holds that employees must prove there was no legitimate business reason for a firm's alleged discriminatory acts.

1989:   Five other close Supreme Court decisions limit remedies for job discrimination, prompting legislation to overturn them.

1990:   Congress passes a civil rights bill; Bush vetoes it and the Senate fails to override the veto by a single vote.

1991:   New York City elects a black mayor, David Dinkins.

1991:   Congress passes, and Bush signs after long opposition, the Civil Rights Act (PL 102–166).

1991:   Clarence Thomas, Bush's nominee for Thurgood Marshall's seat on Supreme Court, is confirmed by 54–46 vote after considerable controversy.

1991:   Racial violence breaks out in nearly all-white Dubuque, Iowa.

1992:   Racial violence in Los Angeles follows the acquittal of white police officers accused in the beating of black motorist Rodney King.

1992:   *Freeman v. Pitts* relaxes school desegregation requirements.

1992:   *Presley v. Etowah County Commission* removes the requirement for Justice Department preclearance of changes in local election districts.

on many phases of policy making. Today, conventional political action has replaced the mass demonstrations and protests of the 1960s. Interest group advocates now seem to have diminished in importance, as evidenced by their inability to oppose even the policies of the Reagan-Bush administrations of the 1980s and 1990s. Yet, they continue to be a force (if now more on the defensive than offensive) in the civil rights policy process.

The importance of civil rights to the general public has varied. Survey data suggest, however, that civil rights attitudes do help shape mass belief systems (Carmines and Stimson 1980, 10). Race, in particular, has contributed to heightened issue consistency and a greater structure of political beliefs today than Philip Converse (1964) found earlier. Race is now increasingly important in differentiating political candidates and parties. Popular support for civil rights among the American population increased until the 1980s (Shull 1989a, 186) but has since declined.

Political parties have played lesser roles than interest groups in later civil rights policy stages, but their platforms and pronouncements over the years have influenced agenda setting. Research has suggested that a "black realignment" occurred in 1964. Although 30 percent of blacks voted for Richard Nixon in 1960, Republican presidential candidates since then have received 10 percent or less of the black vote (Carmines and Stimson 1989, 57). Republicans began as the party supporting black civil rights, but in the modern era Democrats have become the party of racial liberalism and the Republicans of racial conservatism.

The media and elections have each been influential. The media has been both a social critic and an independent agenda setter. Television showed Americans the violence and demonstrations of the 1960s and a quarter century later in Los Angeles in May 1992. Coverage of such events alarms the mass and elite publics and frequently precipitates political action. Election results can influence policy, as they did in 1964 when major legislation followed. Since that time, party differences among voters on civil rights have been growing (Edsall and Edsall 1991). Elected officials are sensitive to civil rights concerns, and studies suggest that civil rights is salient to the electorate.

Those within Government

Unlike other policy areas, the courts initially played a significant role in civil rights. They took the lead in school desegregation by setting the liberal course in the 1954 *Brown* case. By the 1970s, the Court backtracked somewhat due to resistance from the public, Congress, and some presidents. Presidents Reagan and Bush appointed judges who began moving the courts back in a conservative direction at all federal levels (Detlefsen 1991). Yet a unified Democratic government beginning in 1993 would likely reverse that course. Despite obvious influence by the public, Congress, and presidents, the *Bakke* and *Weber* cases (see Table 2.1) demonstrate instances in which final determination of acceptable civil rights enforcement remains the purview of the Supreme Court. The Court's impact on civil rights policy in the United States is undeniable and continuing, if not always the most important.

During the 1970s, the bureaucracy was particularly important in civil rights policy making. Aggressive agency enforcement diminished under Reagan and Bush through their successful manipulation of all executive actions, including appointments, executive orders, budgets, reorganizations, and programs (Shull 1989b). Agencies became more diffused, politicized, and overburdened in the Reagan-Bush administrations, and they had less discretion in civil rights enforcement. Yet, as in other policy areas, bureaucratic power remains considerable.

Congress took the leadership role in civil rights after the Civil War. In the modern era, it has frequently been the most conservative of the three branches. It often blocked civil rights legislation and frequently exempted itself from laws that passed. Of course, many important bills eventually passed, but it remained conservative until Reagan and Bush, when Congress became the most liberal of the three branches of government on civil rights. It passed major legislation over the objections of both presidents, which had profound effects on both policy and legislative behavior. Research tells us that the votes of members of Congress closely correlate with public attitudes in their districts (Clausen 1973; Miller and Stokes 1963). As those attitudes change, congressional behavior also changes. Congress is probably the best policy-making barometer we have to public preferences.

Assessing Policy Roles

Civil rights is a complex policy arena with a whole range of actors. As political conditions changed and as new issues move to the forefront of the political agenda, the influence of these actors has shifted. Civil rights policy making is both dynamic and highly charged.

Although there is ample evidence that presidents often are not the dominant actors in civil rights policy making (Heck and Shull 1983), when they do take an interest in this policy area they move civil rights to the top of the government's agenda (Redford 1969, 107–23). The influence of the president generally wanes as the policy process unfolds. Thus, even when presidents take an interest in civil rights, one may expect their influence on policy modification, adoption, implementation, and evaluation to be limited. On the other hand, no actor can compete with the president committed to a civil rights *agenda.*

The roles of other policy agents vary considerably, and Table 2.3 offers judgments about such roles. Generally, it seems that agents within government are more important through the policy *formulation* stage, while agents outside government generally move to the forefront in evaluation of those policies. Many actors compete in formulating policies, making it more difficult to fix responsibility. Although they often receive outside stimuli, government officials usually are predominant. Congress and the courts play the major role in the *modification and adoption* of policies, although they receive input from interest groups and others in arriving at these decisions. The bureaucracy has the upper hand in the *implementation* of policy, subject to a degree of oversight by Congress and the courts. Except for interest groups (Bullock and Stewart 1984, 409), actors outside government often play little role in implementation but do *evaluate* policies along the lines of their perceived costs and benefits. Later chapters will look more extensively at these anticipated relationships presented in Table 2.3.

Each actor has differing levels of involvement at particular policy-making stages. This involvement and influence are neither absolute nor completely absent at any stage for any actor; considerable overlap exists. However, the overlap of actors and stages can be made more intelligible through the investigation of relations among actors. Presidents, I believe, are especially important in civil rights, having some influence in each policy-making stage.

This book stresses the potential both for presidential influence and for policy change. Leadership by presidents most often comes early in the policy-making process, particularly in agenda setting, where I expect wide differences in attention, support, and symbolism in policy statements. An inverse relationship between presidential statements and subsequent actions may exist. Presidents Reagan and Bush were

Table 2.3

Perceived Actor Roles

	Policy Stage				
	Agenda Setting	Formulation	Modification and Adoption	Implementation	Evaluation
Those within Government					
President	++	+			
Staff	+	+			
Bureaucracy					
Congress	+	+	++	+	
Courts	+	+	++	+	
Those outside Government					
Elections	+				+
Public opinion	+				++
Political parties		+			+
Media	+	+	+	+	+
Interest groups			++	++	++

Key: ++ = major role; + = moderate role; blank = minor role.

the exceptions because they politicized civil rights more than any of their predecessors. Rhetoric may have increased, but this study anticipates fewer tangible legislative actions in policy making under Reagan and Bush than occurred in previous administrations.

This study uses many types of evidence on the presidency, from quantitative data on statements, actions, and results to more impressionistic interviews with government officials. Such materials are important in illustrating the impact of presidents on the political environment, the nature of issues, and the process of civil rights policy making. Incorporated into the study are data such as legislative votes, budgets, and opinion polls on those actors inside and outside government. The study examines the impact (hence the policy change theme) that committed and assertive presidents can make. Subsequent chapters examine the data as precisely as frequently imprecise data allow.

The roles of presidents and other actors also change as the content of issues changes. Although often submerged throughout American history, civil rights issues have never been far from the surface. Racism in many forms is embedded in U.S. society, from the earlier extremes of slavery and lynching to today's more subtle second-generation school and housing discrimination. In the modern era, civil rights has expanded well beyond race. Issues change in salience over time, and the changes in civil rights have been dramatic. Jack Walker shows that it may be "next to impossible to deny a hearing for 'an idea whose time has come'" (1977, 445). With the maturing of civil rights as a policy area has come a shift in the roles of the actors and in the issue areas and groups targeted for civil rights policies.

Summary

Civil rights exists in a highly charged atmosphere. Even a cursory review of the history of civil rights reveals that groups and individuals other than presidents have had much to do with placing civil rights issues on the national policy agenda. While other institutions and officials have played leadership roles, presidents can play a central role in moving civil rights policy throughout the political process. Although research has shown that civil rights is not the most important domestic policy area for recent presidents (Clausen 1973; Kessel 1974; LeLoup and Shull 1979), presidential involvement is likely. When presidents do take an interest in a policy, it moves to a higher level on the government's agenda. Although presidents are more constrained in their ability to control policy in the 1990s than previously, presidents can take the lead for substantial change in civil rights. They are involved in each stage of the policy-making process.

The president operates in a highly complex and interrelated system or policy arena consisting of nongovernmental actors and government officials. If they choose, presidents may be the focal point for policy making. Presidents inherit ongoing policies that serve as a starting point for their administrations. While they may be able to set the agenda and formulate proposals, the modification and subsequent adoption of proposals and eventually their implementation are partly beyond the president's control. The "conversion" process for policies is often not complete until other participants act. This policy arena creates an atmosphere for presidential policy making, a climate for leadership. It helps define the boundaries of what the president can do as well as providing the possibilities for policy change. Presidential relations with those inside government differ greatly from those outside of government. In many policy areas, internal actors dominate, but on the emotionally charged area of civil rights, external factors have enormous influence.

Actors in the political system help establish the boundaries of presidential action in public policy making (Miroff 1979). The discretionary potential for presidents in civil rights varies according to conditions inside and outside of government. Increasingly, presidents "go public" to assert agenda preferences (see chapter 3). Some presidents, like Lyndon Johnson, can achieve their policy preferences primarily through legislation. His successors relied more on nonlegislative strategies, such as budgets, executive branch reorganization, nominations, and executive orders (see chapters 4–5). Such devices, individually and in concert, can lead to dramatic policy change. Reagan and Bush used these and other creative devices to assert their policy preferences. Reactions to their statements and actions appear in chapters 6–7, while chapters 8–9 cover the consequences (results) of policy statements and actions.

Notes

1. These subissues are included in this book, but voting and public accommodations are subsumed in the *other* category.

2. The examples of communications from earlier presidents refer only to race. The key words used to obtain these remarks include Afro-Americans, blacks, civil rights, colored, lynching, minorities, Negroes, slavery, and African slave trade. Many other groups and issues emerged in the modern era. Specific key words for modern target groups and issue areas appear in chapter 3, Tables 3.4 and 3.5.

3. Readers are encouraged to examine these public communications, found in Bardolph 1970 and Richardson 1899 for early presidents and *Public Papers of the Presidents* (usually two volumes annually) for modern presidents. See also Shull 1989a, ch. 3, for more detailed excerpts.

4. Excerpts of remarks by James Monroe, John Quincy Adams, Martin Van Buren, John Tyler, and Zachary Taylor are in Richardson 1899, 2:62, 309–10, 3:620, 4:363, 5:15.

5. Excerpts of remarks by James K. Polk and James Buchanan are in Richardson 1899, 4:609, 5:555.

6. Important documents on civil rights during the Johnson administration are available on microfilm from the University Press of America.

7. For an interesting discussion of the school busing controversy during 1969–72, see *Congress and the Nation*, 3:1973, 512–17.

Part II

Presidential Policy Statements and Actions

3

Going Public through Policy Statements

Public communications by presidents are an important influence on public policy. Research suggests that presidents can use such messages to set their own agenda, if not always the broader government agenda (Shull 1983, ch. 2; Light 1982). Much of what appears on the subsequent government agenda probably can be traced to presidential communications. Public messages give presidents the opportunity to set the stage for policy innovations, which usually come from the White House (Light 1982; Redford 1969; Kingdon 1984; Shull 1983). Communications provide an important opportunity for presidents to "go public" in a highly discretionary policy area.

Language, especially in a political context, is often symbolic. Murray Edelman, whose work reveals the profound and pervasive influence of symbols, sees political decision making as a "passing parade of abstract symbols" (1964, 5). Presidents are focal symbols of government. They use symbols in their language to help control their agendas and to obtain support for past, present, or future policy (Edelman 1964). Symbols may also help presidents persuade those inside and outside government to accept their views. Charles Elder and Roger Cobb define a symbol as "the process of attributing meaning to an object" (1983, 29). Symbols provide little reference to specific (or tangible) actions and policies but represent vague, general principles. Presidential communications should reveal varying degrees of symbolism.

Presidents play a crucial role in shaping civil rights policy through their messages because only with presidential support are major and lasting policy changes likely. (Exceptions are the 1988 Civil Rights Restoration Act and the 1991 Civil Rights Act, both passed after initial presidential vetoes.) Such communications are particularly important early in the policy-making process. Some presidential communications, especially in an emotionally charged policy area such as civil rights, may be more symbolic than substantive (Denton 1982; Lambries 1983; Ragsdale 1984, 971). Yet even symbolism can have important policy consequences by focusing public attention on the problem. Symbolic or not, communications may help presidents obtain support for their policy preferences, especially in a difficult area of social policy such as civil rights (Light 1982). Presidential preferences, as expressed in public communications, are often helpful in resolving societal conflicts (Eyestone 1978, 3; Lindblom 1980, 4). Because civil rights is highly conflictual, presidential remarks may be more symbolic (and perhaps more at odds with actions) than those in other policy areas (Shull 1983, 44).

This chapter begins with a detailed discussion of specific policy statements within public communications by Reagan and Bush as found in *Public Papers of the Presidents*.[1] To place such remarks in perspective, I then compare the degree of attention, support, and symbolic nature of modern presidential communications. Does presidential attention to civil rights represent policy support, or is it merely symbolic rhetoric? The chapter then empirically assesses the policy statements of modern presidents individually and by political party. Calls for legislative and judicial action are also examined. Presidential policy statements are then arrayed according to target groups and issue areas within civil rights. This latter concern should reveal divergent attention within groups and among subissues and tell us about the changing nature of civil rights policy.

Reagan and Bush "Go Public"

Ronald Reagan made public statements supporting the broad principles of civil rights early in his administration. "Guaranteeing equality of treatment is the government's proper function," he said on June 29, 1981, during a press conference. "We will not retreat on the Nation's commitment to equal treatment of all citizens" (*Public Papers of the President* 1981, 117). This statement appears to reflect the political requisites of the 1980s and 1990s: no president (or serious national politician) can consider any stance other than condemnation of racism and bigotry. Reagan also made skillful use of manipulative techniques, for example, in emphasizing his opposition to unpopular issues like busing and quotas. He stated before a group of black Republicans that Great Society programs were "tragic for blacks because they weakened capitalism" (*Newsweek*, October 4, 1982, 62). Reagan appeared vulnerable in his 1984 reelection bid on the "fairness" issue, particularly regarding blacks and women, but it had little impact on the election. An analysis of Reagan's speeches by James Miller (1984, 62–68) found that his statements became more symbolic and moved further away over time from supporting equality.

Following the divisive 1988 election, civil rights supporters were suspicious of the Bush administration. Still, Bush had called for "a kinder and gentler America" and committed himself to equal access for minorities. In a speech to the National Urban League, he stated: "My Administration is committed to reaching out to minorities, to striking down barriers. . . . We will make America open and equal to all" (*New Orleans Times-Picayune*, August 9, 1989, A3).[2] The first months of the administration did not settle the question of Bush's level of commitment. Jesse Jackson said that the president's rhetoric was not enough. Yet, that period saw a much lower gap in white-black perception of Bush compared to Reagan. Reagan had split the races dramatically, but Bush's early months showed much less difference in approval by race in monthly Gallup Polls (see chapter 7).

Whether Bush perpetuated the Reagan rhetoric can be seen in the following section, which examines these two presidents' specific policy statements from *Public Papers of the Presidents*. These excerpts are centered on particular *target groups* (e.g., minorities, Hispanics/Native Americans, women, the elderly, and *others*) and by *issue areas* (e.g., education, employment, housing, and *others*).[3] This analysis allows a preliminary comparison of Reagan-Bush public communications.

Reagan's Policy Statements

Excerpts by Target Groups

Most of Reagan's early statements focused on blacks and women, and statements about blacks appeared throughout the eight years of his presidency. He professed support of civil rights for minorities but qualified such support by opposing quotas. He stated:

There are some today who, in the name of equality, would have us practice discrimination. They have turned our civil rights laws on their head, claiming they mean exactly the opposite of what they say. These people tell us that the government should enforce discrimination in favor of some groups through hiring quotas, under which people get or lose particular jobs or promotions solely because of their race or sex. Some bluntly assert that our civil rights laws apply only to special groups and were never intended to protect every American. Well, they couldn't be more wrong.... That's discrimination pure and simple and is exactly what the civil rights laws were designed to stop. Quotas also cast a shadow on the real achievements of minorities, which makes quotas a double tragedy. (*Public Papers of the Presidents*, June 15, 1985, 772–73)[4]

Issues concerning women were on the agenda early regarding pension rights. Although Reagan said that women should not be discriminated against, he opposed the ERA, saying:

There are numerous ways of rectifying the problem of sex discrimination. As Governor of California, I signed fourteen pieces of legislation eliminating regulations and statutes that discriminated against women. We passed legislation prohibiting sexual discrimination in employment and business matters, established the right of a woman to obtain credit in her own name, and revised laws giving the wife equal rights covering community property. (October 7, 1981, 1099–1100)

Later Reagan stated that "many provisions of the law which discriminated against women have been reformed by our own policies and initiatives." He supported the Supreme Court's *Norris* (1986) decision requiring equal benefits for men and women for pension credits. He stated that he believed equality could be achieved through existing statutory and legal processes, but he said, "We will work for legislative changes consistent with the Court's decision and will continue to seek other ways of guaranteeing fair treatment under the law for the women of America" (July 6, 1983, 980–81).

Native Americans received attention during Reagan's second term. In 1986, he said:

I reiterate my support for the continuation of the Native American programs. I therefore urge the Congress to provide funding for these programs in the fiscal year 1987 continuing resolution and urge that the 100th Congress promptly consider new legislation to authorize appropriations for these programs. (September 26, 1986, 1276)

Reagan supported legislation on Indian self-determination stating that "tribal self-government allows tribes more freedom to design programs to serve the specific needs of their members" (October 5, 1988, 1268). However, later in that same year, he opposed an Indian Land Transfer Act that he said "would have created an expensive and unnecessary new bureaucracy and duplicated currently existing programs. It would not have addressed the underlying problems of economic development in Indian country" (November 2, 1988, 1426).

The oldest president ever, Reagan opposed age discrimination. He stated: "Older Americans possess a reservoir of experience and a depth of knowledge that is a great national resource. . . . I will back legislation which eliminates mandatory retirement requirements in government and private industry based solely on age. The criteria for retirement should be fitness—not age" (April 2, 1982, 420–21). He signed legislation in 1986 ending mandatory retirement at age seventy "because of the need to sustain and enhance our productive capacity, and attain the goal of fairness in employment opportunity for American workers" (November 1, 1986, 1517).

President Reagan spoke about *other* groups as well:

I know there's a growing concern that some universities may be discriminating against citizens of Asian and Pacific heritage. . . . Well, to deny any access to higher education when it has been won on the basis of merit is a repudiation of everything America stands for. . . . Any practice of racial discrimination against any individual violates the law, is morally wrong, and will not be tolerated. (May 3, 1988, 565)

Reagan also supported the disabled, appointing through executive order a Committee on Employment of People with Disabilities that "shall report annually to the president, who may apprise the Congress, and other interested organizations and individuals on the progress and problems of maximizing employment opportunities for people with disabilities" (May 10, 1988, 598).

Excerpts by Issue Areas

Reagan pushed several aspects of civil rights in education. Early on he initiated an executive order and legislation to make black colleges more competitive for federal grants. He stated:

This program shall seek to identify, reduce, and eliminate barriers which may have unfairly resulted in reduced participation in, and reduced benefits from, federally sponsored programs. Each Executive Department will establish annual plans to increase black . . . participation . . . and submit progress reports. The Secretary of Education shall supervise a review of unintended regulatory barriers and identify ways of eliminating inequities and disadvantages. (September 15, 1981, 978–80)

Early in 1982, Reagan announced that the Internal Revenue Service (IRS) would no longer deny tax-exempt status to private, nonprofit educational organizations that engage in racially discriminatory practices but otherwise qualify for such status. He said that agencies should not govern by "administrative fiat," but, in the face of criticism, he submitted to Congress "proposed legislation that would prohibit tax exemptions for any school that discriminates on the basis of race" (January 18, 1982, 36). Reagan received considerable criticism for this decision, but defended it by saying that he did not know such tax exemptions were even possible. Also regarding education, Reagan stated on several occasions that "this administration is unalterably opposed to forced busing of school children" (February 26, 1982, 238).

In the employment area, Reagan signed legislation enhancing "the ability of women to earn pensions in their own right. . . . An end to inequities in the provision of pension benefits to women has been a top priority of this administration" (August 23, 1984, 1161–62). At least two other aspects of employment rights were of concern to the president. One liberal proposal was the creation of minority enterprise zones. Enterprise zones are projects, federally funded in whole or in part, to encourage job creation, particularly among underrepresented groups. In his 1985 State of the Union Address, Reagan stated, "Let us place new dreams in a million hearts and create a new generation of entrepreneurs by passing enterprise zones this year" (February 6, 1985, 132). The other proposal reflected his conservative view that younger workers should have a lower minimum wage than older workers. He justified this stand by stating that "under the current federal minimum wage, many inexperienced and disadvantaged young people are priced out of the labor market . . . This legislation will help provide the first job, with real work experience for many of these young people" (March 25, 1985, 344).

Regarding housing, Reagan said midway through his first term that "in the year ahead, we'll work to strengthen enforcement of fair housing laws for all Americans" (January 25, 1983, 109). In 1984 he followed through on this effort with legislation that

would impose civil penalties of up to $50,000 for the first housing discrimination offense and of up to $100,000 for a second offense, extend the filing time period, allow individual complaints, and extend protection of the Fair Housing Act to the handicapped and disabled. (April 10, 1984, 516)

Reagan signed the Fair Housing Act of 1988 stating "this bill is the product of years of bipartisan work and repairs a significant deficit—or defect, I should say— . . . in our civil rights laws" (September 13, 1988, 1140).

Bush's Policy Statements

Excerpts by Target Groups

Because the 1990–91 civil rights legislation was called a "quota bill" by the Bush administration, it had mostly racial connotations. After vetoing the legislation in the fall of 1990 (case appears in chapter 4), Bush frequently called for a bill that would not "produce" quotas. He stated on numerous occasions that he wanted to sign a civil rights bill but would not sign a quota bill. He also laid out changes he expected in revised legislation and complained that Congress had given his version of the legislation inadequate attention: "We've heard very little about my civil rights proposal, which is really a very good one" (June 14, 1991, 782). Most of Bush's other remarks concerning race dealt with historically black colleges (discussed under issue areas) and minority set-asides.

The only separate reference to gender was in the context of Bush criticizing congressional Democrats for trying to convert the 1990–91 civil rights bill into a "women's issue." On the need for an equal rights amendment, Bush stated: "I don't think that thing's gotten off; I don't really see much steam behind it now. I think we have existing laws to protect the rights of women . . . and I don't think that it's particularly needed at this point at all" (December 8, 1989, 1672).

Bush was concerned about Hispanics, whom he spoke of as being particularly undereducated. In discussing a task force he had created on education for Hispanics, Bush stated: "They have worked to find ways to improve federal education programs. By enhancing the educational opportunities available to Americans of Spanish and Latin descent, we can help promote their continued social and economic advancement" (September 24, 1990, 1141). Bush also signed an executive order "to advise on how to improve efforts at quality education." He stated: "Our administration has made education assistance for Hispanic-Americans one of the top priorities of our campaign to revive educational excellence" (July 18, 1990, 112).

In a single message in 1990, Bush opposed legislation regarding Native Americans, stating that a particular section "authorized racial preferences for native Americans, divorced from any requirement of tribal membership" (May 24, 1990, 839). Bush stated in vetoing similar legislation later in the year that "Senate Bill 321 is so seriously flawed that it would create more problems than it solved" (November 16, 1990, 1831). In criticizing the 1990 "quota bill" on another matter, Bush said it would also discriminate against Asian Americans.

Bush rarely mentioned the elderly in his first three years, but, as with the disabled, he supported increased income limits under social security, thereby allowing continued employment without losing benefits. Bush's remaining statements regarding age were conservative, proposing limited minimum wage increases on young employees. In fact, he sought a "training wage" for those under twenty. In arguing this position, Bush stated:

The issue is not minimum wage, its a question of skills. . . . My difference with the majority in Congress is not about thirty cents per hour on minimum wage legislation; its about hundreds of thousands of people, largely young people—largely unskilled people—who won't have a job to go to if this minimum wage law now before Congress becomes law. (May 17, 1989, 568)

Most of Bush's policy statements concerned *other* groups; the disabled received considerable attention. He stated "we are supporting landmark legislation to extend the nation's civil rights guarantees to those more than 36 million Americans with disabilities. . . . And the workforce of the future can also benefit from the unique abilities of persons with disabilities" (June 30, 1989, 835–36). He later added that "disabled Americans must become full partners in America's opportunity society." President Bush signed the Americans with Disabilities Act (ADA) on July 26, 1990, calling it "the world's first comprehensive declaration of equality for persons with disabilities." The homeless were discussed frequently. Bush spoke against discrimination toward Arab Americans, particularly during operation Desert Storm, and signed legislation to prosecute perpetrators of hate crimes.

Excerpts by Issue Areas

Despite his claim to be the "Education President," Bush gave education relatively little attention. He pushed to increase the Head Start program "to prepare children from disadvantaged families for effective learning" (August 8, 1989, 1070). However, the entire remaining education emphasis was on aiding historically black colleges and universities. He issued an executive order and pushed legislation on the topic in an effort to involve the private sector. He spoke of "six new initiatives, which will help do nationally what you have done historically: enrich education so that education can enrich our lives. I propose that Congress fund $460 million over four years in endowment-matching grants" (March 9, 1989, 202).

Much of Bush's rhetoric on employment dealt with the creation of enterprise zones, which are only tangentially related to civil rights. These initiatives also coincided with his desire to have the private sector take the lead in job creation. Sometimes Bush put enterprise zones into the same context as controversial capital gains tax cuts. Enterprise zones were also tied to the goal of increasing affordable housing, showing the interrelation among issue areas.

In vetoing the 1990 civil rights bill, which concerned employment, Bush stated:

It will lead to years—perhaps decades—of uncertainty and expensive litigation. It is neither fair nor sensible to give the employers of our country a difficult choice between using quotas or seeking a clarification of the law through costly and very risky litigation. (October 22, 1990, 1634)

Under political pressure, Bush later supported the similar 1991 Civil Rights Act. Bush also advocated strengthening the Job Training Partnership Act (JTPA), saying: "For six years now, the JTPA has been equipping the disadvantaged youth to enter the work force. . . . And we are working to make the program even stronger . . . to target it more tightly on at-risk youth, kids with the most urgent need for job training" (August 8, 1989, 1070). He later said: "The quality of JTPA services will be enhanced by providing a support system to enable our most disadvantaged citizens to become employable. Services will be individualized and substantially intensified. Participants will be assessed to determine their specific education and training needs" (July 25, 1989, 1011).

Almost all Bush's statements on housing were directed at the homeless. He stated the administration "authorized additional grants to the states that would be focused on those who are currently homeless and suffer from both substance abuse and mental illness." He also pushed a "service-supported housing program [HOPE] for the frail elderly by coupling housing vouchers with assistance to help pay the costs of the services they need" (November 10, 1989, 1494, 1498). Bush favored expanding emergency shelters, stating the HOPE legislation also "extends dignity of home ownership to people who live in public housing" (May 12, 1991, 578). He sought full funding for the legislation for fiscal year 1991. He also signed the National Affordable Housing Act that "provides opportunity, and it encourages responsibility without the shackles of dependency" (November 28, 1990, 1929).

The Public Communications of Modern Presidents

Expectations

Presidential communications on civil rights suggest several avenues for empirical inquiry. Considerable variation in attention, support, and symbolism is anticipated in presidential statements. Presidents giving greater attention to civil rights should also voice greater support (or opposition) in their communications than will presidents for whom civil rights is less salient. I expect high attention and consistent support or opposition (less symbolism) from Presidents Kennedy, Johnson, Carter, and Reagan especially. Relatively low attention and mixed support (high symbolism) should emerge from Eisenhower, Nixon, Ford, and Bush. Reagan should be the most ideologically extreme president, making many statements but not highly supportive of government action. He probably also called for more legislative and judicial actions than most presidents.

At the polar extreme, Johnson may have considerable attention, but he should be the opposite of Reagan, ranking low on symbolism by being more consistent in attention, support, and calls for action by others in government. Both Nixon's and Bush's statements should be highly symbolic, with only moderate levels of support, but the latter should exhibit less attention to civil rights.

Nathaniel Beck (1982) and Samuel Kernell (1986, 223) believe that policy agendas vary more by administration than by party. Yet, I expect dramatic differences by presidential party. Democratic presidents should reveal greater levels of attention and support (liberalism) for civil rights overall, consistent with the literature on party differences on broad social policy (Wayne 1978; Orfield 1975; Bullock and Lamb 1984, 200). Democrats should more vocally favor expansionist civil rights policies and be more supportive than Republican presidents (Shull 1983, 45–48). This greater Democratic support may be due to ideological reasons or perceptions that presidents are serving their coalitions. Democrats are frequently seen as the party of "inclusive compromise" and Republicans of "exclusive compromise" (Mayhew 1966). Therefore, Democrats probably call for legislative and judicial actions more often than do Republicans. Some of these expectations by individual presidents and by party are expressed in Table 3.1.

Measurement

The content of all presidential speeches, press conferences, letters, and other public messages as recorded in *Public Papers of the Presidents of the United States* was analyzed for presidential attention, support, and symbolism. Presidential statements were located by using *key words* on civil rights selected from the extensive index included in the annual editions of *Public Papers*.[5] Number of *items* refers to the num-

Table 3.1

Expected Nature of Presidents' Statements

President	Characteristic		
	Attention	Support	Symbolism
President			
Eisenhower	Lo	Mod	Mod
Kennedy	Mod	Hi	Mod
Johnson	Hi	Hi	Lo
Nixon	Mod	Lo	Hi
Ford	Lo	Lo	Hi
Carter	Hi	Hi	Mod
Reagan	Hi	Lo	Lo
Bush	Mod	Mod	Hi
Presidential party			
Democrat	Hi	Hi	Lo
Republican	Lo	Lo	Hi

ber of separate documents mentioning civil rights issues.[6] Policy *state-ments*, as opposed to merely vague remarks, were also identified from presidential communications (items).

The number of policy statements per year, like number of items, indicates the changing level of presidential attention. Such statements can be of any length and must specifically advocate policy rather than be simply vague generalizations. The explicit statement is usually a sentence, but supporting wording varies considerably, and number of *lines* (a measure of relative attention) is also reported.[7]

In addition to attention, the research includes a measure of presidential support toward civil rights. Each policy statement was coded as supportive, nonsupportive, or neutral. Favoring policies sought by civil rights activists and minorities is an example of a supportive position. More specifically, support could include advocating legislation or litigation directed against segregation or racial discrimination, as well as seeking such remedial devices as busing or stronger enforcement of civil rights statutes. Supportive positions, then, favor increased government involvement to ensure equality and are equated with the "liberalness" of positions.[8]

These measures help tap the amount of attention and support in civil rights communications. Many scholars view civil rights as highly symbolic (see, e.g., Shull 1983, 45–48; Elder and Cobb 1983, 2–4). Civil rights may be a policy area containing ambiguous referents and emo-

Table 3.2

Presidents' Attention and Support on Civil Rights

	Items (No./Year)	Policy Statements (No./Year)	Length Policy Statements (No. Lines/Year)	Supportive Statements (% Liberal)
Mean	49	23	800	84
By Party				
Democrats	54	27	855	99
Republicans	43	19	745	69
By President[a]				
Eisenhower	16	5	112	97
Kennedy	38	18	453	100
Johnson	60	31	775	100
Nixon	23	15	580	62
Ford	28	14	348	43
Carter	58	29	1,257	96
Reagan	79	17	717	72
Bush	71	42	1,986	69

[a]The number of years for which data are available and upon which calculations are based are Eisenhower = 8, Kennedy = 3, Johnson = 5, Nixon = 5.5, Ford = 2.5, Carter = 4, Reagan = 8, Bush = 3.

tional content, referred to by Edelman as "condensation symbols" (1964, 6–9). To be attentive, presidents must make frequent and lengthy statements. Support will be ideological if it is highly consistent (strongly liberal or conservative). Admittedly, symbolism is the most difficult concept to operationalize but relates to attention and support. Statements are symbolic if they contain many mentions of civil rights without specific policy statements and, thus, are largely devoid of policy content. Statements are also symbolic if they are very brief and rarely call for tangible actions by Congress or the courts. The indicators and results of this analysis are found in Tables 3.2 and 3.3.

Findings

Attention, Support, and Symbolism

Table 3.2 presents several indicators of presidential attention and support. The overall (mean) measures provide a baseline for the various comparisons. On the average, presidents mention civil rights (number of items) forty-nine times per year in office and support civil rights 84 percent of the time. However, fewer than half the mentions of civil rights (items) contain policy statements (45 percent), and thus communications appear highly symbolic. These findings suggest relatively greater support for than attention to civil rights, but with variation explained by different indicators and aggregations of the data. Attention, support, and symbolism vary considerably across presidents and parties.

Civil rights clearly is more salient for some presidents than others; it was salient to Reagan, as expected, and especially to Bush, contrary to expectation (as in Table 3.1). Civil rights policy is increasingly impossible to ignore. Johnson and Carter also show high attention, but among these four highly attentive presidents, Reagan had far fewer policy statements on a yearly basis and, especially, few items containing policy statements. Apart from attention, Johnson and Carter have among the highest support for civil rights (100 percent and 96 percent respectively). Thus they score high on attention and low on symbolism. Surprisingly, George Bush is the most attentive president to civil rights, certainly if one looks beyond mere mentions (number of items, where Reagan scored highest). Bush had by far the greatest number of substantive policy statements per year. He also issued the most lines per year and had the longest average statements among these eight modern presidents. Bush was fairly conservative, ranking well below average in percent support overall and average among Republican presidents (see last column in Table 3.2).

Ford is at the opposite extreme from Johnson and Carter; he said little and took the least liberal positions among these presidents. Thus, he ranks low on attention and high on symbolism, at least on percentage of items with statements. Nixon had the highest percentage of statements to items (65 percent), with Johnson next highest (closely followed by Ford and Carter), making Nixon and Johnson the least symbolic on that measure. Bush and Carter had the longest statements (in relation to number issued per year and average number of lines), while the other presidents were more symbolic on that measure.

The assertion of high symbolism for Reagan deserves further scrutiny, given his higher than expected support. His seemingly high attention (number of items per year) suggests considerable symbolism, especially since he had the lowest percentage of policy statements per items and, as previously noted, had relatively short statements. Reagan shows greater rhetorical support for civil rights than anticipated. In fact, he had more liberal rhetoric than Nixon, Ford, or Bush. Perhaps it follows that a degree of at least rhetorical support is a requisite even for conservative presidents who now must deal with many more highly politicized groups. Thus, on several (but not all) measures, Reagan ranks highest on symbolism, as expected.

George Bush was quite willing to make policy statements and lengthy ones at that; they were by far the longest statements on a yearly basis of any modern president. Thus, contrary to what many might think, Bush was not a moderate on civil rights; he was actually more activist and conservative than was Ronald Reagan, the president to whom some attribute the modern conservative revolution on civil rights. Certainly, the "kinder, gentler" Bush on civil rights does not appear during his first three years in office. The results in Table 3.2 confirm some of the expectations in Table 3.1 on the attention, support, and symbolism of presidential statements on civil rights.

Table 3.2 also reveals dramatic differences by presidential party. Democrats show greater attention on all measures as anticipated. Because Republicans had fewer statements per item and briefer statements (number of lines per year), their remarks appear more symbolic than those of Democrats. A particularly dramatic difference is the 30 percentage points greater support in Democratic versus Republican policy statements. Thus, by being much more consistent in their ideological preferences, Democratic presidents also seem less symbolic (and more substantive) than their Republican counterparts in their public communications on civil rights.

Calls for Action

Note in Table 3.3 that very few calls for legislative or judicial action are made by presidents. The few legislative calls and even fewer judicial calls per year suggest a high degree of symbolism in civil rights statements. Thirty-three percent of policy statements contain calls for legislative action, while only 5 percent contain calls for judicial action. Surprisingly, presidents ask little of other branches in the civil rights realm.

There is a somewhat gradual increase in the tendency to call for legislation (through Carter), while the pattern for judicial calls appears to be in the opposite direction after Ford. The "trend" in legislative calls probably reflects the expansion of the civil rights subissues as

Table 3.3

Presidents' Calls for Legislative and Judicial Action[a]

	Legislative		Judicial	
	No.	No./Year	No.	No./Year
Mean	32	5.8	3.8	0.7
By Party				
Democrats	39	9.8	4.7	1.2
Republicans	24	3.5	2.8	0.3
By President				
Eisenhower	6	0.8	2	0.3
Kennedy	6	2.0	4	1.3
Johnson	38	7.6	9	1.8
Nixon	22	4.0	1	0.2
Ford	9	4.1	6	2.7
Carter	73	18.3	1	0.3
Reagan	62	7.8	5	0.6
Bush	21	7.0	0	0

[a]I was generous in coding calls for both legislative and judicial actions. All the president must do is say that he has proposed such action or take a position on existing actions. Reference to a particular legislative bill or court case counts (including constitutional amendments and measures already passed into law). Even general references to the Supreme Court are tabulated as calls for judicial action.

well as recognition by presidents that they must deal with an increasingly resurgent Congress (Sundquist 1981). The reasons why presidents now ask less of the courts in civil rights is less clear, but the broadening of groups and issues may require comprehensive legislation rather than the case-by-case judicial approach.

Democrats equivocate in calls for action less than do Republicans. These results in Table 3.3 and those in Table 3.2 confirm the much greater symbolism of Republicans' statements relative to those of Democrats. Republicans make only one-third the number of either call than do Democrats. Variation is also considerable by individual presidents. Carter made by far the most calls for legislation—three times the average yearly rate, while Eisenhower made the fewest legislative calls. Calls for judicial action also varied, with Ford making the most per year and Bush making the fewest.[9]

Changing Nature of Civil Rights

Seventy-five percent of policy statements were categorizable into target groups and issue areas, but this is not a particularly large percent-

Table 3.4

Presidents' Statements, by Target Group[a]
(number mentions as % of total)

	Blacks[b]	Hispanics/Native Americans[c]	Women[d]	Age[e]	Other[f]
Mean	55	4	23	8	10
By Party					
Democrats	47	4	33	5	11
Republicans	63	4	13	11	9
By President					
Eisenhower	60	5	15	20	0
Kennedy	56	13	25	0	6
Johnson	69	2	3	9	17
Nixon	78	2	10	7	3
Ford	81	0	19	0	0
Carter	31	4	55	3	6
Reagan	53	7	19	12	9
Bush	43	6	5	12	34

[a]Vague references to "equality for all citizens" or "equal protection under law" were left uncoded.

[b]Color, segregation, busing, and any minority not specified.

[c]Mexican Americans, Indians.

[d]Sex, gender, and any reference to the ERA.

[e]Young and old.

[f]Specific group like religion (or creed), disabled, institutionalized.

age when one recalls that multiple counts are allowed. The remaining policy statements were too general to categorize (see notes to Tables 3.4 and 3.5). These tables show the changing nature of civil rights. The data reveal considerable attention to blacks as a target group (55 percent, but diminishing since Ford) and, thus, relatively low attention to other groups. This finding is consistent with expectations. Limited data on age and Hispanics/Native Americans (but increasing emphasis since Ford) complicate the analysis but still reveal differences by president.

Eisenhower provided relatively much greater attention to age discrimination than any other president, while Kennedy gave more attention to Hispanics (based upon only two policy statements in 1961) than other presidents. (Was this in response to the "Viva Kennedy" movement among Latin Americans?) Attention to blacks reached its height in the 1960s under Johnson, Nixon, and, particularly, Ford. Carter and Reagan distributed their attention much more widely, but they were

Table 3.5

Presidents' Statements, by Issue Area[a]
(number mentions as % of total)

	Education[b]	Employment[c]	Housing[d]	Other[e]
Mean	30	36	20	10
By Party				
Democrats	19	39	20	11
Republicans	40	32	20	10
By President				
Eisenhower	26	16	0	29
Kennedy	19	47	16	19
Johnson	22	30	17	16
Nixon	60	24	10	16
Ford	61	13	6	6
Carter	15	49	28	10
Reagan	34	54	12	4
Bush	20	60	18	3

[a] Vague references to discrimination, equality of opportunity, and intolerance were left uncoded.
[b] General except for specific references to higher education; busing and school desegregation automatically refer to blacks.
[c] Jobs, labor, pensions, affirmative action, federal employment, but not "enterprise."
[d] Federal and private; subsidies; "fair" housing; includes renters.
[e] Other specific issues like armed forces (Eisenhower), health and public accommodations (Johnson), higher education (Reagan and Bush); voting (all presidents but Bush).

also more interested in the plight of women than was Johnson. This pattern partly reflects the changing agenda of civil rights away from race toward gender in the 1970s and 1980s. However, Bush ties with Johnson as giving least attention to gender.

Perhaps more than any other president, and certainly more than his Republican predecessors, Reagan spread his attention more evenly across all groups, giving attention even to newly emerging groups such as the disabled. Bush gave far more attention to other groups (especially the homeless) than did any other president. These recent presidents faced a different environment, perhaps explained by the expansion and maturation of the civil rights policy area in the 1980s and 1990s.

Table 3.5 moves the emphasis from the target group to the issue areas of civil rights. Almost 76 percent of the policy statements were categorized into one or more subissue areas, but recall that multiple counts inflate these percents.[10] Generally, we observe a somewhat more even distribution of policy statements by subissues than was seen for target groups. Employment receives greatest emphasis (mentioned in 36 percent of policy statements) followed by education (30 percent), housing (20 percent), and *other* (10 percent, including higher education, voting, health, public accommodations, and jury discrimination).

It is much harder to spot any trends in subissue emphases than in target groups. Most of these issue areas have had staying power in presidential policy statements.[11] Kennedy focused more on employment but much less on the controversial education subissue than did most presidents. Johnson spread his attention quite evenly and, more than most presidents, delved into other issue areas such as health, public accommodations, and jury discrimination (*other* category). Nixon and Ford focused the preponderance of their policy statements, far more than any other presidents, on education (particularly opposing the increasingly unpopular tool of "forced" busing). Carter gave greatest attention of any president to housing, being least attentive to education and *other*, perhaps because he felt his preferred goals had already been attained in those subissues.

Reagan renewed the controversy of education by taking many nonsupportive positions and increasing its salience relative to what Carter had done.[12] Reagan also greatly de-emphasized the controversial subissue of housing. He was the first president to oppose the Equal Rights Amendment. Bush expounded on housing and employment but significantly reduced attention to education and had the fewest policy statements in the *other* category. Thus, as expected, the most ideologically committed president, Lyndon Johnson, spread considerable attention across several subissues and target groups.

Party differences also emerge by target group and issue area. Democrats (except Johnson) give much greater attention to women and other groups than do Republicans, except Reagan (see Table 3.4). However, Democrats give much less attention to blacks and age than do Republicans. Democrats also emphasize the housing and employment issue areas (see Table 3.5). Republicans, on the other hand, continue to give major attention to education (a subissue that was predominantly black oriented during the time of those particular presidents). Republicans emphasize employment and housing somewhat less than do Democrats. Contrary to target groups, party differences posited by issue areas are substantial only on education.

Summary

This chapter discussed the policy statements of Reagan and Bush in some detail by target group and issue area. It also offered a comparative perspective on presidents' public communications on civil rights on the dimensions of attention, support, and symbolism. Dramatic differences in tone and focus were revealed, suggesting the importance of a time dimension in the salience of civil rights. Other research suggests that presidential communications may be cyclical (Shull 1989a), but this consideration is beyond the present focus on Reagan and Bush. Differences also occurred among presidents and by parties in seeking action by others and in emphasis on target groups and subissues.

The empirical analysis revealed patterns of presidential attention, support, and symbolism in civil rights. Although their communications are frequently general and rather vague, presidents set broad brushstrokes of preference and relative issue salience. Presidential communications have grown in this media age of increased expectations of presidential performance (as evidenced by increasing length of the yearly *Public Papers of the Presidents*). Although often symbolic, these communications provide an opportunity for presidents to provide policy leadership by "going public" (Kernell 1986).

Presidents since the late 1960s had greater flexibility on whether and how much to communicate. Ronald Reagan and George Bush have been perhaps the presidents most adept at using public messages to assert leadership in the civil rights realm. They not only renewed interest in civil rights, they also recast it. As much as any president, Reagan used public communications to change the policy agenda in civil rights. Bush surprised many by being even more attentive to civil rights than was Reagan on just about every measure. He continued and pushed even further the Reagan legacy of going public and taking strong stands on civil rights matters. On most indicators, Bush's statements were less symbolic and less equivocal than were Reagan's.

Johnson and Reagan gave civil rights considerable attention but differed dramatically on the symbolism of their communications. Reagan's and, particularly, Bush's frequent, lengthy, and conservative statements returned civil rights to a prominent place on the presidential agenda[13] and show that individual presidents matter. Although attention generally to civil rights decreased over Reagan's time in office, it was spread more evenly (some would say diffused) to other target groups and issue areas nearer the end of both his and Bush's terms. Bush greatly renewed attention to civil rights in presidential rhetoric. The party variable was also important in differentiating presidents' civil rights communications. Perhaps reflecting David Mayhew's (1966) notion of the "inclusiveness" of the Democratic party, Democrats are more consistent in their civil rights statements than are Republicans.

"Symbols play a vital role in the policy process" (Elder and Cobb 1983, 142). They focus attention, legitimize power, and justify authority. Certainly it is true that the substance of presidential communications may count for less than symbols. At the same time, presidents do make substantive policy recommendations, though they make relatively few calls for legislative or judicial action. Presidents communicate to assert their policy preferences and to establish their leadership position for posterity. Such symbols may encourage political support for their preferences, and they appear to be a viable leadership strategy for the ideologically committed president. Symbolism perhaps is more important in civil rights than in other policy areas.

This chapter only scratches the surface of identifying symbolism in presidential communications. Attention, support, and statement length, as measures of symbolism, constitute useful components of presidential communications. Calls for action by others in government and target group and issue area emphases are less clearly linked to symbolism. Although some of the components fit together well, others are more elusive. Presumably purely symbolic statements are less likely to translate into tangible actions. The linkage among statements, actions, and results is addressed in the remaining chapters.

Notes

1. *Public Papers of the Presidents*, usually in two annual volumes, are available from presidents Herbert Hoover to the present (except for Franklin Roosevelt). When *Public Papers* volumes are unpublished, I use the *Weekly Compilation of Presidential Documents*, which began in 1965 "as a companion publication to the Public Papers to provide a record of Presidential materials on a more timely basis. Beginning with the administration of Jimmy Carter, the Public Papers series has expanded its coverage to include all material printed in the Weekly Compilation. This expanded coverage now provides the full text of proclamations and Executive orders, announcements of appointments and nomina-

tions, as well as selected statements or remarks of senior administration officials" (*Public Papers of the Presidents* 1977, viii). Since Carter, the two documents are essentially equivalent.

2. This and subsequent citations to this local newspaper are to wire service stories and syndicated columnists. It is cited purely for the author's convenience. The *Times-Picayune* and *States-Item* merged on June 1, 1980.

3. The growing AIDS subissue required special coding rules. I included issues that were primarily civil rights rather than health related (e.g., funds to discourage homosexuality or restrict it in any way, or exempting religious facilities). I excluded AIDS concerns that were designed to prevent drug abuse or emergency relief for cities. Other coding rules were as follows: decisions making congressional employees subject to civil rights laws were included but concerns in which the main thrust was not civil rights (e.g., "welfare" of Native Americans) were excluded. Also excluded were racial quotas about criminal sentencing, which I considered crime or civil liberties.

4. All subsequent citations in this section are to *Public Papers of the Presidents*.

5. Key index words used to obtain remarks on race include Afro Americans, blacks, civil rights, colored, lynching, minorities, Negroes, slavery, and African slave trade. More specific words are used for the three issue areas (see Table 3.5 and Shull 1983, 58–61). This analysis expands and updates Shull 1989a, ch. 3.

6. The *type* of message may also be an important research consideration. Light (1982) and Kessel (1974) used State of the Union messages exclusively in their studies of presidential agenda setting. My own research reveals that civil rights is not even mentioned in any of Kennedy's State of the Union messages. Thus a wider array of documents is desirable. Although civil rights is more important in other public messages, even these documents do not tell the whole civil rights story, particularly for an earlier era when civil rights had not reached the public policy agenda. Private communications and other sources from presidential libraries are also useful to scholars seeking to examine presidential policy preferences, but they are, of course, frequently less subject to systematic examination.

7. The print and column size in the *Public Papers* varies. To achieve parity on the number of lines measure, the data for Eisenhower and Ford were multiplied by a factor of 1.8.

8. By categorizing even neutral remarks as nonsupportive (conservative), there is greater assurance that the supportive (liberal) category is relatively pure.

9. Some might say that Ford made a large number of calls for judicial action because he was a lawyer. However, the only other lawyer in the group, Nixon, made the next fewest calls for judicial action. I surmise that Ford, with conservative civil rights views, was frustrated by Congress and turned to the courts.

10. *Public accommodations* was originally included as a category, but perhaps because of its local nature, it appeared in only four presidential statements (all Johnson). Because it has been a more or less closed subissue since the late 1960s, it was subsequently placed in the *other* category. The remaining 24 percent of statements were too general to categorize.

11. Only voting declined dramatically under Reagan and Bush after the extension of the Voting Rights Act; no voting policy statements were made after

1983. Voting dominated Eisenhower's policy statements, but Bush made none at all—hence my decision to eliminate it as a separate category.

12. In contrast to earlier presidents, Reagan and Bush emphasized higher education. Whereas Carter had sought to integrate predominately black colleges, Reagan and Bush took the more popular (less controversial) position of attempting to preserve their autonomy.

13. Reagan's need to defend his civil rights record may account for his higher-than-anticipated level of support, especially since he had the highest percentage of symbolic communications.

4

Presidents' Legislative and Budget Actions

Presidents' actions help formulate public policy, in contrast to presidents' policy statements, which assert a symbolic agenda leadership. But actions may also be symbolic, particularly if they do not match up with statements. Public statements help presidents set the stage, and they may be essential for social problems to appear subsequently on the government's agenda (Light 1982; Lindblom 1980, 60; Redford 1969, 124; Lowi 1972, 302–3; Shull 1983, ch. 2). However, presidents' civil rights actions do not always square with their statements, and there is more civil rights rhetoric than civil rights action (Shull 1983, 160). I expect rhetoric to be greater than tangible actions, particularly for Presidents Reagan and Bush, who were observed in chapter 3 to be quite rhetorical in the area of civil rights.

How important have presidential actions been over the past four decades in affecting civil rights policies? The answer at first glance may seem obvious. Dwight Eisenhower sent federal troops to integrate the schools in Little Rock, Arkansas, in 1957. Lyndon Johnson fashioned major policy innovations by shepherding the 1964 Civil Rights Act and the 1965 Voting Rights Act through Congress. In the 1980s and 1990s, Ronald Reagan and George Bush appointed conservatives to the courts and myriad other government agencies. But what can we state more systematically about presidential policy actions in civil rights? What methods do presidents have, and how have presidents differed in attempting to influence civil rights policy outcomes?

One way to ascertain whether presidents follow up on their rhetoric is to examine their relations with Congress. Civil rights policy often results from hearings, legislation, budgetary decisions, and other actions by and interactions between the executive and legislative branches. Legislative and budget actions constitute major presidential and congressional involvement in formulating public policy. It took presidential and congressional cooperation in civil rights policy making before much change actually occurred (Rodgers and Bullock 1972, 217). These two actors play important, even crucial, roles in the evolution of civil rights policy.

Apart from substantive legislation, budgetary actions are a crucial presidential tool over both Congress and the executive branch. Budgets, of course, change more often than legislation. Although Congress has enhanced its role since the Budget Impoundment and Control Act (1974), the president's role is still paramount in budgeting (LeLoup 1979, 195). Presidents have several opportunities to provide leadership in budgeting. Here I examine presidential budget *requests* for civil rights agencies, while chapter 6 considers the degree of congressional budget cooperation (*appropriations*) and agency *expenditures*.[1]

Perhaps because of the relative ease of proposing rather than implementing or evaluating, presidents come to believe that formulating programs is the best way to assert their leadership and to make a distinctive mark in history. Although Richard Neustadt (1980, 7) calls the president the "Great Initiator," any president finds other actors asserting important roles in policy formulation. Thus, to make their mark, presidents must get other decision makers to respond. Still, the wide variety of policy actions available to presidents (legislative, budgetary, administrative, and judicial) provide considerable opportunities for presidents to formulate civil rights policy should they choose such an active leadership role. The first two actions, legislation and budgets, are covered here. Chapter 5 discusses presidents' administrative and judicial actions.

Legislative Actions

Perhaps the most visible presidential actions in civil rights are legislative ones: requests for legislation and positions on congressional votes. Requests to Congress (specific presidential proposals) and positions on legislative votes provide evidence of policy formulation, showing whether the president follows through on his agenda statements. Presidential initiatives to Congress are important indicators of the policy role of the chief executive. Although we would expect presidents' statements to translate into later actions, legislative requests and vote positions require more commitment and hard choices than do mere public statements.[2] Such specific program initiatives help to clarify the developing relationship between Congress and the president. Requests, vote positions, and their later disposition tell us much about actor strategies, choices, emphases, and power.

This analysis updates and expands upon my previous work on civil rights (Shull 1989a), which also divides roll call votes into amendments and key votes[3] and by target groups and subissues. Additionally, I consider the presidents' *direction* (liberal or conservative) and *magnitude* of support in their legislative positions. This section provides a detailed look at presidents' program *requests* and their *positions* on roll call votes in Congress, overall and by target groups and subissues.

Expectations and Measurement

Because legislative actions require a specific commitment, some falloff from presidential statements occurs, particularly from such presidents as Kennedy, who espouse symbolic rhetoric but take fewer tangible actions. Also, ideologically committed presidents, such as Lyndon Johnson, will see requests and position-taking as their major opportunity to influence congressional decision making directly. I expect presidents to be more assertive in their position-taking than in requesting civil rights legislation. Such a finding allows an assessment of the degree of symbolism in legislative actions because it is easier to take a position on an existing vote than initiate new legislation. Furthermore, I expect more liberal presidential positions on certain target groups (e.g., women) and subissues (e.g., employment). The extent that presidents offer legislative leadership should vary by individual presidents and by political party.

This study contends that the Congressional Quarterly (CQ) box score for legislative requests is a useful measure of presidential policy preferences. It excludes nominations, routine appropriations requests, and proposals by administrative actors other than the president. Also excluded are all but the most definitive and specific legislative requests.[4] Although the box score suffers from several drawbacks, it allows systematic comparison (across time, policy areas, political parties, and presidents) of the public legislative requests of modern presidents. While the box score is no longer collected by CQ, scholars still use this aggregate measure of what the president proposes to Congress in quantitative research (Spitzer 1983; Hammond and Fraser 1984; Rivers and Rose 1985; LeLoup and Shull 1979; Edwards 1980b, 13–18; Shull 1983; Cohen 1982). In an important recent study, Mark Peterson (1990) updated the box score and persuasively argued its usefulness.

The president may also assert leadership by taking positions on legislative votes. The relationship of position-taking and requests is important in this analysis. A large proportion of the former to the latter may suggest a high degree of symbolism in legislative actions. Congressional Quarterly records the extent to which presidents take such positions, another type of assertiveness. One can also determine whether such positions are supportive (liberal) or conservative on civil rights.[5] During the legislative process, some of these votes and positions are actually changed. Although many votes measuring support deal with executive-initiated measures, they are now in the legislative arena in often-revised form. These CQ measures are also representative of all roll call votes (Hammond and Fraser 1980, 42). Taking a cue from George Edwards (1985), I include several *types* of votes on civil rights.

Congressional Quarterly has used the same criteria for more than thirty years to measure presidential victories on its legislative roll call positions, so the measure is at least consistent for time-series analysis. *Number* of requests or positions taken per year in office is a measure of presidential assertiveness of legislative leadership. I adopt this measure (rather than *percent* of total votes where positions are taken) for two reasons. First, number of positions is a standardized measure not dependent upon the vast differences in number of votes in any given year. Second, when few votes occur, the percentage measure is unreliable because of insufficient cases. This is particularly the case when studying subsets of votes (e.g., amendments and key votes). When examining specific target groups and issue areas, I categorize presidential position-taking into pro (liberal) or con (conservative) positions toward civil rights. This score allows an examination of presidents' relative support for target groups and subissues.

Results

General

Quantitative data reveal presidential relations with Congress on civil rights, beginning first with average number of vote positions and legis-

Table 4.1

Presidential Legislative Actions in Civil Rights
(number per year)

		Positions Taken on Votes			Symbolism^d (vote positions as % requests)
	Requests^a	All	Amendments^b	Key Votes^c	
Mean	5.3	6.0	3.8	1.1	88
By Party					
Democrats	9.9	9.3	6.4	1.4	106
Republicans	2.9	3.5	1.3	0.8	83
By President^e					
Truman	4.0	1.5	0.25	0.25	267
Eisenhower	6.7	1.0	0.38	0.38	670
Kennedy	11.8	20.2	0.33	0.67	58
Johnson	1.6	6.9	14.4	4.4	23
Nixon	2.0	0	3.5	1.6	0
Ford	—	1.8^f	—	—	—
Carter	—	2.9	1.0	0.50	—
Reagan	—	8.7	0.9	0.38	—
Bush	—	2.0	1.7	—	—

^a Based on 23 years, 1953–75; see chapter discussion for definition.
^b Based on 35 years, 1957–91.
^c Based on 46 years, 1945–91, but positions coded by author prior to 1957.
^d The greater the value, the less symbolic the action.
^e Number of years are Truman = 8 (key votes only); Eisenhower = 8 (4 for roll calls and amendments); Kennedy = 3; Johnson = 5; Nixon = 5.5; Ford = 2.5 (1.5 for initiatives); Carter = 4; Reagan = 8; Bush = 3 (except requests where no data available after 1975).
^f The values are rounded to the highest number. For example, Carter took positions on seven votes during four years, equaling this figure.

lative requests presidents make per year. Table 4.1 shows that the average number of both per year is similar. Literally thousands of legislative requests were made during the period for which data are available (1953–75), but only 3 percent concern civil rights. Thus, presidents make relatively few requests in the civil rights area (only 5.3 per year). Table 4.1 also shows the results for average numbers of positions taken: on all civil rights votes, on amendments, and on key votes. Relatively few amendments and key votes occur. With some exceptions these results are similar to requests, but presidents do take a higher percentage of positions on civil rights (42 percent) than on all issues (30 percent). These findings clearly reveal fewer presidential legislative actions (*requests and positions taken*) than public statements.

Finally, Table 4.1 provides a measure of symbolism: the ratio of requests to positions. The results overall suggest that presidents request specific legislation nearly as often as they take vote positions (88 percent of the time). Thus, legislative actions do not appear to be as symbolic as were presidents' public policy statements.

Legislative actions are also discernible by target group and subissues, although some vote positions could not be so designated. Generally, presidents take liberal positions (79 percent) on votes targeted to specific groups (see Table 4.2). The target group on which the most conservative positions are taken is Native Americans/Hispanics, where just 14 percent of the few vote positions taken are liberal. The most liberal positions are taken on age discrimination.

Results of the analysis by issue area do not differ dramatically from votes divided by target group. Table 4.3 presents these results; generally all presidents take liberal positions on votes by subissue area 76 percent of the time. Housing is the subissue with the most liberal position-taking (followed closely by employment) and education, at 67 percent, is the least liberal. Thus, differences emerge among target groups and subissues when examining the data overall.

Individual Presidents

Table 4.1 reveals dramatic and interesting differences in legislative actions among individual presidents.[6] On both measures, Lyndon Johnson was the most and Gerald Ford was the least assertive president legislatively on civil rights. Generally, the number of requests increased from Eisenhower through Johnson (who made the most), dropping precipitously with Nixon and Ford. Although these box score data are not available beyond 1975, impressionistic information suggests fairly high activism for Carter (my personal interviews list fair housing as one of six priorities during 1979) and low requests from Reagan and Bush.

Eisenhower and Kennedy took very few positions on civil rights votes but made relatively more requests. Thus, their legislative actions were least symbolic among four presidents. Johnson's figures on position-taking are even more dramatic in comparison with other presidents than are his legislative requests. He took positions on congressional votes nearly three times more often than Bush, the next closest, and twenty times more often than Kennedy. The considerable position-taking relative to legislative requests gives Johnson and Bush higher symbolism than their two predecessors, however. Ford made half the yearly requests of Eisenhower and was the only president not to take a vote position. Carter's legislative actions were less frequent than his civil rights statements, and he ranks lower than Nixon on all indicators. Reagan's very modest legislative activism (such as taking less than one position on amendments and averaging just over one-third of a key vote position per year) is divergent from expectations for an ideologically committed president.

In an examination of individual presidents on all target groups, the Democrats reveal identical liberal scores (see Table 4.2).[7] Johnson took positions on *all* target groups, the only president to do so, while Kennedy confined his legislative positions to blacks. Greater variance on liberalism appears among Republican presidents; surprisingly, Reagan took liberal positions most often and Eisenhower took such supportive positions least often, only 20 percent of the time. Nixon was fairly liberal on votes dealing with women, but, like Eisenhower and Bush, he was conservative on votes related to blacks. Reagan's liberalism, particularly on the *other* category, is surprising, but he was conservative on legislation for blacks, and, particularly, for women and Native Americans/Hispanics. Overall, Bush was much more conservative than Reagan, especially on his positions regarding blacks. His few liberal positions were largely reserved for the *other* category.

The individual president category is little more discriminating than political party when examining issue areas because each of the four Republicans were liberal on a similarly small percentage of legislative votes, just as the three Democrats had perfect liberal scores. Although few cases are available for Republicans, surprisingly Bush was the most liberal Republican at 44 percent, while Nixon took the least liberal subissue positions (see Table 4.3, page 82). Republicans took especially conservative vote positions on education, but they were most supportive of the housing category. These findings generally support expectations.

Political Party

Some of the dramatic differences by presidential party have already been revealed. It is evident from Table 4.1 that Democrats request far

Table 4.2

Liberalism of Presidents' Civil Rights Vote Positions, by Target Group
(% liberal)[a]

	Blacks (%L)	Hispanics/ Native Americans (%L)	Women (%L)	Age (%L)	Other (%L)	Total N[b]	Total %L
Mean	76	14	75	100	89	232/295	79
By Party							
Democrats	100	100	100	100	100	192/192	100
Republicans	39	0	50		62	38/93	41
By President							
Eisenhower	25			0		1/5	20
Kennedy	100					3/3	100
Johnson	100	100	100	100	100	181/181	100
Nixon	44		50		0	18/43	42
Ford						—	—
Carter	100		100		100	8/8	100
Reagan	38	0	0		67	11/18	61
Bush	31		60		83	13/27	48

[a]See Table 3.4 for categories.
[b]Numerator = number liberal positions; denominator = number of positions on civil rights. To simplify the table, the cell Ns are not included but are available from the author.

more civil rights legislation than do Republicans (more than three times as much on a yearly basis). Democrats also are much more assertive on position-taking than are Republicans on each measure, and this is particularly evident on amendments (primarily due to Johnson). Democrats were much less symbolic than Republicans by making even more requests than taking vote positions (see Table 4.1). The three Democrats *always* took positions supportive of civil rights, while Republicans supported liberal votes much less often.

Significant party differences occur whenever Republicans take positions on votes affecting particular groups. Party differences are most pronounced on legislation relating to Native Americans/Hispanics and then to blacks (see Table 4.2). Table 4.3 reveals essentially the same partisan differences by issue area; only 38 percent of Republican positions are liberal. Partisan differences are greatest on education and employment, the former due largely to busing. These findings by political party strongly support expectations.

Table 4.3

Liberalism of Presidents' Civil Rights Vote Positions, by Issue Area
(% liberal)[a]

	Education (%L)	Employment (%L)	Housing (%L)	Other[b] (%L)	Total N[c]	%L
Mean	67	88	90	85	155/203	76
By Party						
Democrats	100	100	100	100	125/125	100
Republicans	30	32	50	39	30/78	38
By President						
Eisenhower	33	0		50	2/6	33
Kennedy				100	3/3	100
Johnson	100	100	100	100	115/115	100
Nixon	29	0		100	9/34	26
Ford					—	—
Carter	100		100	100	7/7	100
Reagan	33	0	100	10	6/21	29
Bush		43	33	60	12/27	44

[a] See Table 3.5 for categories.
[b] Other includes 39 public accommodations subissues under Johnson and 26 voting subissues.
[c] Numerator = number liberal positions; denominator = number of positions on civil rights. To simplify the table, the cell Ns are not included but are available from the author.

Other Legislative Actions

Other legislative actions also are possible. On rare occasions, presidents veto legislation contrary to their policy preferences. There have been only six vetoes of civil rights legislation in U.S. history, one each by Andrew Johnson, Truman, and Carter, two by Reagan, and one by Bush. Reagan's veto of the 1988 Civil Rights Restoration Act and Bush's veto of the 1990 civil rights bill generated negative publicity for their administrations. These vetoes constitute our cases in this chapter. The vetoes allowed these presidents to prevail on policy terms and pleased conservatives yet proved costly in alienating the minority community (Sinclair 1991, 170). Bush, particularly, ended up pleasing no one.

Less visible actions but no less important are informal contacts with congressional leaders through congressional lobbying (legislative liaison), personal persuasion, priority setting, and committee testimony. I now summarize the use of some of these and other legislative devices by Presidents Reagan and Bush.

Both Presidents Reagan and Bush were effective in congressional relations. Despite wide philosophical differences with Congress, Reagan, with his friendly manner, had a better personal relationship with House Speaker Thomas P. ("Tip") O'Neill than had Carter, who was less comfortable with politicians. Bush's relationship with congressional leaders was more restrained. Senate Minority Leader Robert Dole had challenged Bush for the presidency in 1988. Bush's antipathy for some Democratic leaders, especially Richard Gephardt (D-Mo.), is well documented in journalistic accounts.

Reagan and Bush developed strong liaison teams on Capitol Hill, again in contrast to Jimmy Carter. Reagan's staff was headed by veteran Max Friedersdorf but was otherwise not very experienced in congressional relations. Reagan relied on his staff heavily, but Bush preferred a more personal approach. Despite having an experienced team, Bush personally and frequently contacted members of Congress. Perhaps this is one reason for the inordinate success of his vetoes during four years in office (only one of thirty-six was overridden).

The Reagan agenda was clear from the beginning. As had Lyndon Johnson, Reagan moved quickly to transform political values into concrete proposals. Yet he was not able to reduce government the way LBJ had expanded it (Jones 1988a, 56). Reagan's domestic and economic goals were clearer than were Bush's. Compared to Reagan's desire for contraction, Bush give little indication of what agenda direction he wanted, admitting he lacked the "vision thing." He offered little legislation, and although he seemed to react well to international problems, he seemed perplexed by matters outside the realm of foreign policy. Bush proposed few initiatives early but, following criticism late in 1991, brought more domestic and economic initiatives into his 1992 reelection campaign. All in all, neither president hesitated to challenge Congress when they disagreed, as the following cases illustrate.

Legislative Cases

Case I: The 1988 Civil Rights Restoration Act

On March 3, 1988, the House passed the landmark Civil Rights Restoration Act (PL 100–259) broadening protections for women, minorities, the elderly, and the disabled. Some considered the act the most significant civil rights legislation in twenty years. The original bill, S 557, was designed to reverse the 1984 *Grove City* decision narrowing the scope of four major civil rights laws to prevent taxpayer financing of discrimination.[8] The act clarified that all aspects of an organization must comply with civil rights requirements if any part or program of entities receives federal funding. Reagan quickly vetoed the bill in March 1988. The congressional override, just five days later, dealt the administration a severe political defeat. Although the bill was not initially very partisan in Congress, Reagan's views and actions made it more so, and the legislation spurred an institutional struggle between the two branches of government.

As early as 1984, Reagan had spoken out against broad legislation. He opposed the bill Congress passed while voicing support for more limited legislation. In threatening to veto the bill, Reagan charged that it

dramatically expands the scope of federal jurisdiction over state and local governments and the private sector.... It diminishes the freedom of the private citizen to order his or her life and unnecessarily imposes the heavy burden of compliance with extensive federal regulations and paperwork on many elements of American society. (*Public Papers of the Presidents*, March 1, 1988, 287)

The act was very controversial. A disputed abortion provision alarmed Catholic hospitals, which feared they might be required to provide such services, and opponents encouraged these fears. The final bill compromised and had a religious tenets clause that exempted any entity controlled by a religious organization from its provisions. The original bill had encompassed both private and public organizations that received federal funding. Other compromises somewhat diffused controversy. Eventually the bill also exempted farmers, food stamp recipients, and others.

Yet controversies on both substantive and procedural grounds persisted. Supporters argued that the bill did not create new legislation; it was a simple restoration of the four laws. Representative Peter Rodino (D-N.J.) stated that "it merely restores the status quo" (*Congressional Quarterly Weekly Reports*, March 26, 1988, 774). House Speaker Jim Wright (D-Tex.) stated: "The new law will not end illegal discrimination. But it does represent a step forward in making America truly a land of equal opportunity for all" *(New Orleans Times-Picayune, August 23, 1988, A6)*. Others called it a "major step toward eradicating discrimination subsidized by federal money" *(Congressional Quarterly Weekly Reports, March 5, 1988, 563)*, and Representative Augustus Hawkins (D-Calif.) said, "Anyone who accepts federal money should not discriminate" *(Congressional Quarterly Weekly Reports, March 5, 1988, 563)*. Many religious groups (such as the American Jewish Congress, the American Baptists, and the United Methodists) favored the legislation. Women's groups reluctantly supported the bill despite more restrictive abortion provisions.

Some saw Republican opposition to the bill as a continuing anti-civil rights stance. Ralph Neas of the Leadership Conference on Civil Rights stated: "The White House complaints have a familiar ring. They are reminiscent of arguments voiced long ago by Reagan when he opposed landmark civil rights legislation of the 1960s" *(National Journal, March 19, 1988, 756)*. The administration had succeeded in defeating an earlier bill in 1984 that would have banned sex discrimination in colleges receiving federal aid. Here again conservatives effectively used the filibuster in the Senate to thwart civil rights legislation that had passed the House earlier that year by the huge margin of 375–32. The bill died until Democrats captured the Senate in January 1987, but the legislation did not pass both chambers until 1988. By then, supporters could not be denied, since the political environment was ripe for passage.

Perhaps sensing their vulnerability, opponents admitted that the *Grove City* decision needed modification but thought S 557 was far too encompassing. President Reagan stated that the bill "dramatically expands the scope of federal jurisdiction over state and local governments and the private sector, from churches and synagogues to farmers, grocery stores, and businesses of all sizes" *(Congressional Quarterly Weekly Reports, March 5, 1988, 563)*. He also called it "a particular threat to religious liberty" *(National Journal, March 5, 1988, 756)*. Other critics stated it would

bring federal intervention into the churches, synagogues, 'mom and pop' grocery stores that take food stamps, and business enterprises that have never been subject to federal civil rights laws. . . . There would be onerous regulations and paperwork, and the result would be stores who would refuse to accept customers with food stamps and businesses who would opt out of programs that provide federal aid. (*Congressional Quarterly Weekly Reports*, March 5, 1988, 565)

Gary Brauer, the conservative director of Reagan's Office for Policy Development, opposed S 557 because it was vague and poorly written, provided assistance to undeserving persons, and was a backdoor way of affording protection to alcoholics and drug addicts (*National Journal*, March 19, 1988, 757).

The legislation also generated controversy on procedural grounds. Opponents charged that the "no amendment" procedure prevented the House from working its will. "The chance to amend is important," Minority Leader Robert Michael (R-Ill.) said, "to help clarify congressional intent" (*Congressional Quarterly Weekly Reports*, March 5, 1988, 565). Several conservative members saw irony in a civil rights bill debated under a procedure that denied members their rights. Representative Dan Lungren (R-Calif.) said, "Democrats were being overtly political with their no amendment strategy" (*Congressional Quarterly Weekly Reports*, March 5, 1988, 565). Yet opponents could see the handwriting on the wall.

Conservatives in Congress and in the White House made several last-ditch efforts to prevent passage. The president proposed a substitute motion that would allow more institutions to escape regulation on religious grounds. In calling for a civil rights "protection" act, Reagan wanted to "eliminate invidious discrimination . . . while preserving their basic freedom from government interference and control" (*Congressional Quarterly Weekly Reports*, March 19, 1988, 752). Most viewed Reagan's efforts as too little too late. His last-minute substitute was not widely regarded as a serious effort, especially considering it was not offered until he vetoed S 557.

The conservative Moral Majority flooded congressional switchboards and mail rooms opposing the legislation. The spokesperson Jerry Falwell sent a letter saying S 557 "could force churches to hire a 'practicing' [*sic*] active homosexual, drug addict with AIDS to be a teacher or youth pastor" (*Congressional Quarterly Weekly Reports*, March 19, 1988, 709). But the barrage was too highly organized to be interpreted as spontaneous. Even conservative lawmakers thought the Moral Majority had gone too far, and, demonstrating leadership, Congress did not overreact.

The final Senate vote was 73–24, with six votes more than necessary to override a presidential veto. All Democrats present voted for the bill, while Republicans were badly split (21 for, 24 against). The House voted 292–133 to override and, again, Democrats were more united than were Republicans (D: 240–10; R: 52–123). Eight Republican House members who initially supported the bill voted to uphold the president while several Republicans in the Senate also switched to support the president. Considerable partisan splitting occurred over the legislation. Many Republicans feared voting against civil rights in an election year. According to Senator Orrin Hatch (R-Utah), "People are just scared to death to vote against a civil rights bill, no matter how bad it is" (*Congressional Quarterly Weekly Reports*, March 26, 1988, 774). Reagan lost a tough battle that was unwinnable, and thereafter the initiative shifted to Congress, which assumed a greater leadership role in civil rights.

Case II: The 1991 Civil Rights Act[9]

On February 7, 1990, Democrats in Congress proposed legislation to reverse six Supreme Court decisions of the previous year that made it more difficult to prove job discrimination. Edward Kennedy (D-Mass.) in the Senate and Augustus Hawkins (D-Calif.) in the House, chairs of the relevant committees in their respective chambers, introduced the legislation simultaneously. The six decisions affected an 1866 law and Title VII of the 1964 Civil Rights Act and narrowed the remedies to combat job discrimination, particularly limiting damage awards.[10]

The 1990 bill contained numerous provisions to overturn these court decisions. It granted victims the right to recover compensatory damages and, in extreme cases, punitive damages. Either side in a discrimination suit could demand a jury trial. The most controversial provisions were the shifting of the burden of proof from the employee to the employer and expanding coverage beyond race to discrimination based upon gender, disability, religion, and national origin. Many amendments were made along the way to placate critics, among them conservatives in Congress, the White House, and the business community. In the end, even extensive revisions failed to satisfy opponents.

The legislation was initiated in Congress with very little White House involvement early on. It soon took on a partisan tone in the Senate, where most of the debate and controversy took place. Proponents were represented by Senator Edward Kennedy (D-Mass.), who sought the broadest possible scope for the legislation, while the opposition, led by Senator Orrin Hatch (R-Utah), desired more restrictive legislation. These two had represented their respective sides during debates on the 1988 bill, following which the Democrats successfully overrode Reagan's veto. They reflected the ideological extremes: Kennedy said "quotas, schmotas" to Republican charges, and Hatch called the bill a "radical reworking of Title VII" (*Congressional Quarterly Weekly Reports*, July 21, 1990, 2312, and April 17, 1990, 1078).

Through various parliamentary maneuvers, the Senate leadership also became involved. Minority Leader Robert Dole (R-Kans.), who had supported previous civil rights legislation, criticized the Democratic leadership for "ramming [the bill] down our throats." After a cloture vote to cut off debate on July 17, Dole stated: "If we're going to be treated like a bunch of bums on this side of the aisle, there won't be any agreements on anything" (*New Orleans Times-Picayune*, July 18, 1990, A3). Although he directed his ire at Democratic leader George Mitchell (D-Maine), Dole's frustration was aimed partly at fellow Republicans, some of whom supported a cloture motion to cut off debate and also voted for final passage. Dole even threatened to resign. In the House, Republican members walked out of committee meetings on several occasions, criticizing Democratic rules they considered arbitrary. Thus partisanship was substantial and hampered cooperation.

Dole and other moderate Republicans sought more restrictive legislation and pushed an administration alternative. Senator Kennedy and White House Chief of Staff John Sununu met on several occasions to resolve disagreements on the bill. After eight weeks of negotiation, the talks collapsed amid "mutual recriminations." Compromises were adopted along the way, however. Employees would have to show that discrimination resulted from "specific practices," and the dollar amounts of damages were limited. Still, partisan deadlock continued.

Although the Bush administration agreed that some of the Court decisions needed modification, it felt no major response was necessary. The administration seemed to favor most provisions for blacks but not for other groups. Nancy Fulco, human resources attorney of the U.S. Chamber of Commerce, stated, "The Administration has gotten itself caught in a snare" (*Congressional Quarterly Weekly Reports*, April 21, 1990, 1196). But the Bush administration denied inconsistency. Deputy Attorney General Donald B. Ayer said: "Racial discrimination is uniquely abhorrent. . . . There is no question that race is different" (*Congressional Quarterly Weekly Reports*, March 21, 1990, 1197). Other conservatives apparently conceded that Title VII did not allow enough remedies for job discrimination.

The Bush agenda on civil rights was unclear and steered a vague, cautious path. The administration wanted to give more latitude to companies to defend their employment policies and allow practices resulting in "unintended discrimination." Administration supporters of the legislation included Arthur Fletcher, chair of the Civil Rights Commission, and Louis Sullivan, Secretary of Health and Human Services. However, opponents included such "heavy hitters" as Sununu, Attorney General Richard Thornburgh, and Vice-President Dan Quayle. Thus a major struggle arose within the administration over whether to sign the bill; mixed signals frequently resulted. Even Senator Hatch thought an agreement had been reached, but the White House opposed the legislation as passed in the conference committee.

In issuing his veto on October 22, Bush stated, "I deeply regret having to take this action with respect to a bill bearing such a title, especially since it contains provisions that I strongly endorse" (*New York Times*, October 23, 1990, A1). Bush urged Congress to pass the administration version of the act early in its next session. The Democratic party chair Ron Brown stated: "At the cross roads of his presidency, George Bush has made it clear where he and his Republican Party really stand" (*New York Times*, October 23, 1990, A1, B7). Others criticized the administration for "bowing to the right wing of the Republican party" (*Congressional Quarterly Weekly Reports*, April 7, 1990, 1078) and for "failing the litmus test" (*Congressional Quarterly Weekly Reports*, October 20, 1990, 3519) on civil rights.

Many wondered about the possible political implications of these decisions. The veto represented the first defeat of a major civil rights bill in the last quarter century. Voting in Congress had been highly partisan. No Democrats opposed the legislation and several moderate Republicans supported it.[11] Democrats hoped that it would help their candidates for office and hurt Republicans, but it had little effect on the 1990 election result. As is usually the case, incumbents won overwhelmingly. The only incumbent senator losing reelection was Rudy Boschwitz (R-Minn.), who switched at the last minute and supported the legislation. If anything, the Democratic unity was somewhat illusory; many southerners who supported the bill in 1990 were pressured by their conservative constituents. Indeed, Bush aides were confident they would have enough votes to sustain another veto in 1991 if necessary.

Early in 1991 President Bush rebuffed efforts by Senator John Danforth (R-Mo.) to produce compromise legislation. Both sides were at loggerheads. Bush continued to call the legislation a "quota bill," but at least two events began to mute his opposition. First, the debate over Clarence Thomas's nomination to the Supreme Court angered many women who recalled that Bush had opposed expanding the legislation's damage limitations to discrimination against women. Second, some members of Congress feared a no vote would be interpreted as support for the controversial views of Louisiana gubernatorial candidate David Duke. Representative William Jefferson (D-La.) said of Bush, "I think he sensed the changing political climate in the country" (*New Orleans Times-Picayune*, November 8, 1991, A1).

After these events, Republican senators, including John Warner (R-Va.), notified President Bush that they would vote for the legislation, thereby no longer upholding his 1990 veto margin. Finally, both sides reached a compromise that limited damages and defined legal defenses for employers accused of hiring discrimination. Although President Bush compromised the most, senators accepted changes that applied the bill's job protections, and those of other antidiscriminatory laws, to its own employees and those of the White House who had previously been exempt. The long deadlock was resolved by large margins of passage (93–5 in the Senate and 381–38 in the House). Bush signed the legislation on November 21, 1991.

Patterns of Cases

Despite greater partisanship in the 1980s, the 1988 Civil Rights Restoration Act was a genuine example of congressional leadership. Leaders used legislative techniques to overcome delay, amendment, and other dilatory tactics. The case revealed a real power struggle between the branches (even including the judiciary, as Congress used the legislation to overturn Supreme Court decisions with which it disagreed). Congress saw Reagan as vulnerable on civil rights but could not prevail there or on extending fair housing until 1988, Reagan's last (lameduck) year in office. The legislation revealed the strong role of interest groups, particularly the resurrection of liberal ones and the seeming decline of the religious right. It seemed harder than ever to be anti-civil rights, particularly in an election year.

Fear of electoral repercussion was only one implication of the controversy over the Civil Rights Restoration Act. Reagan's overall support in Congress during 1988 dipped to 43.5 percent, the lowest of any prior president since Congressional Quarterly began counting. However, Reagan increased his support from the public; his recovery in the Gallup standings was substantial. The White House was a spoiler rather than a leader, leaving direction on civil rights to Congress. Little leadership came from presidential candidates either. Although concerned that it might prove costly in the election, Vice President Bush refused to depart from Reagan's opposition. Presumably he was uncomfortable with opposing the act but seems not to have suffered politically.

The 1991 Civil Rights Act involved extraordinary efforts at resolution (particularly through secret negotiations), but the initial result was failure and deadlock. The struggle over definition and coverage of civil rights legislation continued well into 1991. Democrats tried to redefine the issue from race to gender, while Republicans continued to raise the specter of quotas. The latter seemed the most important symbolically as polls showed growing black and white division over quotas and affirmative action.

Being anti–civil rights did not hurt Republicans in the 1990 elections. Bush seemed unstoppable following the Persian Gulf War and at the beginning of the 1992 presidential campaign. Extraordinary resolution was possible in late 1991 only when changes in the political environment forced the president to compromise. However, Bush's legislative support in 1990 dropped even lower than Reagan's lowest, setting an all-time record. Although Bush recovered somewhat in 1991, his support dropped again in 1992. The long-running controversy raised the political temperature of civil rights policy.

Budget Actions

Budget Requests

Apart from legislation, budgets are an important part of presidential policy making. Presidents can set priorities and the broad outline of budgets without being greatly involved personally. The Office of Management and Budget (OMB) does nearly all the detailed groundwork in preparing the budget. Truman and Ford as former members of congressional appropriations committees were very active as presidents in budget building, while other presidents, particularly Nixon during the height of the Watergate scandal, were not (LeLoup 1979).

The president is required to submit a budget to Congress each year. One important policy action available to presidents is budget requests, found in *The Budget of the United States Government*. Budget "enthusiasts" are likely to exert personal involvement in budgeting (LeLoup 1979). Such requests can be examined systematically, and I offer this assessment next.

Expectations

What should we expect from a systematic examination of presidential budget requests? Surely substantial differences in the propensity for presidents to commit funds should relate to their legislative actions. Democrats, particularly Johnson, should reveal the greatest budget support, while Republicans, particularly Reagan, should request the least for civil rights agencies. Until Reagan, I expect generally high support for the general civil rights agency, the U.S. Civil Rights Commission, but greater variation for agencies in the three subissues.[12] Republicans probably are more supportive of employment than housing.

Collecting budget data on a policy area like civil rights is a very difficult undertaking.[13] The cynic might think that Congress, presidents, and the OMB go out of their way to make the process complex. Additionally, many changes in the law and the reporting of budgets further confound comparison and systematic analysis. Table 4.4 provides the average growth in presidents' civil rights budget requests in constant dollars. I derived this figure by dividing the current dollar budget authority estimate by the consumer price index. The purpose is to look at average annual growth overall, by president, and by party, controlling for inflation.

Results

The figures in Table 4.4 show generally that presidents have requested budget increases even when controlling for inflation (4.7 percent yearly increase in overall requests). I posited an inverse relationship between legislative and budget actions. Since legislative actions did not reveal this general upward trend, some support exists for the ex-

Table 4.4

Presidents' Budget Requests[a]
(% growth in constant $)

Issue Area Agency[b]	General (CRC%)	Education (CRD%)	Employment (EEOC%)	Housing (FHEO%[d])	Means
Overall	-0.8	6.0	9.1	4.0	4.7
By Party					
Democrats	2.2	10.4	18.5	0.50	9.9
Republicans	-2.0	3.4	5.3	4.0	2.9
By President					
Kennedy		35.0	33.3		35.0
Johnson	7.4	11.4	16.2		17.4
Nixon	8.7	10.3	5.0	4.8	10.0
Ford	4.5	-7.5	7.3	27.9	7.5
Carter	-1.8	3.0	1.5	0.5	2.3
Reagan	-4.6	-0.36	-5.7	6.3	2.8
Bush[e]	-58.7	13.0		-8.9	-60.3

Sources: OMB, *The Budget of the United States Government*, annual, budget authority estimate for requests; Department of Labor, *Handbook of Labor Statistics* (Washington, D.C.: GPO, 1983), 323, consumer price index for all items for constant dollar deflator (1967 = 100), updated by Council of Economic Advisers, *Economic Indicators* (Washington, D.C.: GPO, December 1991), 23. Deflator for 1991 based on June.

[a]To simplify the table the *N*s are not included but are available from the author.

[b]Agencies are the Civil Rights Commission (CRC), Civil Rights Division (CRD) of the Department of Justice (DOJ), the Equal Employment Opportunity Commission (EEOC), and the Fair Housing and Equal Opportunity program (FHEO) in the Department of Housing and Urban Development.

[c]General sources for Civil Rights Division: OMB, *Budget*, App., listed as "civil rights matters" under "Legal Activities"; *Budget* 1957; *Budget* 1984, special analysis, table entitled "Federal Outlays for Principal Civil Rights Enforcement Agencies" under "Division of Civil Rights," Department of Justice.

[d]From line item in the budget under Management and Administration, "Equal Opportunity," research, regulatory and insurance programs. Fair Housing and Equal Opportunity." Fair Housing and Equal Opportunity as a separate program (1971–76), but same figures are listed under Department of Management and Administration, Operation Fund, as a line item.

[e]The data are for FY 1990 based on the FY 1992 budget.

pectation for this type of administrative action. The general trend in budget requests reflects decreases in percentage change requests for each succeeding president but one, however.

Individual presidents make quite different budget requests for civil rights agencies as observed in Table 4.4. As anticipated, Nixon reduced requests in employment drastically from Johnson, but only marginally in education and actually increased requests (even controlling for inflation) in the *general* civil rights category. Except for the single year in education under Kennedy, Johnson, as expected, does reveal the greatest aggregated budget support for civil rights (17.4 percent average on all agencies). We have already seen Nixon's higher than expected requests. Although only two fiscal years are available for Ford, the data reveal dramatic decreases in his requests for three categories but inexplicably huge increases in funds for housing. Although Carter reveals increases over Ford in employment and, particularly, education, he greatly reduced requests in housing and in civil rights generally. The huge inflation rate during Carter's administration swallowed up what was actually a considerable increase in current dollars.

Reagan actually averaged higher total budget requests over the course of his administration than did Carter. He increased requests substantially for housing while decreasing requests considerably for civil rights overall (Civil Rights Commission), controlling for inflation. The Bush data must be interpreted cautiously since only one year's worth of data were available (because of the two-year time lag). His overall cuts are dramatic, particularly for the Civil Rights Commission.

These findings lend support to expectations about differences by individual presidents and presidential party. Overall, Democrats average much greater budget requests than Republicans. Republican presidents have greater budget support than Democrats only for the housing agency, but gave less support to the *general* category, education, and employment.[14] These findings are surprising because Republicans were expected to support only the less controversial *general* and employment subissues more than Democrats. Table 4.4 provides mixed results for budget actions, but overall support by Democrats averages well over three times that of Republicans.

The figures in Table 4.4 reveal considerable differences in presidents' budget requests by issue areas. Contrary to expectation, average growth in presidential budget requests was greatest in employment and least in *general*. While the annual change in constant dollars of only 4.0 percent overall for housing makes that subissue appear to change very incrementally, we have seen that the individual president figures fluctuate wildly.[15] The dramatic decreases for the CRC must be due to its growing controversy under Republicans Reagan and Bush. Also as expected, party differences in budget requests occurred in each subissue.

Other Budget Actions

Besides overseeing the preparation of the annual budget, the president has several opportunities to influence taxing and spending decisions. First, although impoundment is now more difficult, a president can request a deferral (proposal that the funds not be spent that year) or a rescission (proposal that the funds be returned to the Treasury; see Fisher 1975). Deferrals are automatically accepted unless Congress passes a motion to the contrary; a vote of Congress must approve rescissions.

Second, a president has the power to veto appropriations bills, and at least one of the few vetoes observed on civil rights in the modern era (Carter in 1980) was on an appropriations amendment. Although Congress passes its budget in the form of concurrent budget resolutions (which do not need the signature of the president), these do not create spending authority. The resolutions are binding only on the congressional committees that create spending authority through appropriations bills. These bills are subject to presidential veto.

Third, a president can propose emergency spending legislation when regular appropriations bills have not been passed. Although limited empirical research exists on this question, I suspect that emergency and supplemental requests approved by Congress offer considerable discretion to presidents. Presidents also propose various other measures in an attempt to change specific programs, taxes, and spending. Mowery and Kamlet (1984) reveal this enormous diversity of presidential budget strategies.

Reagan's Actions

The first year of the Reagan administration was a model of presidential manipulation of the budget process to achieve political and economic objectives (Burke 1985). Reagan succeeded because of effective use of legislative and budgeting tools. The administration was well organized and moved its proposals quickly to Congress. Unlike Carter, who had many priorities, Reagan concentrated on crucial priorities in his first year. His administration used reconciliation, a previously little used technique, to push its budget priorities and, later in the year, used a continuing resolution (emergency funding bill referred to earlier) to cut spending even further. Reagan also took advantage of his popularity and effective media personality.

Reagan's skill and luck in budgeting did not carry through the entire first term, and civil rights was one of the many areas for which he was criticized for budget cuts. In education, Reagan sought increased funding to cover the costs of pushing higher education suits to a settlement. While some black schools received substantial increases in federal funds, the overall effect for most black schools is debatable, partly because the administration also cut eligibility for student loans and grants.

Reagan said in 1984 that his administration had increased funding for higher education by 11.3 percent and claimed increases for the EEOC in FY 1983. As we saw in Table 4.4, his growth in requests were least in education and greatest in housing. Reagan asserted that he had made a 24 percent increase in overall civil rights activities over the last year of the Carter administration (*Weekly Compilation of Presidential Documents*, July 28, 1983, 1065). Thus, Reagan's budget actions were mixed.

Bush's Actions

No inflation rate and budget data were available beyond 1991 when this book was written, but we can examine estimates of Bush's requests beyond then (see note 13). He did gradually seek increases in the CRC, although estimated requests for fiscal year 1993 were still only about 84 percent of the FY 1987 figure Reagan proposed. Bush proposed a FY 1993 figure of nearly 10 percent higher for the Civil Rights Division (education) than his 1990 figure. In employment, he increased the figure just 4.2 percent over three years, which was, of course, below the rate of inflation. Finally, in housing Bush kept requests at exactly the same level for three years running (again amounting to a cut after inflation). Thus, while some of the figures will be muted over the course of several years, Bush seemed to continue dramatic cuts in budget requests in the civil rights realm.

This overview of budgetary actions in the Reagan and Bush administrations speculates that it is possible for presidents to use the budget effectively as a vehicle for changing national priorities. As the previous section suggests, Reagan and Bush attempted this in civil rights policy. Reagan's policy statements were more supportive (72 percent support) than the budget actions shown here (2.8 percent increase in requests). Bush's assertive statements and actions were, surprisingly, more conservative than were Reagan's.

Summary

This chapter sought a better understanding of presidential legislative and budget actions in civil rights policy formulation. Policy statements were geared largely toward the public (actors outside government); thus, it is perhaps not surprising that we found divergence between statements and the actions (directed exclusively toward Congress) discussed in this chapter. Policy actions put flesh on presidential agenda ideas and move toward specific proposals in policy formulation. These data help sharpen our focus and clarify some of the differences between presidents in the agenda-setting and formulation stages of the policy process.

Timing of civil rights statements and actions has been important in the modern era. While statements generally have increased, legislative actions generally decreased from their high point in the 1960s. Differences occurred by individual president and political party. Gerald Ford, for example, took no positions on legislation but was quite active in budget requests in civil rights. The varied findings reveal the importance of multiple indicators (see Edwards 1985) but also the discretion available to presidents in a myriad of policy actions in the civil rights realm.

Republican presidents are relatively nonassertive in legislative and budget actions. Democrats are far more legislatively assertive, and while presidents' positions on civil rights votes generally are quite liberal, it is the Democrats who exhibit by far the more liberal scores. Republicans are particularly more conservative on the black target group and the education and employment subissues. They especially opposed the Civil Rights Commission (general) in their budget requests, but Republican presidents supported housing at higher levels than expected.

The symbolism of presidential statements and actions is an important consideration. Policy statements often seemed symbolic, while legislative actions were less so. Nixon was the most symbolic, while Kennedy was the least symbolic in legislation among four modern presidents. These dramatic variations by presidents obscure party differences, although Democrats, as predicted, were slightly less symbolic. Republicans requested less funding than Democrats for three of the four civil rights agencies.

Civil rights legislation changed dramatically under Republicans

Reagan and Bush (Stern 1991). Unlike the 1960s, leadership now is most often initiated by Congress. Although not as partisan as economic policy, partisanship in civil rights is growing. Increased conflict could threaten governability similar to what we saw in these two case studies. Legislation on affirmative action and comparable worth, or other issues subject to the charge of reverse discrimination, are likely to further divide the parties and, thus, the governing institutions of our nation.

Presidents have also used budgets to further their goals in civil rights policy, although most requests have proposed only incremental change. Still, there were dramatic differences by party and president and across issue areas. Democrats exhibited greater budget requests than Republicans overall and for each category except housing. If some of these findings are surprising, the one on education is not. Readers will recall efforts by Richard Nixon and Gerald Ford to withhold HEW funds for school busing.

Presidents have been able to influence civil rights policy; Johnson and Reagan probably had the greatest impact, although their strategies varied widely. Johnson used primarily legislative means to encourage Congress and the general public to support equal rights with unprecedented activity and success. Reagan and Bush were assertive in budgeting. Such assertive presidents should receive more of their preferences than nonassertive presidents. Chapter 5 discusses other presidential actions, while chapter 6 reveals how Congress and agencies respond to presidents' statements and actions.

Notes

1. Research has shown an imperfect correspondence among requests, appropriations, and expenditures (Shull 1977), but the connections among these indicators may reveal budget roles and actor relationships in civil rights policy.

2. A positive relationship exists between yearly number of presidential communications (items) and legislative requests ($r = 0.632$, significant at .001 level). This correlation held for all issues, not just civil rights. The latter relationship was much less impressive ($r = 0.292$). The Congressional Quarterly box scores of requests are simply suggestions for legislation, not necessarily actual legislation sent to Congress. Thus they show whether the president follows through on his stated agenda preferences but do not assure us that the request was actually introduced in Congress (see Shull 1983, App.).

3. *Congressional Quarterly Almanac* (1970, 88) defines *key votes* as including *one or more* (emphasis mine) of the following: a matter of controversy; a test of

presidential power; a decision of potentially great impact on the lives of Americans. See Shull and Vanderleeuw (1987) for a critique of Congressional Quarterly's key votes.

4. For an example of the rules, see *Congressional Quarterly Almanac 1974*, 943.

5. A pro-civil rights position is *liberal* on civil rights, supportive of governmental intervention and remedial tools to seek equality and end discrimination. It favors policies sought by civil rights activists and minorities. Mixed or equivocal positions and those opposing busing, quotas, or other governmental remedies are labeled *conservative*, or anticivil rights.

6. To tap the support (liberalism) of presidential position-taking on legislative votes, one cannot rely on Congressional Quarterly's measure of whether the president supports a legislative position. He may, as Lyndon Johnson did often during 1964, take positions against conservative amendments. Thus, I had to examine carefully the paragraph in CQ describing the vote, and sometimes it was necessary to go to more detailed discussions of a particular vote. Although highly liberal position-taking occurs, we shall see that this is due to the assertiveness of Democratic presidents.

7. The Ns for all roll calls in Table 4.1 may not correspond with the total Ns in Tables 4.2 and 4.3 because of *multiple* counting into categories and *deleting* noncategorizable votes from the latter two tables.

8. The original bill overturned the case of *Grove City College v. Bell* (1984). The four statutes are Title VI of the 1964 Civil Rights Act for race; Title IX, the Education Amendment, passed in 1972 for gender; Section 504 of the Rehabilitation Act of 1973 for the handicapped; and the 1975 Age Discrimination Act for age.

9. See Stern (1991) for another detailed case study of the 1991 Civil Rights Act.

10. The six 1989 Supreme Court decisions are *Patterson v. McLean Credit Union; Wards Cove Packing Co. v. Atonio* (the most controversial decision); *Martin v. Wilkes; Lorance v. AT&T Technologies; Federation of Flight Attendants v. Zipes;* and *Price Waterhouse v. Hopkins.*

11. The vote to accept the conference report was 62–34 in the Senate and 273–154 in the House.

12. If it is difficult to define civil rights, identifying issue areas within it is even more difficult. Some agencies and subissues overlap. The Civil Rights Division deals with many subissues even within education (including school desegregation and higher education). Another example is the Office for Civil Rights (OCR), formerly in the Department of Health, Education and Welfare, which was divided into the Departments of Health and Human Services and Education in 1980. It is virtually impossible to separate out OCR's health functions (admittedly a relatively minor component) of this agency before 1981. Accordingly, the agencies selected for comparison in the budget tables in chapters 4 and 6 may not totally reflect budgeting in that issue area.

13. The budget data available have changed over the years. I calculate the indicators for recent years as follows, using fiscal year 1979 as an example: presidential *requests* = what presidents ask for, budget authority *estimates* (from 1981 budget); congressional *appropriations* = what Congress allocates, budget

authority *actual* (from 1979 budget); and agency *expenditures* = amount agencies spend per year, *estimated outlays* (from 1981 budget). Accordingly, the current appropriations data are actuals, while figures for requests and expenditures are estimates lagged two years later in any given budget document.

14. It is Ford's figures in housing that account for Republicans' greater budget support in that subissue.

15. It is possible that comparisons *within* subissues (e.g., types of education funding) may be masking the relatively small budget differences *across* subissues.

5

Presidents' Administrative and Judicial Actions

If presidents do not get their way with Congress in the civil rights realm, and evidence suggests that they often do not (see chapter 6), then potential solutions exist through the courts and bureaucracy. Research (Nathan 1983; Waterman 1989) has shown the increasing proclivity of presidents to turn to administrative actions when proposed legislation is not forthcoming or when they oppose existing laws. This chapter covers a myriad of actions used to influence executive and judicial actors in formulating civil rights policy. Presidents issue executive orders and other directives to obtain their policy preferences. Presidents also attempt to influence agency decisions, such as asking the Civil Rights Division of the Justice Department to initiate or drop law suits.

Presidents also take judicial actions. While judges do not look kindly on overt attempts by presidents to influence their decisions (Scigliano 1971, 62–64), presidential administrations participate in cases through *amicus curiae* briefs and by prosecuting or defending cases in which the government itself is a party (O'Connor and Epstein 1983). President Kennedy, for example, entered "friend of the court" briefs for desegregation in federally impacted areas (*Congress and the Nation*, 1:1965, 1631).

Obviously, a major influence on the decisions of both the bureaucracy and the courts is the presidents' power to appoint like-minded officials and judges. Such long-term appointments can create a policy legacy and, thus, are taken very seriously by presidents. Presidents

Reagan and Bush were particularly successful in this regard, although their conservative nominees drew heavy criticism (Goldman 1991). Their appointments to the Supreme Court had conservative records on most civil rights subissues, and together they appointed more than two-thirds of the entire federal judiciary.

Key administrative appointments in the area of civil rights have also generated much controversy. Reagan's first nominee as chair of the Civil Rights Commission, Sam B. Hart, stirred criticism, particularly in the black community. Hart, a radio preacher, opposed the Equal Rights Amendment, busing, and civil rights for homosexuals. His name was subsequently withdrawn, but others appointed to the commission, such as Clarence Pendleton, were also controversial. Bush also appointed many officials. Among his most controversial nominations were William Lucas to the Justice Department and Clarence Thomas to the Supreme Court. Two early Clinton executive branch nominees drew fire from conservatives for their civil rights views.

I examine here several major forms of administrative actions. The first is executive orders, and I include those from Franklin Roosevelt to the present. Another type of executive action is the appointment power to executive branch positions. Reagan's appointments to the Civil Rights Commission and Bush's to the Department of Justice constitute case studies of these presidents' assertiveness in administrative actions. The representativeness of their judicial nominations and other legal maneuvers are also important policy actions presidents take.

Administrative Actions

Overview and Expectations

Numerous executive or administrative actions are available to presidents. Such actions are often assumed to be taken primarily because legislative actions are unsuccessful. Some presidents, however, such as Roosevelt, Kennedy, and Reagan, may use them simply to avoid the controversy that legislation may entail. The general expectation is for substantial administrative actions when presidents do not push or cannot get legislative actions. Variations are also expected by individual president and by political party.

Ideologically committed presidents probably take more administrative actions to obtain their policy preferences. Thus ideology should relate to activism. Lyndon Johnson was the greatest legislative activist in civil rights policy; presumably he did less administratively but was still active. The civil rights policy area languished somewhat until Ronald Reagan renewed its attention on the government policy agenda (Yarbrough 1985). Reagan's actions were more administrative than legislative, with their foundation in his administration's conservative ideology (Detlefsen 1991). These two activist presidents took nearly opposite stands on the appropriateness of government intervention, however, and party differences should also be a factor.

Chapter 4 showed greater Democratic presidential budget activism, but Nathan (1983) may be correct in asserting greater Republican activism in other administrative decisions. Republican presidents may take more administrative and judicial actions than do Democratic presidents. Chapters 6–7 consider whether presidents receive support from those inside and outside government for these statements and actions. I expect variation in such support by individual presidents and political party.

The type of civil rights subissues may also condition presidential actions. Democratic presidents should emphasize more controversial issue areas (e.g., education and housing) while Republican attention probably will be greater to less controversial subissues (e.g., employment and *general* civil rights). Individual presidential assertiveness should also vary because of changes in salience of issue areas over time. Public accommodations, voting, and portions of education (e.g., school desegregation) have been resolved largely by Congress and the courts. Housing has always been controversial, while employment has been less so (Bullock and Lamb 1984). It may be easier for presidents to support *general* civil rights issues than to take explicit policy stands on controversial subissues (such as housing).

Modern Presidents

Chapter 3 suggested that presidential statements can be symbolic. Actions may also be symbolic, as everything the president does increasingly receives attention. Examples of symbolic but progressive civil rights actions are evident at least as early as Herbert Hoover, who invited a black representative's wife to be a guest at the White House and commuted the sentence of a black man convicted of murder without due process (Day 1980; Wilson 1975, 136). Roosevelt's civil rights actions were exclusively administrative—two executive orders. Truman fought for legislation but generally relied upon administrative actions. He issued several executive orders and also established a commission on desegregation and higher education. He also wanted a permanent Fair Employment Practices Commission, but it was not established until 1964.

Both Eisenhower and Kennedy acted under their authority as commanders in chief by sending federal troops to uphold the law. Eisenhower created a new Government Contracts Committee to reduce discrimination in federal projects, and he issued an executive order on employment (Burk 1984). Kennedy sought to smooth the school desegregation process in, for example, the state of Virginia and the city of New Orleans. He endorsed the extension of the Civil Rights Commission but issued only a limited executive order on housing discrimination. Johnson, of course, had less need to resort to administrative solutions. In 1966 he established a White House Conference on Civil Rights. Studying presidents from Eisenhower through Carter, Paul Light (1982, 70) concludes that the staffs of the Kennedy and Johnson administrations were the only ones to rank civil rights among the most important domestic problems (no. 4, named by 18 percent under Kennedy; no. 2, named by 79 percent under Johnson).

The Nixon administration suggests greater executive than legislative action. Ford, however, is the only contemporary president never to issue an executive order relating to civil rights. The lack of presidential leadership during both presidencies encouraged bureaucratic recalcitrance (*Congress and the Nation*, 4:1977, 661). Nixon backed away from HEW funding cutoffs for education and Ford did not encourage the Office for Civil Rights to enforce the law against discrimination in education (Bullock and Lamb 1984, 200).

Carter consolidated several diverse functions into the EEOC (*Congress and the Nation*, 5:1981, 820). He urged the Justice Department to sue school districts to force compliance with civil rights laws. Perhaps more than any other previous president (and, except Reagan, to follow), Carter used the appointment power to achieve his civil rights objectives (Halpern 1985, 138). He also issued many executive orders.

Reagan's Actions

The Reagan administration reminds us of the interrelationship of policies. More than any other recent president, he linked civil rights policy to broader ideological issues and other policy areas. Most critics do not claim that the administration was overtly racist. Rather, they suggest that the application of the general antigovernment, antiregulation, laissez-faire philosophy to civil rights issues halted progress and eroded previous gains.

The impact of this general philosophy on civil rights reveals itself in the words of William Bradford Reynolds, head of the Justice Department's Civil Rights Division, who stated in an interview, "There's growing awareness that the agencies that enforce civil rights laws have been overly intrusive" (Wines 1982, 536). Reynolds led the administration toward conservative positions in virtually every subissue of civil rights (*Newsweek*, October 6, 1986, 27).

Critics saw these administration arguments as opposing civil rights (Miller 1984; Amaker 1988; Wines 1982; Yarbrough 1985). But President Reagan promised a "positive" program to remedy these shortcomings. In 1983, he proposed the longest extension of the Civil Rights Commission in its history. Because the actions of the administration were so extensive, I summarize them briefly by the three subissues.

Reagan administration actions in education were invariably conservative, as defined earlier. The Department of Justice under William French Smith initially sought to limit Supreme Court jurisdiction and challenged the long-standing IRS ban on tax exemptions for private schools that discriminate against blacks (*Newsweek*, June 6, 1983, 38). The emphasis was on voluntary compliance rather than litigation. The Office for Civil Rights (OCR) in the Department of Education, which previously had been a "prototype of past deficiencies" (OMB 1982, special analysis, J13), became a model of the solution. In 1981, the OCR settled controversies with several state universities by dropping actions. Reagan issued executive orders and presidential directives increasing support for black institutions, but enforcement activities slowed. The *National Journal* (September 22, 1984, 1772) stated near the end of Reagan's first term, "During the last three years the Reagan administration . . . has been less aggressive in identifying discrimination and has tried to narrow the remedies available to correct discriminatory practices."

The greatest level of Reagan administration activity was in the area of discriminatory hiring practices. To eliminate sex discrimination, Reagan issued an executive order establishing a task force on legal equity for women. He continued to oppose ratification of the Equal

Rights Amendment, however, which subsequently died on July 1, 1982. To increase policy coordination, the administration increased the responsibilities of the Justice Department for enforcing the four major statutes requiring nondiscrimination in federally assisted programs. The department was further to coordinate efforts with the President's Task Force on Regulatory Relief. At the Equal Employment Opportunity Commission, the administration claimed to have "tightened management procedures and increased productivity" (OMB 1982, special analysis, J15). The president also asserted that the Department of Justice found 140 statutes that discriminate against women and moved to correct 122 of them (*Weekly Compilation of Presidential Documents,* April 5, 1984, 481).

Less visible administration activity occurred on the fair housing front (Lamb 1985, 81–83), but "antidiscrimination efforts in housing were diluted" (*Newsweek,* October 6, 1986, 27). The Reagan administration pushed regulatory changes that limited the actions available against discrimination. Litigation also slowed dramatically. According to Miller (1984, 66), Carter filed twelve housing suits in 1980 alone, while Reagan filed only six during his first thirty months in office. Additionally, Miller asserts that the Carter suits were more "nationally significant, precedent-setting cases" (1984, 67). The Reagan administration cut housing assistance funds by 60 percent between 1981 and 1985 and proposed no new housing units for fiscal year 1986 (*Washington Post National Weekly Edition,* December 9, 1985, 10–11). The president's approach was that vouchers and the "free market" make for better housing policy. At least in these subissues then, the Reagan administration's modest rhetorical support for civil rights was followed by much less supportive administrative actions.

Bush's Actions

Bush's administrative actions in civil rights were fewer than Reagan's on a yearly basis and on an absolute basis since he served only a single term in office. Most of Bush's activity focused on employment, where he consistently attacked Democrats as favoring hiring quotas. He managed to anger all sides with a controversial administrative directive upon signing the 1991 Civil Rights Act. Controversy mounted when a leaked draft of the directive called for the abolition of all government affirmative action programs and regulations that had built up since

Lyndon Johnson's executive order in 1965. The White House quickly disavowed the directive, saying White House counsel, C. Boyden Gray, had issued the directive without the president's knowledge or permission.

Accordingly, President Bush had to defend his support for affirmative action at the bill-signing ceremony. Critics claimed portions of the directive undercut sections of the new law. Some said the directive was designed to placate Republican conservatives, while signing the act he had long opposed showed Bush was not anti-civil rights. Thus the Bush administration was trying to play both sides against the middle with mixed signals. The controversial directive was to be appended to the bill, but the White House issued a new statement in the president's name eliminating the directive. Presumably President Bush tried to accomplish by administrative means what he failed to do legislatively. One administration official said privately that "there is still strong support for eliminating some affirmative programs later" *(New Orleans Times-Picayune*, November 22, 1991, A8). All in all, the directive was a clumsy action that pleased no one.

Executive Orders

Executive orders, proclamations, and directives are tangible, measurable administrative actions.[1] Some executive orders are purely administrative, while others are real instruments of policy formulation. Ruth Morgan (1970) argues that presidents (Franklin Roosevelt through Lyndon Johnson) were able to bring about policy changes in the civil rights realm through executive orders. Her assertion that their use would decline after Kennedy has not proven to be the case, however.

Table 5.1 presents the detailed executive orders for presidents Franklin Roosevelt through George Bush. Presidents on the average have issued about seventy executive orders per year on all issues during their administrations, so the average of fewer than one per year on civil rights matters constitutes a very small subset of the whole. This finding of fewer executive orders than legislative requests in civil rights supports the anticipated inverse relationship between executive and legislative actions even more strongly ($r = -.293$) than did budgets.

Next, I examine executive orders quantitatively by issue area. Very small Ns appear in Table 5.1 when

Table 5.1

Presidents' Civil Rights Executive Orders, 1941–1992

Franklin Roosevelt

June 25, 1941: EO 8802 bans discrimination in all defense contracts.

May 27, 1943: EO 9346 prevents discrimination in employment in war industries.

Harry Truman

December 18, 1945: EO 9664 establishes study committee to recommend policies on employment discrimination in reconverted industries.

December 12, 1946: EO 9809 establishes Commission on Civil Rights.

July 26, 1948: EO 9980 ends discrimination in government employment.

July 26, 1948: EO 9981 requires equality of treatment in the armed forces.

December 3, 1951: EO 10308 establishes the President's Committee on Government Contract Compliance.

Dwight Eisenhower

August 13, 1953: EO 10479 establishes the Government Contract Compliance Committee.

September 3, 1954: EO 10557 strengthens and revises the nondiscrimination clause in government contracts.

January 18, 1955: EO 10590 strengthens the government employment policy program by establishing a presidential commission.

John Kennedy

March 6, 1961: EO 10925 establishes President's Committee on Equal Employment Opportunity to implement nondiscriminatory policies in government and private employment under government contract.

November 20, 1962: EO 11063 bans discrimination in federally assisted housing.

June 22, 1963: EO 11114 includes Grant-in-Aid Program under nondiscrimination policies.

Lyndon Johnson

February 12, 1964: EO 11141 establishes nondiscrimination on basis of age.

February 5, 1965: EO 11197 creates President's Council to assist and coordinate elimination of discrimination.

September 24, 1965: EO 11246 Requires nondiscrimination in government employment, as well as in contractors and subcontractors.

Richard Nixon

August 8, 1969: EO 11478 implements the Affirmative Action Program to eliminate job discrimination in federal agencies.

January 15, 1974: EO 11758 delegates the authority of the president under the Rehabilitation Act of 1973.

Gerald Ford

None

Jimmy Carter

June 30, 1978: EO 12067 coordinates federal Equal Employment Opportunity programs under the Reorganization Act of 1978.

June 30, 1978: EO 12068 transfers functions of Title VII of the Civil Rights Act of 1964 to the attorney general.

October 5, 1978: EO 12086 transfers to the Department of Labor the function of contract compliance.

December 28, 1978: EO 12106 transfers certain equal employment opportunity functions from the Civil Service Commission to the Equal Employment Opportunity Commission.

May 18, 1979: EO 12138 prescribes additional arrangements for developing and coordinating a national program for minority business.

June 22, 1979: EO 12144 transfers certain equal pay and age discrimination functions from the Department of Labor to the EEOC.

May 2, 1980: EO 12212 establishes the Department of Education.

August 8, 1980: EO 12232 increases participation of black colleges in federally sponsored programs.

November 2, 1980: EO 12250 consolidates powers of the attorney general in nondiscrimination laws.

December 31, 1980: EO 12259 facilitates leadership and coordination of fair housing in federal programs.

Ronald Reagan

June 16, 1981: EO 12310 reforms federally subsidized housing.

September 15, 1981: EO 12320 revokes EO 12232 (see above).

December 21, 1981: EO 12336 establishes task force on legal equity for women.

January 13, 1982: EO 12339 increases membership on President's Commission on Housing to thirty.

April 1, 1982: EO 12355 substitutes Cabinet Council on Legal Equity for Women for Cabinet Council on Human Resources.

January 14, 1983: EO 12401 establishes Presidential Commission on Indian Reservation Economics "to promote the development of a strong private sector."

June 22, 1983: EO 12426 establishes President's Advisory Committee on Women's Business Ownership.

July 14, 1983: EO 12432 requires relevant federal agencies to "provide guidance and oversight for programs for the development of minority business enterprise."

September 21, 1983: EO 12442 terminates Commission on Indian Reservation Economics thirty days after submitting report (unless extended).

December 9, 1983: EO 12450 amends membership on Interagency Committee on Handicapped Employees.

January 21, 1984: EO 12482 adds minor amendments to Presidents's Advisory Committee on Women's Business Ownership and calls for its termination on December 31, 1984 (unless extended).

September 28, 1984: EO 12489 continues advisory committees, including one on Small and Minority Business Ownership.

September 30, 1985: EO 12534 continues Advisory Committee on Small and Minority Business Ownership until September 30, 1987, but revokes EO 12426, which established the President's Advisory Commission on Women's Business Ownership.

September 30, 1987: EO 12610 continues certain Federal Advisory Committees, including Small and Minority Business Ownership, until September 30, 1989.

May 10, 1988: EO 12640 Creates the President's Committee on Employment of People with Disabilities.

George Bush

March 21, 1989:	EO 12672 revises membership of Interagency Committee on Handicapped Employees.
April 28, 1989:	EO 12677 establishes in the Department of Education an Advisory Commission on Historically Black Colleges and Universities.
July 28, 1989:	EO 12685 allows personal assistants of employees with disabilities who are no longer needed to convert to regular federal career appointments.
September 24, 1990:	EO 12729 provides for Educational Excellence for Hispanic Americans by increasing their opportunities to participate in and benefit from federal programs.

Source: Adapted from *Weekly Compilation of Presidential Documents.*

---

looking at the presidents individually. Kennedy was the only president to average one order per year until the substantial increase under Carter and Reagan, who issued by far the most orders per year.[2] Consistently with his nonassertiveness legislatively, Ford issued no executive orders. Reagan's high issuance does correspond with expectations. President Bush's order issuance was lower than recent presidents (none issued during his last two years) but just above average overall.

Some difference exists between the two political parties in the propensity to issue executive orders. The finding of somewhat greater Republican issuance than for Democrats complements existing literature (Morgan 1970, 78–80; Flaxbeard 1983, 12) and supports my expectation. Perhaps Republican presidents issued more executive orders because they faced Congresses controlled by the opposition party and needed to rely on administrative as opposed to legislative actions (Nathan 1983). Republicans emphasize employment and orders in the *other* category just slightly more than do Democrats.

Over half of the executive orders on civil rights issued during the last fifty-nine years concern employment. The next largest category is *other*, where orders were fairly general in the 1960s for Kennedy and Johnson. Three of Reagan's *other* orders concerned the AIDS virus. Presidents infrequently issue orders on housing and education, although the latter has been emphasized more recently (e.g., Carter and Bush). Orders in the *other* category for Carter and Reagan contained quite a few seemingly routine reorganizations. Some of Reagan's orders in this category dealt with Native Americans and the disabled. These limited findings provide little basis for confirming or rejecting expectations by subissue.

Table 5.2

Executive Orders of Modern Presidents, by Issue Area

	Education	Employment	Housing	Other	Total[a] Mean (number/year)
Overall[b]	4	27	4	14	0.83
By Party					
Democrats	2	13	2	6	0.72
Republicans	2	14	2	8	0.96
President					
Roosevelt			2		0.17
Truman			4	1	0.63
Eisenhower			3		0.34
Kennedy		1	1	1	1.0
Johnson		1		2	0.60
Nixon		1		1	0.36
Ford					0
Carter	2	5	1	2	2.5
Reagan		9	2	7	2.1
Bush[c]	2	2			1.0

Source: Table 5.1.

[a]To simplify the table, the total number and number of years served are not included, but they can easily be calculated.

[b]Values are total numbers.

[c]Bush orders through 1992.

Nominations

Modern Presidents

Linkages between nominations to office and presidential civil rights policy preferences are difficult to draw or prove. Some "firsts" stick out as having symbolic importance. Franklin Roosevelt appointed the first female cabinet secretary (Frances Perkins as secretary of labor) and the first black federal judge (William Hastic to the U.S. District of the Virgin Islands). Alternatively, Kennedy's appointees often were moderates, as he attempted to appease conservative southern senators. Kennedy presumably would have liked to have appointed Robert Weaver as the first black cabinet secretary, but that "first" was to fall to Lyndon Johnson, who also appointed Thurgood Marshall as the first black member of the Supreme Court.

Perhaps Carter's most durable achievement is the appointment of more minorities and women to important federal posts than any other president in history. He is the one president to move beyond tokenism in his appointments, at least to the federal judiciary (Goldman 1985, 324–25). Some scholars (Walker and Barrow 1985), however, question the effects of his appointments. Reagan appointed the first female Supreme Court justice. Bush's controversial nomination of Clarence Thomas to fill Thurgood Marshall's seat on the Supreme Court maintained the black seat, but it became a conservative rather than a liberal one.

Reagan's Appointments

Ronald Reagan used the appointment power to place his ideological stamp on civil rights policy. His nominee for head of the Equal Employment Opportunity Commission, Clarence Thomas, met criticism from civil rights leaders, who charged that out of many qualified blacks, the administration came up with poor nominees. Much of this criticism was ideologically based. Reagan's choice of William French Smith as his first attorney general also influenced civil rights policy in the administration. Besides slowing the enforcement process within the Department of Justice for civil rights cases, Smith publicly stated that Congress has a right to limit the original jurisdiction of the Supreme Court but later modified his position. Clearly reflecting administration sentiment on this delicate constitutional issue, Smith's comments had relevance for congressional proposals limiting the court's jurisdiction over desegregation cases and its ability to mandate remedies that include busing. Administration critics were no happier when conservative Reagan adviser Edwin Meese succeeded Smith as attorney general. Meese and his subordinates also redirected the Justice Department's civil rights actions (Ball and Green 1985, 21–25).

Although Reagan claimed to have appointed more minorities to top policy-making posts than Carter, the facts are to the contrary. According to a study by the Civil Rights Commission, "in thirty-three of the categories, minority and female appointments had declined proportionately since Reagan took office; in only eight categories had they risen" (cited in Miller 1984, 67). Although Reagan named some blacks and women to visible positions in government, perhaps his most controversial appointive action was replacing members of the seemingly "independent" Civil Rights Commission (see case in this chapter); only one previous president had sought to oust incumbent members during the agency's thirty-five-year history. Other key Reagan administrative and judicial appointments in the area of civil rights policy generated controversy.

Bush's Appointments

Bush's moderate-to-conservative nominations provide a good example of taking the middle ground on civil rights. George Edwards states that Bush appointed people to federal agencies "more sensitive to the concerns of the black community than were those appointed by Reagan" (1991, 149). Certainly Bush sought the goodwill of blacks and wanted to double Reagan's and his own share of the black vote from 11 percent in 1988 to 22 percent in 1992. Thirteen percent of Bush's senior political appointees were black, including such potent policy makers as Colin Powell, chair of the Joint Chiefs of Staff, and Louis Sullivan, secretary of the Department of Health and Human Services. Bush also appointed more women to high office than had Reagan. Of appointees requiring Senate confirmation, women accounted for 19 percent of Bush's full-time appointees; seven of twelve deputy assistants and thirteen of forty-five special assistants through 1991 were women (*National Journal*, October 19, 1991, 2563). Although conservative, most of Bush's appointees were not very controversial (e.g., Supreme Court justice David Souter). Bush seems to have been more concerned than Reagan about the qualifications of judicial nominees (Goldman 1991, 301).

Certainly Bush's most controversial nomination was Clarence Thomas to the U.S. Supreme Court. Some were surprised that cautious Bush would pick such a divisive nominee. Both the president and Thomas opposed quotas, but the latter had benefited from them (e.g., admission to Yale Law School). Bush insisted that race was not a factor in selecting Thomas, but cynics considered the nomination a brilliant ploy to divide both Democrats and African Americans. The long-drawn-out confirmation hearings led to charges of sexual harassment by a former employee of Thomas's at the EEOC. The hearings engrossed and stunned the nation, with Thomas alternatively characterized as an "insensitive brute" or a "victim of character assassination" (*Newsweek*, October 21, 1991, 27).

Administrative Cases

Case 1: The Pendleton Nomination
to the Civil Rights Commission

During his first term, Ronald Reagan greatly politicized an agency that had previously experienced little controversy. Through a number of challenges, the president succeeded in changing the structure, mission, and, most important, the personnel of the U.S. Commission on Civil Rights. According to legal scholar Norman Amaker, the "Commission ceased acting as the conscience of government" (1988, 169). The first case presented here presents a nomination that greatly helped President Reagan achieve his policy goals in civil rights.

Reagan's nomination of Clarence Pendleton to the Civil Rights Commission was controversial because it coincided with the firing of members who had criticized the Reagan administration's civil rights policies. Only one previous president had sought to oust a commissioner: Richard Nixon requested the resignation of Father Theodore Hesburgh for not opposing busing to achieve racial integration. Hesburgh was replaced by the Republican Arthur S. Flemming, who most assumed would be a less forceful advocate for civil rights. Yet Flemming did not compromise on policy and became a critic of the Reagan administration's policies. Some saw irony in Reagan's effort to replace Flemming with conservative black Republican Clarence Pendleton.

Upon his firing, Flemming held a news conference criticizing both his ouster and the administration's "retreat" from affirmative action. He stated: "Our Commission has consistently been taking positions contrary to the positions of the Reagan administration. The cumulative impact of the civil rights decisions made by the administration are very disturbing" (*New York Times*, November 17, 1981, A22). The Washington lobbyist for the NAACP, Althea Simmons, stated, "What the administration is trying to do is not just put civil rights on the back burner, but take it off the stove completely" (*Time*, November 30, 1981, 29).

During the 1970s the commission was a liberal body supporting busing, numerical goals, and integrated housing. It was the only agency in the federal government that "held consistently to the concept of minority rights that pervaded the federal establishment in the 1960s" (*New York Times*, November 18, 1981, A21). Conservatives countered with their own charges against the Civil Rights Commission. Criticisms came from President Reagan personally and through his appointees in government, particularly in the Justice Department. Members of Congress also reacted. Senator Orrin Hatch (R-Utah) had criticized the commission as "captive of special interests that advocate quotas" (*National Journal*, December 17, 1983, 2624).

Pendleton was one of a rare group of conservative black Republicans. He sometimes described Ed Meese as his "political mentor"; Meese was a friend who had recommended Pendleton for the job. Like many conservatives, Pendleton pushed minority self-help and economic development instead of government programs. He stated during confirmation hearings that he did not believe in goals and timetables. The White House argued that Pendleton "shared Mr. Reagan's opposition to affirmative action hiring programs and to busing to achieve school desegregation" (*New York Times*, November 17, 1981, A22). The Federal Bureau of Investigation conducted lengthy background checks, and the Senate delayed Pendleton's confirmation upon reports of financial improprieties as president of the San Diego Urban League. Blacks in Pendleton's hometown and nationally opposed his nomination. The civil rights community wanted a minority CRC chair but not Pendleton.

Reagan defended his nominations by saying that liberal members appointed by previous presidents had not been accused of compromising the agency's independence: "These appointees are under fire for supposedly doing that. In truth, they are independent. They don't worship the altar of forced busing and mandatory quotas. They don't believe you can remedy past discrimination by mandating new discrimination" (*Weekly Compilation of Presidential Documents*, August 1, 1983, 1080–81). The increased politicization of the commission perpetuated Reagan's image as an opponent of civil rights and shows how important the appointment power can be in presidents' pursuit of policy goals.

The appointment of Pendleton and other conservatives generated criticism of the Civil Rights Commission in Congress. Democrats threatened to cut off funding for the commission and make it part of the legislative branch. With its charter due to expire, Reagan was forced to compromise on a reorganization measure so as not to be blamed for the agency's demise. On November 30, 1983, the president signed legislation reconstituting the commission with the president and

Congress each having the power of appointing four members for fixed six-year terms of office. Members of Congress and other supporters of the commission thought the four members who had criticized the administration were to be reappointed, but the administration disputed that it was bound to any "oral agreement." In the end, Reagan ended up with a 5–3 conservative majority. Later, Chair Pendleton stated, "Those up in arms tend to forget who won control of the Commission" (*National Journal*, January 14, 1984, 81).[3]

President Reagan brought upon himself much greater criticism for his conservative appointees to the Civil Rights Commission and other civil rights agencies than he had anticipated (*Washington Post National Weekly Edition*, May 5, 1986, 8–9). A four-month fight with Congress ensued over the proper composition of the commission, with Reagan favoring a House plan over a Senate version that would have made the agency more independent of presidents by having all members appointed by Congress. The likely unconstitutionality of that Senate plan led to a compromise version that expanded the commission to eight members but gave them fixed terms of office. Although the president was not able to fire all the members he wanted, the reconstituted commission generally supported Reagan's civil rights views (Amaker 1988, 174; Detlefsen 1991, 8–10).

When Reagan appointees on the commission echoed the president's charges and criticized civil rights leaders for "promoting new racism," many civil rights groups responded by breaking relations with the commission in February 1985. At least two black Democratic representatives excluded from discussions with the administration attacked Pendleton as "a presidential puppet" and "administration lackey." Ralph G. Neas, executive director of the Leadership Conference on Civil Rights, criticized CRC efforts to cease using remedies used in the past. He and other critics said that "the President has robbed the Commission of much of its legitimacy and its reputation for independence" (*National Journal*, January 14, 1984, 81).

Previous legislation extending the life of the agency in five-year intervals had seldom generated controversy.[4] We have already seen, however, the conflict that ensued over extension of the CRC in 1983. Although the Civil Rights Commission is still an independent agency, its character changed greatly under Ronald Reagan. During the early years of the administration, the agency criticized the president for hiring far fewer minorities and women as full-time employees than had

Carter (Thompson 1985, 183–88). For a period, the Reagan appointee chair (Pendleton) was the lone administration supporter at the CRC. Despite drawing the wrath of civil rights interest groups, Pendleton and later Reagan appointees made a difference in policy. The CRC "retreated from conscience" and no longer opposed administration policies (Amaker 1988, 175). Policy recommendations by the new conservative majority were dramatically different from those of previous commissions, which were more liberal in composition. For instance, both the chair and vice-chair voiced strong support for a Supreme Court decision curtailing affirmative action plans that conflict with seniority.

Case II: The Lucas Nomination
to the Civil Rights Division

On February 24, 1989, the name of William Lucas was forwarded to the White House for consideration as assistant attorney general. This position as head of the Civil Rights Division (CRD) of the Department of Justice is the premier civil rights position in the federal government. Lucas immediately drew criticism from civil rights groups, and his subsequent nomination, which was delayed for several weeks, triggered heated controversy. After much rancor, the Senate Judiciary Committee on August 1, 1989 (with one Democrat voting yes), defeated Lucas's nomination by a 7–7 party-line vote, causing an embarrassing defeat for President Bush. The case is an example of pervasive conflict resulting from pressures of interest groups and ideology.

Reagan's head of the Civil Rights Division, the controversial William Bradford Reynolds, had been highly visible in seeking narrow enforcement of civil rights laws. Presumably, the White House saw Lucas as symbolizing a more tolerant White House attitude toward civil rights. He was the highest-ranking black Republican elected official and had been mentioned previously for several federal positions, including head of the U.S. Marshal's Service and aide to the drug czar. Under President Carter, Lucas had even been one of five finalists for FBI director. He became the first black candidate for federal office rejected by the Senate after being formally nominated. How could the appointment of a visible and seemingly qualified African American attorney have gone so awry?

During the confirmation hearings, Lucas became controversial for at least three prior actions. First, he claimed on a resume to have been an assistant attorney general in the Justice Department but had been only a legal assistant without even passing the bar exam. Second, a federal district court held Lucas in contempt for "Knowingly, intentionally, and deliberately failing to improve overcrowded jail conditions" (*Newsweek*, May 8, 1989, 20). The court criticized the fact that he reprimanded no one for these abuses and cited his "toleration of illegal brutality" (*New York Times*, March 1, 1989, 24). Finally, Lucas clashed with customs officers in 1985 and was cited for failing to pay duties on jewelry shipped into the United States. These actions and his confirmation testimony heightened Senate opposition.

Lucas was a rare black conservative who opposed quotas and supported segregated private schools seeking federal tax exemptions. He was chided for inexperience, having only recently practiced law part time and never having appeared in court. During the confirmation hearings, Lucas uttered confused testimony and said, "I'm new to the law" (*Congressional Quarterly Weekly Reports*, July 29, 1989, 1964). He also stated that he did not think the court rulings during the Reagan administration were very significant roadblocks to equal opportunity. These statements and actions diminished support for his nomination. Even his early sponsor, Representative John Conyers, Jr. (D-Mich.), who had introduced Lucas to the committee, withdrew his endorsement.

Jesse Jackson quickly withdrew his previous support for Lucas. Although the Southern Christian Leadership Conference continued to support Lucas, several liberal organizations immediately opposed the nomination. Mayor Coleman Young of Detroit criticized Lucas's civil rights record, and Elaine Jones of the NAACP Legal Defense Fund stated, "It doesn't appear at first glance that he has had any substantial experience in the area in 20 years" (*New York Times*, February 25, 1989, L10). The executive director of the Leadership Conference on Civil Rights, Ralph Neas, was among the many critics of the appointment. The *New York Times* (March 1, 1989, A24) stated in an editorial opposing the nomination that "for this job, a symbolic appointment is not good enough." Other groups and individuals spoke out as the hearings wore on. Norman Amaker found it "incredible that the administration would even contemplate having someone in that position who does not on his record appear to know very much about the civil rights field" (*New York Times*, March 12, 1989, E5). The Leadership Conference on Civil Rights, an umbrella group of 185 organizations, expressed "deep disappointment and concern" (*Congressional Quarterly Weekly Reports*, April 15, 1989, 830).

Conservative groups rallied to Lucas's defense, seeming to want a nominee in the mold of Reynolds. The International Associations of Chiefs of Police and National Sheriffs Association supported the nomination (*Congressional Quarterly Weekly Reports*, July 22, 1989, 1872). Patrick B. McGuigan of the Free Congress Foundation stated:

It is brilliant. Bill Lucas is a fine, courageous man who, in his career, has been willing to put himself on the line. . . . He understands that the purpose of American civil rights is to provide equal opportunity for all. . . . He is being opposed because he will not recognize the infallibility of the reigning civil rights establishment in the nation's Capitol (*Congressional Quarterly Weekly Reports*, April 15, 1989, 831).

Although President Bush expressed disappointment with the opposition that developed, he took little personal role once the Senate received the nomination. Attorney General Richard Thornburgh became the chief administration spokesperson on the nomination but angered senators because of his partisan appeals. Bush may have deferred too much to his friend Thornburgh, who stated, "What's wrong here is that Mr. Lucas's critics seem to have forgotten the results of the election last year" (*Congressional Quarterly Weekly Reports*, July 29, 1989, 1964). One Thornburgh aide called Lucas a "groovy appointment." After criticizing "political partisanship that had taken over and twisted the nomination process" (*New Orleans Times-Picayune*, August 2, 1989, A7), Senate Minority Leader Robert Dole suggested that Lucas should receive an interim appointment to the position during the congressional recess.

When this possibility leaked, the Bush administration was not interested in such a ruse that might perpetuate the controversy. Instead, it appointed Lucas as head of Liaison Services for the Department of Justice, a job paying the same salary but not requiring Senate confirmation. The nomination suggests that the Bush administration missed a chance to convince minorities of its sincerity. Although we will see in chapter 7 significantly greater early black support for Bush than existed for Reagan, Bush too became suspect.

Like its nominee, the Bush administration did not believe that the

1989 Supreme Court cases signified a major civil rights retreat (*Washington Post National Weekly Edition*, January 15–21, 1990, 7). Administration officials admitted that differences with the Reagan administration on civil rights were, "more in style than in substance." The later nomination of another black conservative, Clarence Thomas, outspoken chair of the EEOC, to be a federal court of appeals judge and then Supreme Court justice, promised to keep civil rights activists vigilant. Melanie Verveer of People for the American Way stated that the organization planned to "send a signal to the Bush administration that we need a recommitment to civil rights, not a retrenchment" (*National Journal*, August 5, 1989, 1992).

The Bush administration was under considerable pressure to find an acceptable replacement for Lucas. It nominated former New York state senator John Dunne, who had little experience but whom columnist Tom Wicker called "personally and politically courageous" (*New Orleans Times-Picayune*, January 30, 1990, B7) for his prison reform efforts. It also helped that Dunne appeared less controversial than Lucas. Bush's nomination problems continued when the Civil Rights Commission floundered due to a lack of a quorum; four of its eight commissioner positions were vacant at the beginning of 1990. Liberals wanted former commissioner Arthur S. Flemming appointed as chair. The Leadership Conference on Civil Rights Executive Director Ralph Neas stated, "Certainly everyone in civil rights gives Bush high marks for access and rhetoric but this [appointment] will be a measure of his commitment" (*New Orleans Times-Picayune*, January 15, 1990, B1). Instead, Bush pushed for moderate-to-conservative Arthur Fletcher as chair.

Patterns of Administrative Cases

The Pendleton nomination to the Civil Rights Commission perpetuated conflict with Congress over the agency. In addition, many African Americans were furious with Reagan over his criticism of black leaders (*Newsweek*, January 28, 1985, 30). The National Urban League President John E. Jacob called Reagan's remarks "insensitive and insulting." He called the administration's record in excluding blacks from key administration posts the worst in a quarter of a century and accused Reagan of "fanning the flames of racial polarization with ill-tempered attacks on black organizations" (*Newsweek*, January 28,

1985, 30). The head of the Southern Christian Leadership Conference, Rev. Joseph Lowery, also faulted President Reagan for degrading black leaders: "I think it does not serve any useful purpose for Reagan to continue to pour fuel on the fire" (*Washington Post National Weekly Edition*, May 5, 1986, 8). White writers responded similarly. Jack Germond and Jules Witcover stated that "the President only deepens resentment in the black community, and diminishes his chances to have his ideas listened to seriously, when he derogates the black leaders who demonstrably address the broad range of black concerns in the 1980s" (*National Journal*, January 26, 1985, 224).

Besides criticizing black leaders, Reagan had no major discussions with them as president. Even black Republicans agree that his 1985 meeting with a new group called the Council for a Black Economic Agenda was an unnecessary snub by excluding traditional black organizations. Arthur S. Flemming, former chair of the Civil Rights Commission (before his ouster by the Reagan administration), joined with other prominent government officials and established and became chair of the Citizen's Commission on Civil Rights. Pro-civil rights groups coalesced around these attacks by the president and actions by his appointees to the Civil Rights Commission. Reagan's statements and actions unnecessarily angered Congress and civil rights supporters.

The Lucas nomination to the Civil Rights Division is another example of interbranch conflict. Interest groups and Congress sent President Bush the message that they would not allow a Reagan-style retreat on civil rights. Congress's newfound support for civil rights, at least from 1988, continued through Bush's term. The rejection of Lucas seemed to have little effect since Bush appointed him to another, less visible position in government. Bush cut his loss with the defeat and did not try to alienate the Senate further. But the message had been sent that Congress wanted strong enforcement of civil rights.

The Lucas case also shows the Senate's power to approve presidential nominations. Congress did not initially want to fight the president but received outside criticism about the qualifications of the nominee. Liberal Democrats voted against even an African American whom they considered unqualified. Attorney General Thornburgh's announcement of the nomination while President Bush was in Japan angered the White House. It had supported another candidate and criticized the Justice Department for inept handling of the matter (*Washington Post National Weekly Edition*, January 15–21, 1990, 7).

Although the case also revealed considerable conflict between Congress and the president, it was not as long lasting as Reagan's disagreement over the Civil Rights Commission.

Judicial Actions

The relationship between administrative and judicial actions may be quite close. The appointment of judges and the enforcement of judicial decrees relate to the president's responsibility to ensure that the laws are faithfully executed. Following upon the nomination discussion of the previous section, I begin with the characteristics of appointees to the federal courts and then discuss other judicial actions presidents may take on civil rights matters.

How Representative are Judges?

One important type of representation is symbolic, with representatives largely mirroring characteristics found in the electorate. The concern with judicial appointments in this chapter is on this *symbolic representativeness*. The background characteristics of district and appellate court appointments in Table 5.3 reflect symbolic representation. The results show (in percent) some interesting differences in the types of judges presidents choose. Appointments by Presidents Johnson and Ford tended to have more political and government experience than those of other presidents. Moreover, these characteristics were even more important for district than for appellate court judges.

Prior judicial experience appears to be more important for contemporary presidents, however, and was a concern to Johnson and Ford. These two presidents appointed the highest proportion of district court judges with previous political and government experience; Carter appointed those with least. Sheldon Goldman finds that 22 percent of Reagan's district court nominees were millionaires versus only 4 percent for Carter (1985, 330). Goldman also finds that more judicial selections attended public law schools than had previously.

Presidents seek like-minded justices (Heck and Shull 1982; Scigliano 1962); they overwhelmingly choose justices from the same political parties as themselves. Only Ford dropped considerably below the mean, while Reagan made the most partisan appointments at the appellate level. Presidents are also inclined to nominate federal judges with past party activism. Bush's appointees at both levels had particularly high prior party activity. As might be expected from party clien-

Table 5.3

Characteristics of Federal District and Appellate Court Judges
(% of appointees having listed characteristics)

Characteristics	Johnson D[a]	Johnson A[a]	Nixon D	Nixon A	Ford D	Ford A	Carter D	Carter A	Reagan D	Reagan A	Bush[b] D	Bush A
Political and government experience	21	10	11	4	21	8	4	5	13	9	10	11
Judicial experience	34	65	35	58	42	75	54	54	47	60	50	56
Attended public-supported law school	40	40	42	38	44	50	51	39	42	40	48	22
Same party	94	95	93	93	79	92	93	82	93	97	94	94
Past party activism	49	58	49	60	50	58	61	73	59	55	63	67
Protestant	58	60	73	76	73	58	60	61	60	97	65	56
White	95	95	97	98	90	100	79	79	92	97	96	89
Male	98	98	99	100	98	100	86	80	92	96	90	89
Exceptionally well qualified[c]	7	28	5	16	—	17	4	16	54	59	58	78

Source: Sheldon Goldman, ''The Bush Imprint on the Judiciary,'' *Judicature 74* (April/May 1991): 298-99, 302-3.

[a] D = district; A = appellate.

[b] Through 1991.

[c] American Bar Association rating; for Reagan and Bush also includes well qualified.

tele support, Johnson and Carter selected a high percentage of Catholics and Jews to the federal judiciary, and only Carter appears to have made much effort to recruit women and minorities. His use of judicial selection committees was specifically designed to increase the representativeness of minority groups in the courts. Carter even sought the advice of black and female organizations of lawyers in the selection process.

During his first three years, Bush appointed more women district court judges than any president but Carter but far fewer nonwhites (14.3 percent) than Carter (*National Journal*, January 25, 1992, 203). In an earlier article, Sheldon Goldman saw Carter as the president most committed to affirmative action but also believed that the "Reagan administration is the 'most determined since the first [Franklin D.] Roosevelt administration' to mold a judiciary to its liking" (1985, 34). Reagan's and Bush's judicial appointments were ideologically conservative on civil rights (see chapter 7). One study found their appointees agreeing just 13 percent of the time with plaintiffs filing desegregation suits, compared to 59 percent for Carter appointees (cited in *National Journal*, January 25, 1992, 205). Finally, a decline after Johnson occurs in the extent that presidents seek to appoint judges considered *qualified*, as determined by the American Bar Association.[5] All in all, judges seem to reflect presidents' experiences and preferences, but their backgrounds are not very representative of the American population as a whole. Thus, little symbolic representation occurs in judicial appointments.

Other Legal Maneuvers

What other judicial actions are available to the president assertive in civil rights policy? Presidents rely heavily on the advice of their legal advisers in the executive branch (e.g., attorney general, solicitor general, head of the Civil Rights Division). They may be quite passive in following up on rulings of the courts, as Eisenhower was, or they may be more aggressive in filing suits or in taking positions on *amicus* briefs, as were Kennedy, Carter, and Reagan. An assertive president knows that the government wins most of the cases in which it (the Office of the President) takes a "friend of the Court" position (Puro 1971, 224–26; Scigliano 1984; Sigel 1988).

President Reagan settled out of court most of the desegregation suits against southern state higher education systems that the Carter administration had initiated. Concerning elementary and secondary education, William Bradford Reynolds, head of the Civil Rights Division under Reagan, stated: "Forced busing has largely failed to work and to gain the public acceptance it needed to work and to enhance educational achievement" (*New Orleans Times-Picayune/States-Item*, September 21, 1981, sec. 1, p. 31). Overall, Reagan filed fewer desegregation suits than had Carter (Miller 1984, 64), but Reagan claimed his Department of Justice filed more cases charging sex discrimination than did the previous administration during a comparable time period.

We saw in chapter 3 that Bush's policy statements were not geared toward the judiciary; he was the only president not to call for any judicial actions during his first three years in office. It was not for want of important cases. Two important Supreme Court cases were decided early in 1992. In January, the Court declared that black elected officials could no longer count on the federal courts to prevent local governments from dodging the intent of the Voting Rights Act. In March, the Court determined that school systems are not responsible for *resegregation* caused by demographic factors. Critics said the Court was endorsing white flight to the suburbs, whites thereby avoiding having to attend schools with blacks. I can find no evidence of the Bush administration taking a position on either case. Finally, Bush said, "The court system has worked" (*Newsweek*, May 11, 1992, 42) upon hearing that an all-white jury in Los Angeles acquitted four white police officers charged with brutality against black motorist Rodney King. After being criticized for insensitivity, Bush quickly modified his position in a more conciliatory statement.

Reagan's and Bush's judicial actions and appointments are reminiscent of Richard Nixon. By relaxing other federal pressures, Nixon returned to less comprehensive "case-by-case litigation as the major weapon for enforcing compliance" (Bardolph 1970, 465). We shall see the results and effects of these varied judicial actions in chapter 7 (particularly appointments and litigation) taken by modern presidents to pursue their civil rights policy preferences.

Summary

Presidents have been able to influence civil rights through their policy actions. Johnson and Reagan may have acted most often, although their strategies varied widely. Johnson used primarily legislative means, with unprecedented activity and success, to encourage Congress and the general public to support equal rights. Reagan was surprisingly active in civil rights, although his activity was manifested primarily in budgetary and judicial action rather than through direct legislation (Nathan 1983). He provides the best example of legislative inaction but administrative leadership. All in all, Reagan was among the presidents most adept in the skillful use of myriad actions to attain his civil rights policy goals.[6]

Perhaps more than any other president, Ronald Reagan used administrative and judicial actions to influence civil rights policies. This activity contrasts to Reagan's legislative inactivity (except through lobbying and other informal means) and shows how ideology guided his administrative and judicial actions. Reagan's conservative nominations to the Supreme Court, Civil Rights Commission, and other agencies show how important appointments can be. The filling of more Supreme Court vacancies in Reagan's second term made judicial appointments comparable to the substantial influence of executive appointments in his first. He also pushed government court suits in the civil rights realm.

Beginning in the 1970s, administrative actions, such as executive orders and presidential nominations, largely supplanted legislation.[7] Administrative actions have also had important policy consequences in civil rights. Contrary to legislation and budget requests, Republican presidents are more assertive than Democrats on administrative actions. Executive orders are one such administrative device, and most focus on employment. Executive order issuance increased dramatically under Carter and Reagan,[8] and such administrative actions as appointments have also become more important to recent presidents. Perhaps Carter used judicial appointments to obtain representativeness, while Reagan sought to obtain ideological purity.

The fact that the direction of most Reagan actions was conservative —bucking a longstanding trend toward greater government enforcement to ensure equality—testifies to the effectiveness of this president. Presumably Reagan took risks in politicizing civil rights to a greater degree than done heretofore, but he suffered little political damage for it. Reagan used many administrative and judicial actions to further his policy preferences, such as putting hundreds of civil rights cases on hold. Ideology played a greater role in Reagan's policies on civil rights than, perhaps, it did in any other administration.

Bush, too, seemed ideologically conservative in his policy actions, except perhaps regarding gender. Only Carter appointed more women to top positions in his administration. Bush was much more assertive rhetorically and legislatively than administratively and on judicial matters, however. He was almost entirely uninvolved in the latter. Thus his policy actions were inconsistent.

The key question, of course, is whether legislative, budget, executive, and judicial actions by a president make a difference. Most such actions (perhaps apart from executive orders) do not create policy themselves but must be acted upon (modified, adopted, and implemented) by other governmental institutions. Chapter 6 explores whether presidents get their way with Congress and the rest of the executive branch, while chapter 7 covers responses to presidential statements and actions from the courts and those outside government.

Notes

1. One can find executive orders in the *Federal Register*, in the *Codification of Presidential Proclamations and Executive Orders*, and in the *Weekly Compilation of Presidential Documents*.

2. Flaxbeard (1983) asserts that as a result of the Reorganization Act of 1978, President Carter issued some executive orders that were administrative in nature, such as calling for the reorganization of civil rights agencies. These executive orders were issued for the purpose of streamlining the bureaucracy. Reagan, too, made several purely administrative changes, and, therefore, it is debatable whether I should have used all of their orders in calculating the number of executive orders.

3. The *Washington Post National Weekly Edition* (May 5, 1986, 8–9) criticized Pendleton for fiery rhetoric and for "baiting" black leaders. Several excerpts from statements by Pendleton appear in the article.

4. Those extensions were 1967 (PL 90–198), 1972 (PL 92–496), and 1978 (PL 95–444) (*Congress and the Nation*, 2:1969, 375, 3:1973, 510; 5:1981, 798).

5. The data in Table 5.3 for Reagan and Bush also include *well qualified and thus are not fully comparable.

6. The relationship between number of policy statements and some presidential actions is moderately high (e.g., executive orders $r = 0.470$; legislative positions $r = .723$), whereas for others it is nonexistent (e.g., legislative requests $r = 0.075$).

7. LBJ's focus on legislation seems natural because he was faced with a situation where legislative authority was needed for further government action. After LBJ, civil rights languished somewhat, fitting what one would expect from

Anthony Down's (1972) "issue-attention cycle." Before significant legislation is passed, administrative actions may be the only way to pursue a policy; after laws exist to be enforced, they need not be so numerous. Thus, while issues are on the legislative agenda, administrative actions should be fewer.

8. The great increase in executive orders under Carter and Reagan may also be fairly symbolic, since many of their orders do not seem very substantive.

Part III

Reactions to Presidential Statements and Actions

6

Responses by Congress and Agencies

This chapter examines the responses of legislative and executive officials to presidential decisions. How do these actors view presidents' statements and actions? Although presidents may help set the agenda and formulate policy, other agents often have the final say on the shape of policy. Their responses may alter presidential priorities and agendas and the entire public policy agenda. The president does not always take a leadership role; the impetus for civil rights policy may come from these officials inside government.

Resultant policy may substantially differ from what the president initially had in mind or formally proposed. Even if his ideas gain acceptance, they may be greatly modified prior to or after adoption. Because of the perceived high controversy of civil rights policy, there is a good chance that presidents will not attain all civil rights policies they favor. Yet, because leadership must come primarily from the president, ideologically committed presidents should obtain more of their policy preferences.

The main responses to the president in adopting and implementing policies come from Congress, the courts, and the bureaucracy. If the president dominates agenda setting and formulation, modification and adoption are much more under the purview of Congress (Jones 1984, 116). Congress has many opportunities to place its stamp on, greatly redefine, or reject presidential initiatives. The decentralized, diffused nature of power in Congress requires constant majority building by the president to prevent defeat of his policies.

Congress' predispositions often differ from the president's. It also has many ways of monitoring executive proposals, including committee and floor votes and amendments, administrative oversight, and committee hearings on confirmations and investigations. Legislative liaison is also important.[1] Although these legislative techniques are major components of leadership and response, the quantitative analysis here focuses on responses to presidential legislative requests and positions on votes in Congress.

Budget appropriations are another legislative response to the president (see chapter 4, note 13, for definition). Congressional approval of presidents' budget requests (appropriations) varies by president. The scholarly literature has long debated the degree of presidential leadership in budgeting, most often concluding that Congress makes only incremental (small) changes in presidential requests in its appropriations (Neustadt 1955, Gordon 1969, 62; Wildavsky 1984; Ripley 1972, 172; Ripley 1969, 34). A counterview is that legislative dependence is less obvious today than it once was. Research suggests that, more often than not, Congress cuts presidential budget requests (Ott and Ott 1972, 50). This was not true under Reagan and Bush generally, but these actor roles may vary in the civil rights realm.

Presidential actions and responses to them must be implemented to have any policy impact. Implementation (or execution) of policy consists of the activities conducted by the government to carry out its programs. Implementation is particularly critical to attain compliance with the intent of the law and presidents' preferences (Rodgers and Bullock 1972; Ripley and Franklin 1986; Edwards 1980a; Mazmanian and Sabatier 1983). The bureaucracy is such a crucial, even dominant, actor in implementation that I cover both budget and program responses.

Legislative Responses

Legislation is an important response to the policy actions of presidents. Disagreement over the ability of Congress to initiate policy abounds. Some writers charge that policy formulation is a function that Congress increasingly is unwilling and unable to perform (Spitzer 1993). According to one researcher, the fragmented and diffuse nature of

Congress cannot allow it to compete with the president as "Chief Initiator" (Gallagher 1974, 231). Others argue, however, that Congress is not powerless in policy formulation; it still shares power about equally with the president (Chamberlain 1946; Moe and Teel 1970; Orfield 1975, 20; Schwarz and Shaw 1976). Congress plays a more important role in policy making than is often recognized, certainly in policy modification and adoption, if not in setting broader national goals or in policy formulation (LeLoup and Shull 1993).

This section begins with expectations about how Congress reacts to presidential requests and vote positions (the two Congressional Quarterly measures introduced in chapter 4). I posit expectations on presidents' legislative success (on requests) and support (of vote positions) generally, by individual presidents and political party, and by target group and subissue, after which some assessments of legislative responses are made.

Expectations

Congress supports presidents' vote positions a high percentage of the time. One study found that among the six policy areas, civil rights experienced the least modification (Shull 1983, ch. 4). On the other hand, Congress adopts relatively few of presidents' requests compared with those in other issue areas (Shull 1983, 103, 132). Thus presidents obtain greater *support* on vote positions than receive *success* on their legislative requests. Presidents often take positions on votes that may pass only one house, while requests for legislation must go through many more hurdles (several committees, two chambers) before adoption. In addition, presidents should receive greater legislative support for their positions on all votes than for those on amendments or key votes because of the greater controversy of the latter two.

Dividing the data by target groups and issue areas should further illuminate differences in modification and adoption, which relate to controversy and support. African Americans are expected to be a more controversial target group of governmental action, particularly in contrast to age or gender groups, while housing and education should be more controversial subissues than employment. The greater the controversy, the less legislative support expected.

Civil rights should reveal considerable differences among individual presidents in legislative responses. Ideologically committed presidents (e.g., Johnson, Kennedy) should obtain more of their policy preferences. Although Johnson took liberal and Nixon conservative positions (*National Journal*, March 27, 1982, 538; also see chapter 4), Congress responds to such executive leadership, and it, too, became more conservative on civil rights into the 1980s (Baum and Weisberg 1980). Thus, individual presidents should fare differently: high legislative support for more ideological Johnson and Nixon, low support for less ideological Reagan and Bush (based upon policy statements in chapter 3).

Party differences in legislative success and support should occur even though civil rights was not highly partisan in congressional voting in the 1960s and 1970s (Turner 1970, 52–54, 86–88; Clausen 1973, 80, 97; Vanderslik 1968, 723). Still, Democratic presidents have had much larger legislative majorities and should have greater legislative success and support than Republican presidents (Orfield 1975; Bullock 1984a, 200; Shull 1983, 45–48; Kessel 1984, 498).

Measures

It is not easy to determine legislative modification and adoption of presidential policy preferences. Many avenues exist for interaction where *modification* could occur; however, rather than the number of requests and vote positions per year, I use percent approval by Congress even though there are few votes upon which to base the percentages. Modification is the *support* of presidential positions on legislative votes on civil rights: generally, on amendments, and on key votes. These subsets of votes may differ significantly from the universe of all votes. Support occurs when Congress votes yea on a measure the president favors or nay on one he opposes. Thus, low modification would be high support of presidents' positions, and support is *reactive* to his positions on Congress's agenda.

Adoption by Congress is probably somewhat easier to tap, measured by the percentage of presidential requests that are approved (*success*). Unlike positions on votes, which originate in Congress, requests are the presidents' proposed legislation. They are *proactive* to presidents' legislative priorities. Congressional Quarterly collects these measures, and the literature identifies problems with their use (Shull 1983, 195–99; Wayne 1978, 168–71; Edwards 1989; Edwards 1980b, 13–18; Edwards 1985; Peterson 1990, 303–5, 323; Spitzer 1993; Cohen 1982, 516).

Results

General

The most obvious finding in Table 6.1 (page 136) is that Congress generally goes along when the president takes a vote position, and this is particularly true on amendments, for which presidents' positions prevail 89 percent of the time. On the other hand, *presidential* requests, as opposed to positions on *congressional* votes, are adopted only one-third of the time. Thus, presidential success is relatively low.[2] These general findings support one expectation, but amendments were *not* supported less by Congress than are all votes.

Table 6.2, on page 137, divides support of presidential position-taking by target groups.[3] Presidents' positions on women and the *other* category receive the greatest overall legislative support while votes on age questions and especially relating to Hispanics/Native Americans are supported least. Recall that I expected votes on gender to be upheld more than votes on blacks. The various other aggregations reveal considerable differences, but the small *N*s, especially for Hispanics/Native Americans and on age, frustrate interpretation of the results.

Table 6.3, on page 139, examines congressional support by subissues. Support does not exist for the expectation that the presidents' positions on employment issues and issues in the *other* category (largely voting, public accommodations) would be approved more than positions on education and housing. Employment is the most controversial subissue, while housing, surprisingly, generated the least controversy (e.g., most congressional support of presidents' vote positions).

Individual Presidents

Looking at presidents individually is the first grouping of the data (see Table 6.1). Not only can we compare similarities of legislative support for the nine presidents (Truman for key votes only), but we can also examine trends over a forty-seven-year period. Truman is supported least among these presidents in obtaining his positions on key votes. Notice, too, that, after Kennedy, the trend is for Congress to uphold such key vote positions. Eisenhower was supported the least of all presidents on amendments and in the category *all* votes, and Congress adopted only 25 percent of his civil rights requests.

Table 6.1

Presidents' Congressional Support and Success
(% success of requests and support on vote positions)

	Requests[a]	Vote Positions		
		All[b]	Amendments[b]	Key Votes[c]
Mean[d]	33	80	89	80
By Party				
Democrats	33	95	94	83
Republicans	32	62	79	74
By President				
Truman				
Eisenhower	25	50	0	50
Kennedy	5	67	0	100
Johnson	42	98	97	100
Nixon	56	66	84	82
Ford	33			89
Carter		71	50	100
Reagan		52	86	25
Bush		69	67	60

Source: *Congressional Quarterly Almanac*, yearly.
[a] Based on 23 years, 1953–75.
[b] Based on 35 years, 1957–91.
[c] Based on 47 years, 1945–91, but positions prior to 1957 coded by author.
[d] % = means based on the number of times Congress supports the presidents' positions divided by number of presidents' positions. To simplify the table, *N*s are not included but are available from the author.

Congress upheld just 5 percent of Kennedy's requests, by far the lowest success rate for any president. Kennedy also fared poorly on his positions on all three types of votes. Johnson received high approval among presidents for his civil rights positions on *all* votes and amendments but not on key votes. His huge legislative majorities in Congress gave him only 42 percent adoption of his program requests, a success level Nixon exceeded by a considerable margin.

Nixon was more assertive in taking positions than in requesting, although he was the most successful of all recent presidents when he did make legislative requests. He was also able to prevail more often on his controversial amendment and key vote positions than on *all* votes, but he still got his way two-thirds of the time on the latter. Requests reveal Ford's nonassertiveness (even though only one and one-half years of data are available), but he was also the only president never to take a position on a legislative vote in the

Table 6.2

Congressional Response to Presidents' Vote Positions, by Target Group[a]

	Blacks (%)	Hispanics/ Native Americans (%)	Women (%)	Age (%)	Other (%)	Total	
						N[b]	%
Mean	75	33	85	40	88	232/298	78
By Party							
Democrats	92	100	94	33	94	177/192	92
Republicans	54	20	67	50	57	52/98	53
By President							
Eisenhower	0				0	0/5	0
Kennedy	0					0/3	0
Johnson	96	100	93	33	96	171/181	94
Nixon	64		50		33	26/43	60
Ford						—	
Carter	67		100		50	6/8	75
Reagan	45	20	100	100	100	11/6	52
Bush	52		75	0	57	18/28	64

[a]See Table 3.4 for categories.

[b]Numerator = number times Congress supports presidents' positions; denominator = number presidents' positions. To simplify the table, the cell Ns are not included but are available from the author.

civil rights realm during two and one-half years in office.

Since no data on requests exist after 1975, there is no systematic way to compare legislative success for recent presidents.[4] Neither Carter nor Reagan was very assertive on vote positions, but Bush was; thus, some comparisons are possible. Carter received about average support for his positions on all votes and amendments but received support on each of his key votes positions. Reagan lacked assertiveness on amendments and key votes but received much greater support on the former than the latter. Bush's overall support on many positions taken was the greatest among Republican presidents.

The support of individual presidents' vote positions by target group reveals interesting similarities and differences (see Table 6.2). Neither Eisenhower nor Kennedy was able to get congressional approval for the few positions he took, regardless of the target group focus. Johnson, of course, did inordinately well on his positions for all groups except for votes concerning age. Nixon's positions were supported much less, especially for women and *other*. Recall that Ford took no positions, and Carter and Reagan took few, despite more opportunities to do so (e.g., increasing number of roll call votes in Congress). Bush's support was greatest in positions taken on women.

The data for issue areas also reveal differences in legislative support among individual presidents (see Table 6.3). Kennedy was not supported at all, while Johnson received 100 percent support for his vote positions in education and employment but was supported least in housing, perhaps due to white fear of blockbusting. Subsequent presidents received 100 percent support for their few housing positions. Nixon was supported much more in education than employment, while Carter, except on his single position on housing, was infrequently supported. His contrast with Reagan is stark and further supports the assertion that the latter was much more effective than the former in persuading Congress to support his policy preferences. Bush ties with Nixon in receiving support for his positions, particularly in housing and the *other* subissue.

Political Party

Political party of the president distinguishes modification of vote positions well but not adoption of presidential requests (see Table 6.1). The greatest party differences are on *all* votes, where Democratic presidents, as expected, are supported 33 percentage points more than Re-

Table 6.3

Congressional Response to Presidents' Vote Positions, by Issue Area[a]

	Education (%)	Employ-ment (%)	Housing (%)	Other (%)	Total N[b]	Total %
Mean	73	69	87	82	167/214	78
By Party						
Democrats	87	100	83	83	112/125	90
Republicans	68	42	100	55	55/89	62
By President						
Eisenhower	33	0		50	2/6	33
Kennedy				0	0/3	0
Johnson	100	100	82	97	109/115	95
Nixon	71	33			23/34	68
Ford						—
Carter	50		100	0	3/7	43
Reagan	67	100	100	27	12/22	55
Bush	67	43	100	87	18/27	67

[a]See Table 3.5 for categories.
[b]Numerator = number of times Congress supports presidents' positions; denominator = number of presidents' positions. To simplify the table, the cell Ns are not included but are available from the author.

publicans. Obviously, much of this support relates to Democratic partisan majorities in Congress during most of the period under consideration. It may also help to be assertive; Democratic presidents take many more positions than do Republican presidents. The least partisan difference (9 percentage points) is on key votes.

Party differences in support for positions on target groups are dramatic and along the lines expected (see Table 6.2). Generally, Democratic presidents' positions on votes are upheld 92 percent versus just 53 percent for Republican presidents. Party differences in congressional approval are substantial for all categories, particularly for blacks.

Although Republicans took few positions by issue areas, party contrasts in approval rates in employment are especially stark (see Table 6.3). The only exception to Democrats' doing substantially better on vote positions than Republicans is the housing category. Thus, party differences are greatest on employment and least, but still substantial, on education and housing subissues.

Assessment

What can we conclude about congressional support of presidents' vote positions and the success of their legislative requests? The most assertive presidents are not always the most successful. Johnson was highly successful on his vote positions but received much lower support for his legislative requests. Kennedy was also assertive on civil rights requests, if not on legislative votes, with disastrous consequences on the former (one in twenty initiatives adopted). Assertiveness in taking positions diminishes greatly after Nixon. One might conclude from Johnson's example that presidents fare better with Congress by taking liberal positions, but conservatives Nixon and Bush also do very well. Thus, a strong liberal commitment by the president (e.g., Johnson) usually bodes well for support and success since conservative presidents fare much more poorly. Certainly Johnson was the most effective legislative president ever in civil rights. At least for all votes, these findings generally support expectations. Target groups and subissues help illuminate these differences among presidents.

Budget Responses

Budget appropriations are another congressional response to the president. The expectations are similar to those previously posited; that is, congressional budget growth will decline over time and will be greater for ideologically committed presidents, especially Democrats, and on less controversial employment and *general* (nonspecified) subissues. Although presidents probably are supportive of agencies more often than is Congress, generally the two actors agree (Shull 1979, 234; Stewart, Anderson, and Taylor 1982). One anticipates this norm of cooperation in civil rights also, although it may vary by aggregations of the data. The specific expectation is that presidential-congressional budget agreement will be greater for ideologically committed presidents, especially Democrats, and on less controversial employment and *general* subissues.

First I present congressional appropriations in constant dollars and then offer a more direct comparison of presidential-congressional relations by showing the difference between presidential budget requests and the amount appropriated by Congress. This difference provides a measure of presidential-congressional budget cooperation, and this level of agreement should reveal how Congress responds to presidential budgetary leadership.

Congressional Appropriations

Chapter 4 revealed fairly incremental presidential budget requests in civil rights. The figures in Table 6.4 show that congressional appropriations in constant dollars average 9.5 percent per year overall and change more annually than did requests. Yearly growth in congressional appropriations averages nearly 11 percent for all categories but housing, where the figure was 6.3 percent.

For the included agencies, appropriations data for Eisenhower and Kennedy exist only on education.[5] Both presidents experienced substantial (nonincremental) growth in appropriations. Appropriations grew under Johnson, too, especially for employment. As with his requests, considerable growth occurred in appropriations under Nixon, particularly in employment and housing. Under Ford, growth in appropriations was small except for housing, but even it grew at only slightly more than half of the rate as under Nixon (see Table 6.4). Under Carter, dramatic decreases in appropriations occurred from the Ford levels (except for employment); appropriations for the housing agency dropped the most of any issue area. Congressional appropriations under Reagan were lower than for any president except Carter. Considerable increases occurred in general (Civil Rights Commission), and the greatest average cuts were for housing (−2.1 percent). Increases in appropriations averaged 7.3 percent for Bush and, like Reagan, were greatest in general and least in housing.

Table 6.4 reveals much less congressional support under Reagan and Carter, but appropriations under Bush returned to the Ford levels. Agencies in all four subissues revealed steady declines through Carter in legislative appropriations in civil rights. Such declines in housing have continued, while other agencies, particularly the CRC (general), have recovered somewhat.

Contrary to expectations, appropriations are greater (by 3.4 percentage points) under Republican than Democratic presidents. Perhaps greater congressional generosity is not surprising because, except under Reagan for six of eight years, Democrats controlled both houses of Congress. Congress may have been trying to counteract Republican presidential conservatism. Appropriations increases were greater under

Table 6.4

Congressional Budget Appropriations
(% growth in constant $)

Issue Area Agency[a]	General CRC (%)	Education CRD (%)	Employment EEOC (%)	Housing FHEO[b] (%)	Means N[c]	Means %
Overall	10.9	10.6	11.0	6.3	964.3/101	9.5
By Party						
Democrats	5.4	10.4	16.6	-14.5	248.3/33	7.5
Republicans	14.0	11.0	8.4	8.9	716/68	10.9
By President						
Eisenhower		27.3			109/4	27.4
Kennedy		18.3			55/3	18.3
Johnson	14.0	12.7	26.5	22.7	239.5/14	17.1
Nixon	10.7	10.4	21.0		388.5/24	16.2
Ford	6.5	5.0	6.0	12.5	60/8	7.5
Carter	-5.4	1.6	6.8	-14.5	-46.2/16	-2.9
Reagan	18.7	2.9	-1.0	-2.1	129.2/12	4.6
Bush[d]	16.1	14.2	2.9	-3.9	29.3/4	7.3

Source: OMB, *Budget of the U.S. Government.*

[a] Agencies are the Civil Rights Commission (CRC), Civil Rights Division of the Department of Justice (DOJ), the Equal Employment Opportunity Commission (EEOC), and the Fair Housing and Equal Opportunity (IFHEO) program in the Department of Housing and Urban Development.

[b] Data from 1977 on are listed in the budget under Management and Administration as "equal opportunity and research programs."

[c] Figures are aggregated yearly averages derived by subtracting year 1 from year 2 and dividing by year 2. Numerator = average appropriations per year; denominator = number of years for which data are available. To simplify the table, the cell Ns are not included but are available from the author.

[d] Values are for 1990. FY 1991 estimates were used instead of actuals to compute growth.

Republican presidents in controversial housing but also somewhat larger in education and *general*. Appropriations for Democrats in employment averaged two times greater than for Republicans. These findings yield mixed results for my expectations by subissue.

Presidential-Congressional Cooperation?

The data from chapter 4 on presidential requests (see Table 4.4) can be compared with the appropriations data in Table 6.4 to assess executive-legislative correspondence in budgeting. No difference would suggest maximum presidential strength, while high positive or negative values indicate congressional strength in budgeting. Overall, Congress gave presidents more than requested, but differences are dramatic by issue area. Congress gave *general* 10.1 percent more than presidents requested, while housing obtained very close agreement between the two actors.

Dramatic differences in budget agreement also appear for individual presidents. For Johnson, differences between requests and appropriations were greatest in the *general* category (Civil Rights Commission) and employment. Congress appropriated more for every agency than Nixon requested. Ford wanted greater funding for housing than Congress was willing to provide.[6] Carter had little budget "success"; just the opposite from Nixon, Congress gave him less than he wanted in every instance.

Congress appropriated far more for education but less for housing than Reagan requested. Reagan had proposed deep cuts in the former but increases in the latter. Overall, Congress appropriated just 1.6 percent more than Reagan requested. Although limited data exist for Bush, Congress appropriated more than he requested in every instance, particularly for the CRC. Again, interpretation is difficult; Congress was probably expressing its dissatisfaction with conservative Reagan and Bush policies, such as when it cut Civil Rights Commission appropriations in fiscal year 1987 and later.

Differences in budget cooperation are also dramatic by presidential party and across subissues. Overall, Congress cut Democrats' requests 2.4 percent but increased Republican requests by 7.0 percent (compare Tables 4.4 and 6.4). Democrats obtained closer correspondence on education and employment, but not on *general* or, particularly, housing (14 percent difference). However, Carter is the only Democrat for whom housing appropriations data are available. Republican presidents ask for little but obtain far higher budgets than they desire in the housing subissue. Thus, housing reveals much less presidential-congressional agreement by party than does any other issue area. Party differences in appropriations are least in employment (see Table 6.4).

Both Congress and the president face limits to their influence in the budgetary process. Neither is able to judge all programs comparatively, and nonsystematic decision criteria have continued in both executive and legislative budget calculations. Budget formulation is an area in which Congress and the president have some power and discretion, largely because it constitutes policy initiation and development. Budget implementation, however, may be more removed from their influence. Next, I show that agencies themselves have considerable, perhaps inordinate, control over their own expenditures and programs (Fisher 1974, 3–4; Shull 1977; Shull 1989b).

Bureaucratic Responses

The civil rights bureaucracy that has developed since the late 1950s is a legal arrangement that presidents inherit when they take office. Civil rights enforcement involves many departments of the federal government. These numerous executive branch actors play a role in civil rights policy making, ranging from the president and his staff, to cabinet officers and their subordinates, to officials at various levels in the agencies themselves. The latter may reside in line agencies, like the Justice Department's Civil Rights Division (CRD), or in agencies supposedly independent of departments, such as the Equal Employment Opportunity Commission (EEOC).

In an effort to gain fuller control over implementation, presidents increasingly have sought larger administrative roles for agencies in the Executive Office of the President (EOP). One EOP agency, the Office of Management and Budget (OMB), does oversee both budgets and programs. President Reagan's interest in civil rights enforcement allowed a greater role for the White House staff than normally exists in the implementation of public policy. But staff is only part of the equation. Presidents may find they cannot do all they might wish; they can change programs and procedures only gradually or not at all. Others in the executive branch often have discretion in filling in details of policy, and the president does not preside as chief executive with as much authority or expertise as is commonly presumed. Often the bureaucracy becomes an obstacle to presidential influence and policy change.

Expectations

According to some studies, civil rights has not been high priority for recent presidents (Clausen 1973; Kessel 1974; LeLoup and Shull 1979). Although it had limited salience for Presidents Reagan and Bush as well (Bullock 1984a, 198; Stewart 1993, 337), their strong rhetoric and actions returned civil rights to a place of prominence on the public policy agenda (Wines 1982, 536–41; Amaker 1988; Shull, 1989a). But civil rights implementation is very fragmented. Resources have not grown, but the breadth of enforcement has greatly expanded and overburdened the agencies (Bullock and Stewart 1984). This situation may have allowed these presidents' vastly different policies—more conservative and assertive than most other presidents—to prevail.

By the 1970s inflation sharply limited agency budget and program growth. Presidents Reagan and Bush were conservative, pushing to limit agency implementation. Enforcement probably corresponds more closely with actions of ideologically committed presidents such as Johnson and Bush. The aversion to quotas characterized the Bush administration (Stewart 1993, 338). Moreover, greater enforcement efforts should occur during Democratic administrations than during Republican administrations.

Implementation efforts should also vary by issue areas. Government seems largely to have resolved some concerns. Education, for example, has had greater enforcement effort than has housing (Bullock 1984a, 188); but because housing is controversial, it should reveal varied enforcement. The school desegregation dimension of education largely left government's agenda by the mid-1970s, replaced to a considerable degree by problems in housing and employment (e.g., affirmative action, quotas, and comparable worth in the latter subissue).

A major goal of this chapter is to assess whether presidents have succeeded in obtaining their brand of implementation in civil rights policy. Did Reagan and Bush, in particular, get what they wanted? The assumption is that presidential influence is less in implementation than in the other policy stages; thus, bureaucratic responses should diverge more from presidential preferences than do legislative or judicial ones. This expectation is based partly on the assumption that agencies have wide-ranging discretion and responses. Such discretion appears in their spending and program activities.

Agency Expenditures

Most agencies need both presidential and congressional support to survive, let alone prosper, in the budget process. However, an agency's budget support from both Congress (appropriations) and the president (requests) is only partially related to its expenditures (outlays; see chapter 4, note 13, for definitions). Agencies can "smooth out" changes in annual appropriations by carrying over funds, requesting future funding, and using other creative devices to regulate their outlays. Although expenditure data for the individual agencies are surprisingly elusive, some interesting data on aggregated civil rights activities are available that did not exist for requests and appropriations.[7]

Total Spending

The *Budget of the United States Government* provides a wealth of information on the government. The *Special Analysis* of the budget (which regrettably is not available for civil rights after 1987) often includes information on agency activities, outlays, and personnel, revealing some of the magnitude of governmental activity in the civil rights area. The average change in civil rights expenditures over the eighteen-year period ending in FY 1988 revealed a 4.5 percent decrease in current dollars but a 4.5 percent decrease in constant dollars. Civil rights averages 8.2 percent of total federal expenditures, but the proportion was lower during the earlier and later years and higher during the middle years (Shull 1989a, ch. 6). These findings support the expectation of reduced expenditures over time.

Spending by Issue Area

Although agencies do not divide neatly into subissues, I provide expenditures for agencies in general civil rights and in each of three issue areas. Unfortunately, I was not able to use the same agencies for expenditures as for requests and appropriations. Exhaustive searching could not uncover sufficient data for the Civil Rights Division of the Justice Department. Accordingly, I substitute the Office for Civil Rights (OCR) for education. The other agencies remain throughout the budgeting analysis.[8] Note, too, that expenditures data on these agencies are not available before Johnson.

Overall, agencies average 4.7 percent yearly growth in expenditures (see Table 6.5). Only the Commission on Civil Rights (*general*) has shown a decrease in expenditures *growth* (−5.5 percent), while the other agencies have experienced increases, particularly the EEOC. This finding partially supports the expectation that enforcement would be greater in employment than in housing. Agency budgets themselves

Table 6.5

Agencies' Expenditures
(% growth in constant $)

Issue Area Agency[a]	General CRC[b] (%)	Education OCR[b] (%)	Employment EEOC (%)	Housing FHEO[c,e] (%)	Means N[d]	Means %
Overall	-5.5	6.2	14.3	3.5	325.6/90	4.7
By Party						
Democrats	7.3	-1.3	20.7	-71.6	124.7/25	5.0
Republicans	-12.7	11.1	10.3	12.3	300.9/66	4.6
By President						
Johnson	16.6		46.8		270.5/9	30.1
Nixon	9.3	19.2	22.0	15.5	377.5/23	16.4
Ford	-107.5	3.0	6.2	-2.7	-202.1/8	-25.3
Carter	-4.3	-1.3	5.0	-71.6	-145.1/14	-10.4
Reagan	-5.2	3.4	0.9	18.8	125/26	4.8
Bush	-5.9	-1.0	13.6	-28.2	-21.5/4	-5.4

[a] Agencies are the Civil Rights Commission (CRC), the Office of Civil Rights in the Department of Health, Education and Welfare (OCR), the Equal Employment Opportunity Commission (EEOC), and the Fair Housing and Equal Opportunity (FHEO) program in the Department of Housing and Urban Development.

[b] Department of Health, Education and Welfare and/or Department of Health and Human Services until 1979, Department of Education thereafter.

[c] FHEO data were "zero" in FY 1980, leading to the dropping of FY 1980–81 from the analysis. Note that Carter is the only Democrat for whom education and housing data are available.

[d] Figures are aggregated yearly averages derived from subtracting year 1 from year 2 and dividing by year 2. Numerator = average expenditure (outlay) per year; denominator = the number of years for which data are available. To simplify the table, the cell Ns are not included but are available from the author.

[e] Data for 1977–79 for FHEO from OMB, *Budget, Special Analysis*, and may not be comparable to other years from *Budget App.*

change over time, due partly to the life cycles of agencies and environmental conditions of issue salience and institutional support (Downs 1967).

Agency expenditures differ among individual presidents. As expected, greatest growth by far occurred under Johnson (for agencies where data are available); the least growth occurred under Ford (overall and *general*) and Carter (housing). Inexplicably, expenditures under Reagan increased overall—the first time since Nixon—and did not decrease as much for the CRC as had been anticipated. Also, growth in housing expenditures under Reagan was substantial (18.8 percent). Expenditures under Bush (based on limited data) are more in line with expectations; they greatly decreased for *general* and housing. The trends are for decreasing civil rights outlays over time across these administrations.

No differences by political party are evident in Table 6.5. Contrary to expectation, greater growth in expenditures occurred under Democrats in *general* and employment but under Republicans in education and housing. Perhaps the bureaucracy was countering conservative Republican requests. Note that the education data for Democrats exist only for Carter; had they been available for Kennedy and Johnson, growth in education expenditures for Democrats would no doubt have been considerably higher. The greatest party differences were in housing and the least in employment and education.

Considerable data have been presented on civil rights expenditures. Although the Reagan administration curtailed growth, it did not slash budgets from previous levels as much as many had anticipated. The administration argued that the civil rights bureaucracy provoked unnecessary confrontations, were unduly detailed, duplicated services, and expended money on procedures of dubious value (OMB 1982). Expenditures under Bush were dramatically lower for every issue area but employment.

Agency Programs

Data on implementation often are sketchy and difficult to quantify. Still, agency annual reports and other government documents are valuable sources infrequently tapped by scholars.[9] I examine several types of implementing activities for these agencies, such as formal rulings and cases received or resolved. Some agencies, like the Civil Rights Commission, make recommendations only, while others, like the Civil Rights Division of the Department of Justice, can initiate suits or settle them out of court.

Agency program activities occur after the budget process. These actions are literally the activities the agency pursues as it implements programs. Because the activities are so varied, and because this area of policy research is largely uncharted (Shull 1977), I sought activities that were relatively common to all agencies. These activities often include hearings and complaints brought by people charging civil rights violations. I tried to measure what the agency actually did. On how many of these cases did it act, and what was the result? Although the latter suggests impact, the present meaning of the term is more constricted. Did the agency succeed in settling the cases or grant a monetary settlement? These are some of the questions posed in ascertaining agencies' program responses.

Table 6.6 compares four agencies on a similar (but not identical) implementing measure. Because the Civil Rights Commission has no implementing responsibilities, the data presented in Table 6.6 are for all the civil rights activities (*general*) of the Department of Justice. It is hard to see a trend in implementation (number of cases terminated), and enforcement efforts may be no less now than in earlier periods. Implementation was most vigorous under Kennedy and Bush and least under Nixon. Contrary to expectation, enforcement in all subissues is relatively low for Johnson[10] but not necessarily so for Reagan (except for reductions in employment).

Implementation levels under Reagan and Bush exceed those of Carter in the *general* subissue area. Enforcement in employment was greatest under Carter (declining drastically under Reagan and, especially, Bush). Education implementation effort was greatest during the Nixon administration. The data for Carter and Reagan on education are not equivalent to earlier presidents but do seem to reveal greater activity under the latter president than the former. Obviously implementation data are extremely limited for the Bush administration (see note 4 in chapter 8).

Contrary to expectation, implementation efforts were not greater for Democrats than Republicans. In each of the subissues, enforcement efforts were greater during Republican than Democratic administrations. This finding would be inexplicable except for Nathan's (1983) argument that Republicans emphasize administrative actions more than Democrats. Or one can argue that presidents do not completely control the bureaucracy. Perhaps agencies resist Republican presidents' reduced enforcement efforts. However, no judgment is made about whether such agency actions are pro— or anti–civil rights.

Alternative explanations are timing and external pressures. For example, increased enforcement under Nixon may have been due not to his preferences but because HEW and other agencies were empowered by recent legislation to increase the pressure. Thus, implementation (perhaps at different levels) would have increased under any president, regardless of party. Nixon could not or would

Table 6.6

Civil Rights Agencies' Implementing Actions,[a] by Issue Area

Issue Area Agency[b]	General[c] (DOJ) N	General[c] (DOJ) X̄	Education[d] (DOE) N	Education[d] (DOE) X̄	Employment[e] (EEOC) N	Employment[e] (EEOC) X̄	Housing[f] (FHEO) N	Housing[f] (FHEO) X̄
Overall	4161/26	160	115/13	8.8	1159/25	46.3	38.4/11	3.5
By Party								
Democrats	1972/12	164	35/8	4.4	335.1/8	41.8	13.4/4	3.4
Republicans	2189/14	189	80/5	16.0	823.5/17	48.4	24.9/7	3.6
By President								
Kennedy	771/3	257	22/3	7.3				
Johnson	604/5	121	13/5	2.6	16.1/4	4.0		
Nixon	664/6	111	80/5	16.0	106/5	21.2	8.1/3	2.7
Ford	416/2	208			121/2	60.5	7.8/2	3.9
Carter	597/4	149	(57/1	57)[g]	319/4	79.8	13.4/4	3.3
Reagan	1206/8	151	(256/4	64)[g]	453.9/8	56.7	9.0/2	4.5
Bush	853/3	284			142.6/2	47.5		

[a]Values are means and = total number of actions (numerator) divided by number of years in office for which data are available (denominator).

[b]Agencies are the Department of Justice (DOJ), Department of Education (DOE), the Equal Employment Opportunity Commission (EEOC), and the Fair Housing and Equal Opportunity (FHEO) program in the Department of Housing and Urban Development.

[c]Number of all civil rights cases terminated, both civil and criminal; estimated for 1990–91. Source: OMB, *Budget*, annual, App.

[d]Number of school litigation cases closed. Source: U.S. Department of Justice, *Annual Report* (Washington, D.C.: GPO, 1974), 79, Civil Rights Division.

[e]Number of completed investigations in thousands; values after 1974 refer to number of Title VII charges resolved. Source: U.S. Equal Employment Opportunity Commission, *Annual Report* (Washington, D.C.: GPO, 1987), App., I-Z17.

[f]Number of complaints closed in thousands; Department of Housing and Urban Development Title VII complaint activity. Source: for 1973–77, C.M. Lamb, "Equal Housing Opportunity," in *Implementation of Civil Rights* (Monterey, Calif.: Brooks/Cole, 1984), 165; for other years, U.S. Department of Housing and Urban Development, *Annual Report* (Washington, D.C.: GPO). Report not available after 1984.

[g]Percent Department of Education complaints closed. Source: OMB, *Budget,* annual, *Special Analyses* (e.g., 1987, J6).

not gain control quickly of the Office for Civil Rights (in HEW). However, just because more cases were closed under his administration does not mean civil rights was more vigorously pursued. Nathan's (1983) interpretation above may be partially correct in that these conservative Republicans seem to have figured out that one can use the administrative process to appear to be enforcing the law while accomplishing little. In short, implementing actions has different meanings at different times, and ascribing party differences may obscure other dynamics of civil rights policy making, like such external factors as court orders. Such an interpretation relates closely to the policy change theme of this book.

Expectations are difficult to test because of the earlier caveat that the quality of the data varies greatly by agency. Also, the particular indicators used for each may not be comparable across agencies (or even within a single subissue such as employment; see Shull 1989a, app. D). What I can say is that changes in enforcement efforts do not appear to be as great in *general* civil rights and, surprisingly, housing, as they are in education and employment.[11] Thus, agency responses are in accord with expectations in *general* and education subissues but not in employment and housing. While Table 6.6 does not present the data, Reagan reduced fair housing suits (Lamb 1985, 95–98) but vastly increased the number of housing cases referred to state and local agencies (OMB 1985, *Special Analysis*, J25). Thus, even the nature of enforcement efforts is changing, further confounding systematic comparisons.

Implementation under Reagan

I now step back from the large amount of data presented in this chapter and assess civil rights policy enforcement in the Reagan and Bush administrations. Generally, less enforcement occurred under Reagan, but there are considerable gaps in the data available.[12] Critics have suggested greatly reduced civil rights enforcement under Reagan (Wines 1982, 536–41; Carter 1986; *Washington Post National Weekly Edition*, January 3 1984, 12, and April 13, 1987, 31; *Newsweek*, April 25, 1983, 96; and March 7, 1988, 21; Amaker 1988; *National Journal*, September 22, 1984, 1775).

The Reagan administration shifted the course of civil rights policy implementation. Attorney General William French Smith admitted that "the Justice's Civil Rights Division under Reagan has departed from its 'traditional role' of forceful advocacy" (*National Journal*, January 23, 1982, 164). Litigation also changed. Reagan's assertions that more cases were filed than under previous administrations (*Public Papers of the Presidents* 1983, 1081, and 1982, 1156) refer to specific criminal violations of civil rights. Moreover, litigation moved from broader class action suits to the individual level. Ideology guided these shifts in policy and, unlike the active liberalism seen under Johnson, this was "a conservative administration being activist in the opposite direction" (*National Journal*, March 27, 1982, 538).

Implementation under Bush

The Bush administration continued conservative policy implementation. It barred college scholarships awarded solely on the basis of race but allowed race to be considered as "one factor to encourage diversity" (*New Orleans Times-Picayune*, December 2, 1991, A7). Civil rights supporters said, "It is deplorable that the administration would ignore the educational crisis facing minority students and instead take a position based purely on racial politics" (*New Orleans Times-Picayune*, December 2, 1991, A7). However, conservatives said, "The Education Department is going in the right direction" (*New Orleans Times-Picayune*, December 2, 1991, A7).

The federal directive on affirmative action based upon the 1991 Civil Rights Act reveals Bush's uncertainty in domestic affairs. It was prepared in secrecy without consulting others in the administration or Congress. The columnist Anthony Lewis called it "making policy without accountability, to run things from within the White House." Lewis believes that the directive "shows how profoundly the Republican Party has changed on racial justice" (*New Orleans Times-Picayune*, November 26, 1991, B7).

In the employment area, the administration seemed to implement civil rights policy more vigorously. Although it would not conduct the audits itself, the EEOC accepted for investigation charges brought by private groups testing for bias in hiring by private firms. Although most employment suits concern firing and promotions rather than hiring, the agency showed continued enforcement effort (*National Journal*, October 26, 1991, 2598). In December 1991, Bush's own appointee to head the Civil Rights Commission criticized the administration for giving mixed signals on minority hiring.

Summary

What role has Congress played in the modification and adoption of civil rights policy over the last half century? It was often the most conservative branch and supported presidential initiatives in civil rights less than practically any other policy area, approving only about one in three proposals. However, when presidents took positions on legislative votes, Congress tended to go along. Historically, civil rights has not been particularly partisan or conflictual in congressional voting (Shull 1983, ch. 4), but it became more so by the 1970s. Moderately high support for Nixon's and Bush's conservative vote positions is illustrative of increased presidential and legislative conservatism in civil rights. Except for the 1988 Civil Rights Restoration Act, Congress often blocked civil rights advances, sometimes exempting itself from laws passed. Permitting members of Congress, but no one else, to discriminate, led to characterizations of Congress as "the last plantation." By the late 1980s, Congress became more liberal and resumed some lost civil rights leadership.

Congress can also exert leadership in the budgetary realm, where its potential for policy impact is substantial. This is evident from the often nonincremental changes (appropriations) made in presidential budget requests. Somewhat more legislative conservatism was revealed on "socially oriented" civil rights legislation (e.g., housing) than toward more "enforcement-oriented" attempts (e.g., education and employment). Both the legislative and budget roles of Congress in responding to presidents are potentially more important than they are in actuality. Thus Congress lets presidents get away with much of what they want (Orfield 1975).[13]

The history of civil rights in the United States illustrates the importance of implementation in the policy-making process. Actors in the executive branch are diffused; there are many of them. Agencies have discretion largely because implementation is complex and nonexecutive actors are less involved than at other stages of policy making. It is hard to tell whether presidents get what they want from agencies.[14] Most agencies are able to adapt to different presidential preferences over the years, but some agencies had a more difficult time under the dramatically different civil rights policies of Ronald Reagan (Detlefsen 1991). Reagan probably had the greatest impact on civil rights enforcement; agencies were responsive to him. This conclusion is hard to prove, however, since data are elusive and Reagan often cited statistics different from those of his critics.

There has been some decline in implementing actions by agencies over time even if it is not certain whether such changes result from presidential wishes. Civil rights expenditures as a proportion of the total federal budget have been reduced dramatically. Employment and housing have increased in salience, compared with education and *general* civil rights.[15] As presidents have come and gone, so has the salience of subissues relative to others changed. Reactions by the courts and those outside government to presidents' statements and actions are presented in chapter 7.

Notes

1. My personal interviews with most of President Carter's liaison staff proved invaluable in understanding his relations with Congress. Although not easily subject to quantification, this background information is helpful in understanding presidential relations with Congress.

2. In a related study, only antitrust exceeded this low success rate on civil rights requests among six domestic policy areas (Shull 1983, 133).

3. The Ns forming the percentages for all vote positions in Table 6.1 may not correspond with the total Ns in Tables 6.2 and 6.3 because of *multiple* counting into categories or *deleting* noncategorizable votes from the latter two tables.

4. The debate over whether Congressional Quarterly should have stopped collecting the box score measure may be seen in Shull (1983, 195–99). Problems of equivalence could occur, but Peterson (1990) has updated the box score. The widely different findings for key versus *all* votes support arguments about their inherent differences (see Shull and LeLoup 1981; Shull and Vanderleeuw 1987).

5. The Civil Rights Division of the Justice Department enforces laws in many areas besides education. Under Eisenhower and Kennedy it played a limited role but it was involved in considerable school litigation. For that reason these education data have been retained.

6. A possible explanation is that, at the time, moderate Republicans tended to take the position that if segregated housing could be eliminated, many other problems would be solved relatively easily.

7. The correlation between appropriations and expenditures (for the average percent change in constant dollars across the civil rights agencies) is $r = 0.766$. The cynic might think a plot is afoot to prevent studying agency accountability. Budget categories and information change often, sometimes on a yearly basis, making comparability and time-series analysis difficult if not impossible.

8. Analyzing budget data can be an exasperating experience for scholars. The

9. Annual reports of agencies often provide a wealth of data unavailable from any other source. Unfortunately for scholars, they are, of course, idiosyncratic to

each agency. Also, data series are not always continued once begun. They decreased under Reagan and Bush in particular.

10. The finding of low agency implementation under Johnson is probably due in part to the long lead time needed following presidential and legislative actions.

11. Table 6.6 does not present these data (see Shull 1989a, app. D, table 3), but complaint investigations for the Office of Federal Contract Compliance Programs dropped precipitously to less than half the numbers in 1985–86 from levels of just a few years earlier (e.g., 1981–82; see OMB, various years, *Special Analysis*).

12. Problems of comparability are considerable as evidenced from the data presented. Education data for Carter and Reagan are not compatible to those for previous presidents. As another example, the data collected from EEOC reports change over time (see Shull 1989a, app. D, table 3). During the mid-1970s the number of EEOC charges resolved is reported, but it is not clear how comparable that data might be to the other variables. In addition, the Reagan administration concentrated on dollar values awarded for discrimination, a variable unavailable for earlier years. Indicators reported for the 1980s are under a category called *complaint processing* and include receipts, closures, and monetary settlements. Implementing data are much more limited after 1985.

13. The correlation between requests and appropriations is $r = 0.374$ (average percent change controlled for inflation for all agencies).

14. Except for budget requests ($r = 0.217$), all presidential statements and actions are negatively related to agency program actions.

15. Education was not even listed as a separate category in the *Special Analyses* during the 1980s, and by the late 1980s, the EEOC spent about 50 percent more than *any* agency on civil rights.

7

Responses by Courts and Nongovernmental Actors

We saw in chapters 3 and 5 that calling for action by the courts, making appointments to the judiciary, and having the government enter cases constitute presidential stimuli directed at the judiciary. The courts respond to such stimuli by voting individually and collectively on cases. Complicating the transition from stimulus to response are the independence of judges once appointed, the separation of powers doctrine, the discretion the Supreme Court exercises over its docket, and the lack of complete presidential control over the solicitor general.

Some of these responses are beyond the scope of this book, but I focus on two related to presidential statements and actions—litigation and appointee voting. Litigation defines the Court docket by deciding which cases the Supreme Court will hear, and appointee voting reveals whether presidents' preferences will be upheld by their appointees. These responses are important because the Supreme Court rules on the constitutionality and legality of many important domestic policy questions. Presidents often seem disappointed in decisions of the courts in high-profile cases where presidential positions are not upheld. Even though presidential appointees do not always support presidential preferences, the courts have much more commonly invalidated actions of Congress than actions of presidents (Scigliano 1984, 408–9).

This chapter also analyzes the responses from those outside government: interest groups, political parties, the media, elections, and public opinion. We have observed the substantial impact of the institutional and external environment on the fragmented civil rights policy process. Interest groups were particularly strong in getting civil rights policies enacted and in keeping decision makers aware of continued inequities. They did the most to make civil rights a movement. The general impact of political parties, while seemingly less than that of interest groups, is more important earlier in the policy process (e.g., agenda setting rather than implementation). Of course, civil rights, particularly race, largely defines our modern parties (Carmines and Stimson 1989; Edsall and Edsall 1991).

Such party differences also appear in election results. Elections usually do not turn on civil rights but can be affected by popular attitudes and actions of government officials. The media also are affected by and influence civil rights. The media cover dramatic events, which affect the attitudes of both the mass public and elite decision makers. Public opinion has shifted toward greater tolerance and acceptance of civil rights in principle but with growing concern about compensatory actions, which have particularly split the races and the political parties (Edsall and Edsall 1991, ch. 1). Although roles of those inside government probably have been more important in civil rights than those outside government, influences of the latter appear frequently in examining the evolution of civil rights policy.

Judicial Responses

Among governmental actors, the judiciary often plays the leading role in civil rights. The Supreme Court has almost total discretion over the cases it hears. Larry Baum and Herbert Weisberg (1980) credit the Court with deciding 267 cases on issues relating to blacks from 1949 to 1976, and many of these cases preceded actions by Congress and presidents. Baum and Weisberg also found the Supreme Court taking more liberal positions than the House of Representatives, at least until about 1973, when Nixon Court appointees began to influence civil rights outcomes (1980, 23–25). Robert Scigliano (1971, 205) also views the Supreme Court as more liberal than Congress on civil rights. Since presidents also have been fairly liberal, their preferences probably influence judicial decisions more than they influence legislative decisions. Therefore, judicial actions probably are more reflective of presidents' positions than are legislative actions.

Rights rather than property issues increasingly dominated the

Court's agenda in the post–World War II era. Baum and Weisberg (1980) find both the House and Supreme Court exhibiting declining support for civil rights but for different reasons. They see member replacement and the evolution of issues as more important for the Court, but region and constituency as more influential for changes in House voting patterns (1980, 42–43). Their study reveals that agendas change and that policy content can be an important influence on actor behavior. (See Brady and Sinclair 1984 for a related analysis of agenda change in the House.) The Court became much more conservative than Congress by 1989 (Eskridge 1991, 683). This changing policy content as it affects target groups and subissues is the next topic.

Policy Content

Target Groups

The agendas of presidents, Congress, and the Supreme Court differ dramatically on some issues but may be more similar on civil rights. Target groups and subissues are, of course, intertwined. For example, rights for African Americans and women are both similar and different. Where blacks were arguing against a *legal* tradition that kept them subservient, women were arguing against a *social* tradition that sought to protect them. The Supreme Court has often justified paternalism against women (e.g., exclusion from the draft) while gradually chipping away at many other barriers to greater equality with men (e.g., pensions).

Thus, the Court's positions vary across target groups. It has taken more liberal positions of late toward women but not toward blacks. The Reagan appointee Sandra Day O'Connor reflects this trend in more recent years. Baum and Weisberg find that nearly 100 percent of Court outcomes were favorable to blacks in 1961–64, but only 32 percent in 1973–76 (1980, 44). The Court took conservative positions during Reagan's first term but was more moderate after 1985 (*Washington Post National Weekly Edition*, July 22, 1985, 32, and August 24 1987, 23). The elevation of William Rehnquist to chief justice and the addition of Antonin Scalia brought more conservative positions, while Anthony Kennedy's views are more moderate.

George Bush's appointees to the Supreme Court were just as conservative as Reagan's. Liberal groups saw Clarence Thomas as among the most conservative justices (*Washington Post National Weekly Edition*, March 9–15, 1992, 32). Thomas voted with the most conservative member, Scalia, on each of the first eight cases in which he participated. Only one of those was a civil rights case. Ironically, the Bush administration took a liberal position of broadly interpreting the Voting Rights Act, but Thomas voted with the Court majority against the administration.

Issue Areas

Judicial responses also vary by subissues. Baum and Weisberg (1980) identify fifty-eight education, twenty employment, and thirteen housing cases heard by the Supreme Court from 1949 to 1976. They believe growing prominence of employment and housing subissues, as well as change in Court membership, help explain the Court's decreasing liberalism into the 1970s on civil rights. The following discussion summarizes responses by issue areas important on the Court's agenda.

Education. The Supreme Court generally resisted efforts by Congress and presidents to weaken school desegregation enforcement, and it received much criticism for its busing orders (*Congress and the Nation*, 3:1973, 512). In May 1983 the Court ruled against a Reagan administration decision to allow tax exemptions for private schools that segregate. A White House aide called the Court's decision "dead wrong," (*Newsweek*, June 6, 1983, 38). In 1985 the Court also let stand a Philadelphia decision to transfer teachers to achieve better racial balance among elementary and secondary school faculty, a decision also opposed by the administration. Court rulings in both school desegregation and equal employment have considered numerical underrepresentation as evidence of discrimination. A near-unanimous Court handed the Reagan administration a victory in October 1986, however, refusing to reinstate crosstown busing to racially segregated elementary schools in Norfolk, Virginia. In an 8–0 vote, the Court in *Freeman v. Pitts* (1992) relaxed some school desegregation decrees.

Employment. This issue area was the main civil rights battlefield in the 1980s and early 1990s, especially over affirmative action and quotas (Edsall and Edsall 1991, 186). In January 1984, the Court unanimously upheld a court-ordered plan for the Detroit Police Department despite a Civil Rights Commission proposal against it. However, in a case the Reagan administration considered reverse discrimination, the Supreme Court determined that whites cannot be laid off before blacks with less seniority (*Memphis Fire Department v. Stotts*, 1984). Several cases in 1986 and 1987 went against the administration. The Supreme Court agreed to confront the issue of comparable worth after a December 1983 ruling by a federal district judge against the state of Washington, which ordered back pay for women doing work requiring essentially equal skills as those required of men. Cases in 1989 during Bush's first year (e.g., *Richmond v. Croson* and *Ward's Cove v. Atonio*) were also controversial. Congressional dissatisfaction with conservative Supreme Court decisions in employment led to legislation to overturn them (e.g., the 1988 Civil Rights Restoration Act and the 1991 Civil Rights Act; see chapter 4).

Housing. Until 1970, the Supreme Court generally took a back seat to Congress and presidents in housing policy. Cases upheld the position of advocates of fair housing (e.g., *Jones v. Mayer*, 1968, and *Reitman v. Mulkey*, 1967). There have been few subsequent cases on fair housing, but a series of Supreme Court decisions during the 1970s upheld as constitutional exclusionary devices developed by local governments (Lamb and Lustig 1979, 177–223). In *Freeman v. Pitts* (1992), the Court determined that school districts need not overcome racial imbalance due to residential housing patterns. The controversial nature of housing reflects this diminishing Supreme Court support for civil rights.

What types of judicial responses to presidents' civil rights policies are possible? One possible response is public positions by Supreme Court justices, although these are very rare. On September 13, 1987, Justice Thurgood Marshall told the journalist Carl Rowan in a television interview that he placed Ronald Reagan at the bottom of U.S. presidents in concern for racial justice. This statement was a highly unusual criticism by a sitting Supreme Court justice. A second possible response comes when the courts uphold or reject government suits or positions taken in cases in which the government is not a formal party. A third type of response is from presidential judicial appointees themselves. How closely do they adhere to the appointing president's policy preferences?

Litigation

Litigation is a major weapon for enforcing compliance with civil rights laws. Chapter 5 revealed differences among presidents in their propensity to resort to the courts, not only in bringing suits in the first place but in enforcing the resultant decisions. The Reagan administration dramatically slowed pursuit of civil rights violations in education and housing and against institutionalized persons (Wines 1982; Lamb 1985). In December 1984 the Department of Justice filed a friend of the court brief stating that school boards should be allowed to abolish court-ordered busing programs and return to neighborhood schools even if the result is increased racial segregation. This brief was clearly an effort to implement Reagan's opposition to busing to achieve school desegregation.

Ironically, the Bush administration took the liberal *amicus* position in 1991 of requiring Justice Department preapproval of changes in election districts. In late January 1992 the Court decided black officials could not count on federal courts for help if local governments try to dodge the intent of the Voting Rights Act. The decision (*Presley v. Etowah County Commission*) no longer required preclearance by the Justice Department of such changes. None of the conservative Reagan and Bush Supreme Court appointees, including Clarence Thomas, had supported the Bush administration's moderate position.

How successful are presidents in obtaining their preferences from the courts? Presidents usually get their way, because the courts must depend upon the goodwill of the president to enforce judicial decisions. Research finds the executive branch (through the solicitor general) on the winning side about 75 percent of the time. One study determined that the government's appeals are accepted more often (66 percent), and on 80 percent of *amicus* briefs, than "the appeals of the executive's defeated opponents" (only 3 percent; Scigliano 1984, 400). The Reagan administration won 87 percent of cases in 1984, 80 percent in 1985, but only 72 percent in 1986 (*Washington Post National Weekly Edition*, July 21, 1986, 13).

Steven Puro finds higher success rates in civil rights than for most policy areas (1971, 224–26). However, at a later time period, Jeffrey Sigel finds that the president does less well on civil rights than on every other issue area but one (1988, 139). He, too, observes the president winning most cases on which the executive takes positions.

Reagan won at much higher levels than Nixon, Ford, or Carter but less often than earlier presidents (1988, 139). Thus, litigation remains an important weapon in the presidential arsenal. The courts recognize that presidents' increasing use of *amicus* reflects their preferences on public policy (Puro 1971). Thus, presidents intervene in cases through the solicitor general's legal briefs. It seems to pay off. Sigel concludes that "solicitors general are responsive to the presidents they serve and not to their own policy preferences" (1988, 138).

Appointee Voting

A variety of judicial actors participate in civil rights policy. Apart from judges, presidents appoint officials in the Department of Justice and other relevant agencies. Reactions by Congress and nongovernmental actors to executive appointments may be just as controversial as to judicial appointments. An example in the Reagan administration was the confirmation of Edwin Meese as attorney general by the largest number of dissenting votes (31) of any cabinet official in the prior fourteen years. Critics also charge that far too few women and minorities were appointed to vacancies in the Department of Justice and other agencies relevant to civil rights (Boles 1985, 73). Nevertheless, Meese quickly echoed the president's opposition to hiring quotas.

Civil rights groups also opposed Reagan's nomination of William Rehnquist to be chief justice of the Supreme Court. The Leadership Conference on Civil Rights charged that "he had fought to keep this country segregated and ruled by whites" (*New York Times*, September 5, 1986, A22). Rehnquist subsequently was confirmed but by the fewest votes ever for a successful nominee for chief justice. In summer 1987, a large coalition of at least 185 organizations opposed Reagan's nomination of Robert Bork to the Supreme Court. The contest centered on Bork's conservative ideology and turned out to be an old-fashioned grass-roots lobbying campaign that even pitted presidential candidates against one another. A second nominee withdrew for personal reasons prior to a confirmation vote, while Reagan's third nominee for the position, Anthony Kennedy, was confirmed unanimously.

We saw in chapter 5 (especially Table 5.3) that Bush appointed more women and minorities to executive and judicial positions than did Reagan. Most Bush administrative appointees were more moderate than were Reagan's. Among Bush's most visible cabinet appointees was Elizabeth Dole, who, as secretary of labor, was also the first cabinet member to resign. She was quickly replaced by another conservative Republican female, former representative Lynn Martin. Although Bush's first Supreme Court appointee, David Souter, was not controversial, his second, Clarence Thomas, a black conservative, was particularly so. After weeks of rancorous hearings, including charges of sexual harassment, Thomas was confirmed by the smallest margin ever for a Supreme Court justice.

Chapter 5 examined the demographic characteristics of those selected to district courts, which suggests degree of *representativeness* to the general public. The votes of Supreme Court justices examined here suggest their degree of *responsiveness*, at least to the appointing president.[1] Can presidents shape judicial policy through their power to nominate Supreme Court justices? The assumption is that presidents seek Supreme Court justices who reflect presidential preferences on major issues that are brought to the Court (Tate 1981; Handberg and Hill 1984; Gates, Cohen, and Shull 1988).

Responsiveness

Virtually every president has recognized that judicial appointments offer important opportunities for pursuit of presidential goals.[2] The appointment power does not, of course, assure success in shaping a judiciary hospitable to those goals. There are many tales of presidents who were disappointed by their appointees' voting records (see Abraham 1985). Yet the nature of the relationship between presidential preferences and judicial votes has received little systematic examination. Despite its scarcity, existing research commonly concludes that perhaps three-fourths of the justices have satisfied the expectations of the appointing presidents (Scigliano 1971, 146; Rohde and Spaeth 1976, 107–10; Heck and Shull 1982, 334).[3]

This section examines the basic relationship between presidential preferences and the voting records of the Supreme Court justices whom they appoint. I relate presidential preferences in their policy statements (see chapter 3) to judicial votes on cases, expecting a positive relationship in level of support for civil rights between a president and his Supreme Court appointees.

Correspondence of Preferences

Both presidents and justices have been supportive of civil rights more often than not during recent decades (Heck and Shull 1982). The

Table 7.1

Rank Order of Presidential and Judicial Support Scores on Civil Rights

Rank	President	Score (%)	Rank	Appointees	Score (%)
1.5	Johnson	100	1	Johnson	91.9
1.5	Kennedy	100	2	Eisenhower	76.8
3	Eisenhower	97	3	Kennedy	71.2
4	Reagan	72	4	Ford	65.2
5	Bush	69	5	Nixon	50.0
6	Nixon	62	6	Reagan	41.9[a]
7	Ford	43			

Note: Spearman's rho = 0.679.

[a]The data for Sandra Day O'Connor are 1982–85; see J.B. Gates, J.E. Cohen, and S.A. Shull, "Presidential Policy Preferences and Supreme Court Appointment Success, 1954–1984," paper presented at the annual meeting of the Western Political Science Association, San Francisco, March 1988. Recall that Carter, whose liberalism score was 96%, had no Supreme Court appointees. These data are through 1985 for Reagan; unavailable for Bush appointees. Presidents' liberalism scores are based upon last column in Table 3.2.

agreement between presidential preferences and judicial votes is analyzed chiefly on the relative position of presidents (compared with other presidents) and on the rank orderings of presidential support scores and the support scores of the justices appointed by each president.

Only limited correspondence exists between the civil rights support scores of presidents and those of the justices they appoint. Table 7.1 ranks seven modern presidents from most supportive to least supportive and compares this ranking to a similar rank ordering of the voting records of their appointees. A positive relationship exists, but it is based on only seven cases and is probably not a strong enough correlation to confirm the expectation. Still, Gates, Cohen, and Shull (1988) find presidential liberalism a far better predictor of appointees' votes than either party or previous judicial experience.[4]

Recent Judicial Appointments

Carter was the only president to complete a full term in office without the opportunity to nominate a Supreme Court justice. However, during those four years, he did appoint about 40 percent of the federal judiciary, due to newly created district and appellate judgeships. According to Stidham and Carp (1986, 15), his district court appointees had liberalism ratings of only 52 percent.

Reagan had an even more profound impact on the judiciary; in two full terms, he named about half the federal judges. His district court appointees were the most conservative among contemporary presidents (31 percent liberal; Stidham and Carp 1986, 15). He also seems to have fared well with his first Supreme Court nominee, Sandra Day O'Connor. Very conservative on blacks' if not on women's issues, she departed less from Reagan's views on civil rights than did Eisenhower and Ford appointees (Abraham 1985, 333, 337; Goldman 1985, 328). Reagan's two Supreme Court nominees in 1986 were activists for his agenda and conservatives on civil rights. Both opposed quotas, and Scalia expressed the opinion as an appellate court judge that the Supreme Court had gone too far on busing.

Bush's selection of Clarence Thomas was the most controversial Supreme Court nomination in U.S. history. After choosing conservative but noncontroversial David Souter, what possessed Bush to take such a chance and engage in the kind of political conflict he seemed to abhor? Politically speaking, the nomination was brilliant, for it split Democrats and blacks badly. Also, according to *Newsweek* (July 16, 1991, 16), Bush "provided himself with a political cover to rail against racial quotas." But, what kind of justice did Bush get, and was it worth risking losing the perception that he was a civil rights moderate? Thomas reflected a small but growing element of conservative civil rights activists. He opposed affirmative action, promoted black self-help, and rejected broad class action suits rather than specific cases of discrimination. Thomas supported Scalia on 85 percent of cases in his first year on the Court (including the conservative position on the abortion case). Thus, he seemed to be a safe, conservative appointee, giving Bush the advantage of placing his opposition off guard.

How salient was civil rights to the Supreme Court appointments of Presidents Reagan and Bush? Probably no single policy area dominated their thinking in appointing justices to the Court. Despite their party's pledge to appoint judges "who respect traditional family values and the sanctity of human life" (Republican Platform, reprinted in *Congressional Quarterly Weekly Reports*, July 19, 1980, 2046), both probably approached appointments from a broader ideological base than abortion specifically or even civil rights generally. Ideologues like Reagan and Bush had to cover many bases and were probably more concerned with overall ideological perspective than with positions in a single policy area.

It is unrealistic to expect that presidents would succeed every time in sending to the Supreme Court justices who consistently support their policy preferences. In addition, there are measurement problems in trying to test this relationship. For example, a president's public statements are an imperfect reflection of his policy preferences, and judicial votes act more as responses to the stimuli presented in specific disputes than as reflections of attitudes per se (see Howard 1968).

Two conclusions follow from this analysis of relationships between recent justices and presidents in the area of civil rights. First, presidents often succeed in appointing justices who share their views on civil rights (see Table 7.1), a conclusion consistent with earlier studies (Scigliano 1971; Rohde and Spaeth 1976). Furthermore, presidents who are attentive to civil rights (such as Johnson) are more likely to appoint justices who reflect their policy preferences. Random turnover complicates interpretation. However, presidential-judicial correspondence is probably largely due to the likelihood that a president with strong views will search diligently for like-minded Supreme Court nominees; once on the Court, justices' votes often reflect their own policy preferences.

Assessment

Congress stymied Reagan's efforts to reverse affirmative action programs. He could not weaken the Voting Rights Act but then took credit for its extension when his partisans in Congress refused to support his position. During 1986, Congress threatened to cut off funding for the Civil Rights Commission that Reagan had weakened and, some say, politicized. Court decisions supporting his preferences were overturned by Congress through the Civil Rights Restoration Act. These examples show that the Reagan administration could not control the legislative or perhaps even the judicial agenda in civil rights. The Democratic-controlled House initiated each measure and got many Republicans to support compromised versions. A reluctant president eventually accepted most. Gradually, however, Reagan's conservative judicial appointees began to support his preferences (Detlefsen 1991, 8). The situation was somewhat similar for Bush. A much more conservative Supreme Court seemed to support his conservative preferences, but a liberal Congress overturned many such decisions. Although Bush obtained his Supreme Court nominee, Clarence Thomas, the confirmation had considerable political consequences. Bush's motives were questioned and Republicans were painted as more anti–civil rights than ever. Some say the president even engaged in race-baiting, more like the openly divisive Ronald Reagan rather than the supposedly "kinder, gentler," more pragmatic George Bush. Minority group suspicion of Bush grew during 1992.

Responses from Those outside Government

Civil rights policy in the 1980s and 1990s differs markedly from that of a generation ago. The Reagan and Bush administrations pursued a large number of actions to limit government's role in fighting discrimination and overcoming the effects of past discrimination. These actions crystallized opposition by some civil rights interest groups. Liberal groups were unified against both administrations, and some anti–civil rights groups, like the Moral Majority, all but disappeared. Other actors, however, have expressed more varied reactions to presidential statements and actions. Such unofficial (nongovernmental) participants have no legal authority in policy making (Anderson 1979, 41), but they can influence later stages in the policy process, particularly implementation and evaluation.

Some commentators thought the presumed moderate George Bush would garner support from those outside government in support of a "kinder, gentler" civil rights policy. Surely he had a better chance to obtain black support than the more ideologically diverse Ronald Reagan. That was the early projection. We have already seen that Bush's statements and actions actually were more ideologically conservative than were Ronald Reagan's. Accordingly, the civil rights community was as critical of Bush's statements and actions as of Reagan's. First I discuss interest groups and then other actor responses during these two administrations.

Interest Groups

Reagan Administration

The leaders of civil rights organizations have often been at odds with one another. The uneasy relationship, or total lack of dialogue, with the

Reagan administration probably helped unite these groups. Reagan's statements and actions contributed to these tensions, especially his direct attacks on black leaders themselves. These criticisms came from the president personally and through his appointees in government, particularly in the Justice Department and on the Civil Rights Commission.

A major question, of course, is whether all this rancor had any effect on administration policy. Criticism by civil rights groups and disputes between the EEOC and OFCCP did delay relaxed affirmative action hiring rules from going into effect. But rhetoric on both sides was unusually strident. Although giving the administration some good marks, the 1984 annual report of the National Urban League said that "the Reagan administration's record on civil rights was 'deplorable' and threatened to divide the country into a 'prosperous majority and an impoverished minority'" (*National Journal*, January 26, 1985, 224). Reagan found civil rights interests weak and divided; thus he was able to operate from a position of strength.

Bush Administration

The fumbled White House directive designed to interpret the 1991 Civil Rights Act was criticized by many types of interest groups. Business organizations believed they had received mixed signals. The directive raised new questions about Bush's leadership on domestic issues generally and civil rights specifically. Even Republican Senator John Danforth (Mo.) insisted the directive be withdrawn. Rights groups threatened to go to court if the Bush administration did not enforce the act, charging that he was seeking to undermine the bill even as he signed it. Representative Maxine Waters (D-Calif.) stated that Bush is "trying to send a message to the conservative right that he does not believe in affirmative action" (*New Orleans Times-Picayune*, November 22, 1991, A8). Much criticism was directed at the White House staff (particularly against C. Boyden Gray, its author, and Chief of Staff John Sununu) for underestimating the political fallout of the president's action. Soon thereafter, Sununu resigned. Pressure from civil rights supporters continued, and even Bush's appointee to head the Civil Rights Commission criticized the White House action.

The Los Angeles riot in May 1992 resulted in the worst destruction and loss of life of any civil disturbance in U.S. history. Civil rights groups reacted strongly when the Bush administration blamed it on the social programs of the 1960s and 1970s. Many blamed the president for lack of leadership. Bush quickly retreated from his position, soon visiting the area and offering programs to aid in the recovery. Forty-three percent approved versus 49 percent of the public disapproved his response to the situation (*National Journal*, June 6, 1992, 1376). Shortly thereafter, rights groups (including the American Civil Liberties Union) filed a lawsuit to compel the U.S. Department of Agriculture to declare a food emergency (to expand food stamp distribution) in South Central Los Angeles, the area hardest hit. Overall, interest group tension heightened during the Bush years to the extent that racial and ethnic disagreements were studied by the Civil Rights Commission. Minority groups were not very enthusiastic about Clinton in the 1992 election, but quickly coalesced around his presidency.

Other Actors

Reagan Administration

Reactions by political parties, the media, public opinion, and election results were more mixed than those of interest groups. The Democratic party is commonly viewed as more supportive of civil rights than the Republican party, taking the view that desegregation must be mandated. The parties have clearly differed on this point (*Washington Post National Weekly Edition*, January 14, 1985, 38). Many of the tools for achieving desegregation, such as quotas and busing, have been unpopular. The Republican party seemingly has been closer to the public pulse, which some think has made a difference in presidential elections despite overwhelming black support for Democrats (Edsall and Edsall 1991). As Seymour Lipset (1985, 35) states:

> The blacks, who gave Walter Mondale over 90% of their vote [in 1984] were slightly more Democratic than in 1980. Their continued opposition to the Republicans was based on the perception that President Reagan and his party were against black interests with respect to civil rights legislation.

Republican leaders worried that Reagan's veto of the Civil Rights Restoration Act would heighten this perception in the 1988 election. However, Republican opposition to civil rights did not hurt his successor, George Bush.

The Democratic party, identified as the party of such special interests, seems to have suffered somewhat as well (Edsall and Edsall 1991, 150). Accordingly, the "party is assessing its next moves, pondering such questions as whether the time has come to begin distancing itself from organized labor, blacks, and other traditional constituency groups" (*Washington Post National Weekly Edition*, December 10, 1984, 25). Party differences on civil rights, at least among rank-and-file voters, probably have not been all that different anyway. Besides, whatever the party differences, Pomper and Lederman (1980) show civil rights among the least implemented platform positions. Thus, political party responses have had limited impact on the modification and adoption of civil rights policy (Miller and Stokes 1963; Sinclair 1985; Stone 1980). The mass media criticized Reagan on civil rights occasionally.

If the amorphous phenomenon we call public opinion has not found great differences between Democrats and Republicans, differences in attitudes on civil rights do exist between blacks and whites and between northern and southern whites. During the 1984 election, the "issues most important to blacks in voting for president were unemployment (65%), helping the poor (45%), and civil rights (38%)" (*National Journal*, January 26, 1985, 224). Generally these were not among the most salient issues to white voters. Blacks continued to perceive unemployment as a more serious problem (*Washington Post National Weekly Edition*, March 3, 1986, 32). Whites supported Reagan's opposition to mandatory quotas and busing. The "white majority feels government would be overstepping its boundaries by pushing desegregation—"trying to protect one group by damaging another"" (*Washington Post National Weekly Edition*, January 14, 1985, 38). Nor was equal access to desegregated public schools seen as a desirable social end.

Although it may have been more an economic than explicitly a civil rights issue, analysts suggest that Walter Mondale's best issue in the 1984 election was "fairness" (Drew 1983, 83; Lipset 1985, 29). The Gallup organization revealed vast differences in public assessments of the ability of Mondale and Reagan to handle various issues. Reagan rated higher on handling the economy and in renewing respect for the United States, but Mondale, despite lower support generally, was seen as superior to the president in keeping the nation out of war, attending to the environment, and improving conditions for minorities and women. Table 7.2 provides these data on the latter two groups, controlling for a variety of demographic conditions. Although the public generally was more liberal than Reagan on domestic issues, the strong support he received on handling the economy and overall leadership overrode his weakness in civil rights and related policy areas. In short, the "Great Communicator" suffered little in the polls. He successfully defused the civil rights issue, and, according to Miller, the electorate wanted to believe that he was not anti–civil rights (1984, 68).

Bush Administration

We have already discussed the vast differences in the perceptions of the parties' handling of civil rights. In 1964, voters gave Democrats the advantage on this policy area 81 percent, to just 2 percent for Republicans. Seventeen percent saw no differences between the two parties on this "most important problem" of handling civil rights in that year (Asher 1988). Blacks and whites differ dramatically, however, in their support for presidents. Bush initially hoped to double black support in the 1992 election from 11 percent in 1988 to 22 percent. However, after the controversial Thomas nomination, the 1991 Civil Rights Act, and the Los Angeles riot, blacks did not have much regard for his handling of civil rights issues. Bush received the identical 11 percent black vote in 1992. Women and Hispanics, however, voted Democratic at higher than normal levels.

Even media opinion of Bush was less positive than it had been for Reagan. Conservative and liberal columnists railed against him, and one of the former, Pat Buchanan, actually ran against him in the 1992 primaries, but later endorsed the president. Coverage of the *Freeman* case, which relaxed school desegregation requirements, shows these divergent media opinions. The columnist Tom Teepen said, "Between them, Presidents Bush and Reagan in order to kill abortion and other rights they dislike, have created a court so reactionary that, on other matters, it now embarrasses even the Bush administration in its excesses. Poetic Injustice" (*New Orleans Times-Picayune*, February 3, 1992, B5). The conservative columnist George Will defended the Court's decision, citing the opinion written by Justice Anthony Kennedy: "Congress did not mean to subject such routine matters of governance to federal supervision." Will went on to say that "in this case, six members of the majority . . . knew it was right not to rectify a wrong that was beyond the reach of the law at issue" (*New Orleans Times-Picayune*, February 2, 1992, B-7).

Table 7.2

Public Support for Reagan and Mondale on Handling of Civil Rights

Question: Regardless of which man you happen to prefer for president—Walter Mondale or Ronald Reagan—please tell me which you feel would do a better job of handling these problems.

	Minorities[a]			Women's Rights			
	Reagan	Mondale	No Difference/ No Opinion	Reagan	Mondale	No Difference/ No Opinion	Number of Interviews
National	25%	54%	21%	20%	63%	17%	1,585
Sex							
Men	24	56	20	20	64	15	774
Women	25	53	22	20	62	18	811
Age							
Total under 30	21	60	19	16	73	11	327
30–49 years	22	56	22	16	67	17	560
Total 50 & older	30	49	21	26	55	19	695
Region							
East	23	60	17	19	66	15	409
Midwest	27	50	23	19	63	18	428
South	25	52	23	21	61	18	452
West	22	57	21	19	65	16	296
Race							
Whites	27	51	22	21	62	17	1,391
Blacks	6	82	12	7	83	10	169
Hispanics	18	67	15	19	72	9	70

Education							
College graduates	20	64	16	14	72	14	320
High school graduates	24	55	21	21	62	17	517
Less than high school graduates	28	49	23	22	62	16	359
Politics							
Republicans	44	33	23	39	40	21	497
Democrats	10	72	18	8	81	11	649
Independents	23	55	22	16	65	19	408
Occupation							
Professional & business	25	58	17	16	69	15	454
Clerical & sales	24	60	16	24	59	17	115
Manual workers	23	53	24	21	64	15	537
Income							
$40,000 & over	28	54	18	18	65	17	253
$20,000–$29,999	20	58	22	20	64	16	269
Under $10,000	22	55	23	21	63	16	339
Religion							
Protestants	26	52	22	21	63	16	956
Catholics	25	55	20	21	62	17	408
Labor Union							
Labor union families	18	61	21	15	70	15	276
Nonlabor union families	26	53	21	21	62	17	1,309

Source: Gallup Report 228/229 (August/September 1984): 25–26.
[a]Including blacks and Hispanics.

Table 7.3

Extremes in Public Support for Candidates Bush and Dukakis, 1988

| | Opinion of Candidate[a] | | | | Understands Concerns[b] | | | |
| | Very Favorable | | Very Unfavorable | | Yes | | No | |
	Bush	Dukakis	Bush	Dukakis	Bush	Dukakis	Bush	Dukakis
National	20	16	18	22	44	59	44	23
Sex								
Men	22	16	18	23	49	59	43	28
Women	19	17	18	20	40	59	45	25
Age								
18–29	24	14	14	24	47	63	45	25
30–49	19	13	18	22	42	58	49	27
50+	20	20	21	19	46	59	39	19
65+	21	22	23	19	45	59	37	17
Race								
Whites	22	13	16	24	46	61	11	23
Blacks	5	35	37	4	31	49	15	27
Hispanics	24	24	14	22	25	46	15	28

Source: Gallup Report 278 (November 1988): 8–9, and 271 (April 1988): 24–25.
[a] November 3–6, 1988.
[b] April 21–23, 1988.

Public opinion is an important barometer of support for the president. Although the exact equivalent of Table 7.2 is not available for the 1988 election, overall polls during that year do reveal variation in support by different target groups for candidates Bush and his Democratic opponent, Michael Dukakis. Table 7.3 provides data on two polls, in late April and just before the November election. The earlier poll shows Dukakis leading Bush by a substantial margin on response to the statement "He understands the concerns of people like me." Both candidates received considerable support among whites, males, and young voters.

By the time of the election, however, the political climate had shifted dramatically. Bush then led or tied Dukakis in the percentage of *very favorable* ratings from every group but those over age sixty-five and blacks. From the latter, Bush received only 5 percent *very favorable* but 37 percent *very unfavorable* opinions. Republican conservatives continued to receive virtually no support from African Americans.

Initially, a much lower gap occurred in white-black perception of

Figure 7.1. **Public Approval of the President, by Race, 1953–1992**

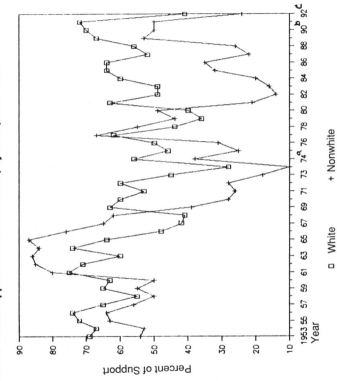

□ White   + Nonwhite

Source: George C. Edwards III, *Presidential Approval: A Sourcebook* (Baltimore: Johns Hopkins University Press, 1990); updated after 1988 from the *Gallup Report*.
a. Value for Ford.
b. Beginning in 1990, Gallup began to split nonwhite opinion into black and other.
c. Through October 1992.

Bush compared to Reagan. Presumably blacks wanted to give Bush's more moderate policies a chance. Figure 7.1 shows that Reagan split the races dramatically, while Carter and Bush experienced much less difference in approval by race. Bush's initial high support from blacks is surprising for a Republican president. At first his tone seemed more conciliatory than Reagan's, but it did not last. The gap soon widened for Bush as it had for Reagan (see Figure 7.1). In fact, by late 1991, the gap between white and black support for Bush was nearly as large as it had been under Reagan.

Assessment

There is some muting of racial differences in public opinion. The attitudes of blacks and whites have grown closer, and we now see more generalized support for the once-controversial notion of racial equality (Sniderman and Hagen 1985, 112). A poll by the National Opinion Research Corporation (NORC 1984) shows the narrowest gap ever of 5 percentage points in 1984 on the question of whether black and white children should go to the same school. Another poll showed that the gap between the attitudes of northern and southern whites on several racial issues is also closing (*National Journal*, January 12, 1985, 63). Perhaps the narrowing of racial and regional differences increased President Reagan's latitude, despite the apparent gap between public support for improving conditions for blacks and his diminished civil rights actions. His personal support from the public continued to be high during his second term, despite criticism on the "fairness" issue.

During his administration, Bush's support from the general public varied by policy area. In June 1991 not quite twice as many people felt Bush was doing a good job in foreign policy compared to domestic policy, but by the end of that year the difference margin was over three times and his overall popularity rating was under 50 percent for the first time in his presidency (*National Journal*, January 18, 1992, 180). Clearly the long honeymoon was over as Bush entered the 1992 presidential campaign. His handling of domestic policy was poorly regarded. In May, only 33 percent of whites and 13 percent of blacks approved his handling of race relations (*National Journal*, June 6, 1992, 1376).

Table 7.4 presents data on racial differences in perceptions of status by issue area. In 1990, fewer Americans perceived equal treatment of the races than in 1978, but more saw equal chances of getting a job and less need to move if minorities move into their neighborhoods. In just one year, from 1989 to 1990, voters saw improvements for minorities in every issue area. However, as the 1990 data indicate, blacks perceived much greater discrimination (by as much as 30 percentage points) than did whites in each subissue.

In theory, white support for integration and racial equality is higher than ever (Table 7.4: *Newsweek*, May 6, 1991, 30). Some say, however, that the Republican party and Bush purposely divided blacks and whites. We now see declining support for civil rights among working-class whites; witness the emergence of civil rights opponents David Duke and Patrick Buchanan in early 1992. According to civil rights attorney William Taylor, "A climate was created in the 1980s that

Table 7.4

Racial Differences on Perceptions of Status, by Issue Area
(% agreeing)

Issue Area	Year		
	1978	1989	1990
General			
A lot of progress in civil rights has occurred		11	16
Equal treatment of races exists	65	61	63
Blacks			37
Whites			66
Education			
Equal chance to get a good education		80	83
Blacks			68
Whites			85
Employment			
Equal chance of getting job	67	65	70
Blacks			43
Whites			73
Housing			
Equal chance to get housing			72
Blacks			47
Whites			75
Would move if minorities came to live next door	4		1

Source: Composite of various polls from *Gallup Report*, June 1990, 24–28.

made discrimination more acceptable, a climate created by the Reagan administration and now [continued] by the Bush administration as well" (*National Journal*, October 26, 1991, 2599).

Subissues vary in their controversy. Edsall and Edsall (1991, 186) conclude, "Of all the civil rights issues, none proved to be more racially polarizing than race-based affirmative action." As an illustration of this divisiveness, in mid-1991, 19 percent of whites versus 48 percent of blacks say qualified blacks should be given preference over equally qualified whites (*Newsweek*, May 6, 1991, 24). Although 80 percent of whites are opposed to black preferences in job hiring, upwards of 60 percent of blacks favor such preferences (Edsall and Edsall 1991, 186). Thus, employment has become the most controversial issue area; education and housing are much less controversial than formerly.

This discussion of responses from those outside government is confined to the Reagan and Bush administrations. While these outside actors do not directly modify or adopt policy, they can influence the decisions of governmental officials. The extent to which Congress, for example, modifies presidential preferences depends upon many aspects in the political environment. Party affiliations of Congress and the president, constituency attitudes and reelection prospects, and the views of interest groups, the media, and the general public are important conditions affecting modification and adoption of public policy. Thus, those outside government greatly influence what those within it do.

The number of actual primary policy makers is small since final power remains largely in the hands of the elected elite and their appointees. In the area of civil rights, political parties are more distinguishable than in perhaps any other policy area. Civil rights also remains highly salient to the general public. While interest groups have varied levels of influence in policy formation, the public itself and the media seldom are dominant (Light 1982, 93; Lindblom 1980, 121). Determined policy makers limit the influence of actors outside government, but these actors do respond to presidential stimuli.

Summary

This chapter has considered responses to presidents' policy statements and actions (stimuli). Reactions from the legislative and executive branches were observed in chapter 6. Coverage here is of responses from the judiciary and those outside government. The primary focus of judicial responses is on the Supreme Court (through litigation and appointee voting). Reaction from those outside government is limited to the Reagan and Bush administrations. All these actors both inside and outside government have responded to presidents' statements and actions in civil rights and influenced the extent to which presidents obtain their policy preferences.

The courts have often played crucial leadership roles in civil rights, certainly since the 1950s. Responses to presidents' positions on cases (litigation) overall usually are as supportive of presidents as are their own appointees' votes. Supreme Court justices are fairly responsive to their appointing presidents' wishes. Presidents seek like-minded judges, especially for the Supreme Court. Eisenhower, and perhaps Kennedy and Ford, did not get the kind of justices they wanted, but Johnson apparently did. Yet even if a president is careful to nominate those who share his general philosophical persuasion, he cannot be sure that the justices he appoints will vote in agreement with his position on any particular set of issues.

Perhaps the real test of policy leadership is whether presidents inspire others to accept their preferences. Presidents obtained greater support (but not success) from Congress than from the Supreme Court. This is especially true for Democratic presidents, since their party has dominated Congress. At this writing all but one member of the current Supreme Court were appointed by Republican presidents. Supportive responses are also more likely for ideologically committed presidents because they are more assertive with all actors. Thus, Congress and the Supreme Court generally are responsive to presidential statements and actions in civil rights policy making.

Actors outside government varied in their responses to Reagan's and Bush's civil rights policies. Interest groups have been among the most significant nongovernmental actors in civil rights, but quantitative data are scant. The influence of the media and political parties was perhaps the least among these external actors, and both parties seem to be reassessing presidents' positions and their own civil rights views. The influence of public opinion seems greater, with increased support for general civil rights actions but not for specific compensatory actions, particularly busing and quotas.

Reagan initially seemed vulnerable to public criticism on the "fairness" issue, but it had almost no impact on the 1984 election results, nor, presumably, on the 1986 midterm contests, even though his candidates for the Senate fared poorly. Reagan and black groups attacked each other during his first term, and pro–civil rights groups coalesced in opposition to the administration. All in all, Reagan seemed more aware of groups during his second term than he had during his first.

Under Bush, numerous opinions were also expressed from the outside environment. The civil rights community considered the 1990 civil rights bill and the subsequent 1991 Civil Rights Act its first priority, but the act did not receive broad, bipartisan support as had the 1988 Civil Rights Restoration Act. The weak economy increased the business community's fears of the legislation. Members of Congress did not feel much constituency pressure for the bill, but business opposition was real. Civil rights groups yielded little ground because they doubted Bush would veto civil rights legislation in an election year. They miscalculated, but Bush got little credit for compromising on the legislation. Business and minority interests all provided mixed signals. Although black organizations became more unified, other interest groups split on specific issues (e.g., organized labor on quotas) and on whether to oppose the administration overtly. The media, too, felt Bush lacked leadership on civil rights.

The Reagan and Bush experiences suggest that ideologically committed presidents can influence actions of Congress, the courts, and the rest of the executive branch. Yet bureaucratic responses are less close to presidential preferences than are those of the Supreme Court or Congress, supporting earlier expectations. This relationship is difficult to prove, but several examples are helpful. Congressional actions are correlated more highly with presidents' positions than are the positions of the Supreme Court or agency implementing actions. Finally, actions by both the Supreme Court and Congress correlate more closely with bureaucratic actions (both expenditures and programs) than do most actions by presidents.[5] These two ideological conservatives, Reagan and Bush, pushed their civil rights preferences, which were responded to by those inside and outside government.

Notes

1. Ken Meier (1975, 542) discusses this distinction and claims that, even where representativeness is achieved, responsiveness does not necessarily follow.

2. This section is drawn and updated from Heck and Shull (1982), which examines measures of presidential and judicial position-taking and correspondence more fully.

3. Correspondence between the views of judges and appointing presidents also exists at lower levels of the federal judiciary. See, for example Songer (1982) for courts of appeal and Carp and Rowland (1983) and Rowland and Carp (1983) for district courts.

4. Gates, Cohen, and Shull (1988) found that liberalism in presidential policy statements explains 47 percent of the variance in judicial appointee votes.

5. The specific correlations with the liberalism of presidential statements are Supreme Court liberalism ($r = 0.155$), congressional support of presidents' vote positions ($r = 0.433$), and agency expenditures ($r = -0.074$). The correlations between expenditures and actions by others are as follows: Supreme Court ($r = -0.132$), Congress ($r = 0.118$), and the president (liberalism above and presidents' legislative requests) ($r = 0.093$).

Part IV

Evaluating Presidential Influence

8

The Impact of
Reagan-Bush Policies

For presidents, civil rights policies are discretionary. The branches of government often cooperate on civil rights, but that is not to say that civil rights policies are bipartisan. Although not as political as economic policy, partisanship over civil rights is growing. Charges of reverse discrimination increasingly are dividing the parties and, thus, the nation (Edsall and Edsall 1991). This situation has occurred with the president changing from a civil rights liberal (Carter) to civil rights conservatives (Reagan and Bush).

Almost immediately upon assuming office in January 1981, Reagan suspended Carter's affirmative action guidelines and reduced their enforcement. During the same year he decreased the number of contractors required to file written affirmative action plans, saying that smaller companies need not comply. Many companies cut back their equal opportunity offices (Edsall and Edsall, 1991, 163). During 1985–86, the administration debated whether to overturn a 1965 executive order on equal employment opportunity (*Washington Post National Weekly Edition*, January 27, 1986, 37, and January 11, 1986, A3).

Reagan also abolished the merit selection panels for district court judgeships and reduced litigation efforts. Carter had targeted specific industries for compliance, but Reagan ended this practice. Reagan drastically reduced the budget of the Office of Federal Contract Compliance Programs and cut its personnel by 52 percent. One scholar charges that "the Reagan administration was more concerned with protecting employers rather than victims of discrimination" (DuRivage

1985, 366). As the first president to retreat on civil rights dramatically and on a broad scale, Reagan undercut much of what Carter had done. Still, Reagan was unsuccessful in revising Executive Order 11246 prohibiting employers from discriminating. Toward the end of his administration, Congress took a more active leadership role in civil rights, countering many of Reagan's actions.

Following racially divisive television ads in the 1988 presidential campaign, civil rights advocates were suspicious of Bush. But Bush fostered hope for greater racial and ethnic peace by promising "kinder, gentler" policies. Thomas Edsall and Mary Edsall (1991, 229–30) forecast more moderate rhetoric and policies under Bush. Yet Bush proved even more conservative than Reagan in his statements and actions (e.g., giving public messages, making controversial nominations, invoking the specter of quotas in legislation). His efforts were frequently challenged by Congress and occasionally even by his own appointees to the Civil Rights Commission and the Civil Rights Division of the Justice Department. Ironically, Bush's two Supreme Court nominees were even more conservative than he was and did not always support his positions.

The Carter, Reagan, and Bush administrations demonstrate considerable presidential effort to attain sometimes opposing goals, especially in federal employment. A possible explanation is that civil rights now is the most distinguishable feature of the parties (Carmines and Stimson 1989). Such increasing partisanship and diffused support generally for civil rights may lead to greater interbranch conflict in the future, as has occurred since 1988. The Civil Rights Restoration Act of that year was less partisan than was the 1991 Civil Rights Act. However, legislation on affirmative action and comparable worth, or other issues subject to the charge of reverse discrimination, could further divide the parties. Some say Bush exacerbated already bad relations with further race-baiting.

Previous chapters have demonstrated that presidents' legislative, administrative, and judicial decisions are important. This chapter is the first of two on the policy consequences of presidential statements and actions. It focuses on results and begins by reviewing and then discussing the impact of the civil rights cases, both legislative and administrative. Next it seeks to examine the impact of civil rights policies on both government and society, especially to see whether the changed policy direction from Carter to Reagan to Bush has had political and policy consequences.

Policy Consequences of Cases

The cases analyzed in the following discussions reveal the complexities and mixed motives in policy making, especially in the highly charged, emotional realm of civil rights. The legislative cases show greater congressional leadership on important legislation after years of internal bickering and followership. Although initially partisan and controversial, the legislation in both instances became much less so, passing both chambers by wide margins. The administrative cases involved nominations of African American conservatives to influential civil rights positions in the executive branch. These cases also reveal seemingly unnecessary and continuing conflict with Congress. In all four cases, presidential leadership was lacking.

Legislative Cases

Overview

The Civil Rights Restoration Act of 1988 reversed a 1984 Supreme Court decision that had narrowed the scope of four civil rights laws. Supporters called the legislation a simple restoration of existing laws, while opponents argued it broadened coverage too extensively. Coverage was indeed expanded in a real power struggle among parties and interests. Democrats in Congress supported the legislation unanimously, while Republicans were badly split. Congress saw President Reagan as vulnerable in his last (lame-duck) year in office. In the end, Reagan was criticized even by members of his own party for stonewalling what the vast majority considered necessary policy change. By being a spoiler rather than a leader, the chief executive relinquished leadership to Congress.

The 1991 Civil Rights Act also reversed Supreme Court decisions, four of which had made it more difficult to prove job discrimination. The legislation expanded coverage to women and provided greater ability to recover damages. As with the other legislative case, influential Senators Orrin Hatch (R-Utah) and Edward Kennedy (D-Mass.) opposed one another, leading the fight for their respective positions. Rhetoric over quotas and other symbols affected the struggle over coverage of the law. As with the 1988 act, the 1991 act was initially vetoed. That veto, too, would have been overturned had not President

Bush compromised at the last minute. After twenty months of controversy, he chose the more pragmatic approach, forced by external events to accept congressional will.

These two legislative cases reveal numerous similarities and differences. Congress saw both presidents as vulnerable on civil rights and may have used these bills as opportunities to assert leadership. As these acts overturned Supreme Court decisions, Congress had to act in the face of strong opposition from both other branches. As of this writing there is no evidence that Congress intends to give up its new-found leadership. Surely conflict among the branches, over civil rights at least, will diminish with Clinton's election as president in 1992.

Impact

The 1988 Civil Rights Restoration Act achieved what its supporters intended. It standardized the laws and sent a clear message to the Supreme Court about congressional intent. The law broadened rights to cover many groups besides blacks and should help reduce discrimination. It passed by overriding the first presidential veto on civil rights legislation since Andrew Johnson. The time for legislation had clearly come, yet the conflict was an exception to the cooperation that often occurs in civil rights. In this instance, President Reagan's ideology got in the way of the pragmatism evident early in his administration. Congress took on a leadership role but, as often happens, could do so because of perceived vulnerability in the presidency.

Although data on compliance are not yet available, Congress clearly achieved its goal of reversing the *Grove City* decision. Colleges that receive federal aid now again must prove compliance with anti-discrimination statutes. The act was also one of the first to include the disabled under the nation's civil rights laws. It had political consequences as well, setting the tone for a Congress anxious to assert its leadership against the lame-duck president. It also raised support for the civil rights bill as a possible campaign issue in 1988. George Bush, who had supported President Reagan's actions during the preceding eight years, would have his own battles with Congress over civil rights.

The 1991 Civil Rights Act reveals the importance of symbolic politics in the decisions made. The charge of quotas led to emotional reactions. Genuine ideological differences on public policy also arose over how specific the charge of discrimination must be; what kind of victim can recover damages and how much money can be awarded; and when affirmative action plans can be challenged. The existing agenda also influences policy. President Bush supported similar remedies in the Americans with Disabilities Act of 1990 but not for other groups in this legislation. Did the president seek to take advantage of growing conservatism of white voters or simply seek support for his own version of the legislation? The columnist Anthony Lewis suggests the more cynical view, claiming that Bush actually wanted to veto the legislation again and, thus, was not acting "presidential" (*New Orleans Times-Picayune*, April 16, 1991, B7). That the legislation was initially unsuccessful shows how hard it is for Congress to overturn decisions of the Supreme Court, even when overwhelming majorities favor so doing. External events ultimately forced President Bush to sign the 1991 act. By so compromising, his political vulnerability was amplified.

What are the results and consequences of the 1991 legislation? It is too early to gauge its long-term impact on discrimination in hiring, criteria for employment, and the ease of proving bias on the job. Several changes were immediately clear, however, particularly the ability of women and religious minorities to collect punitive damages in cases of discrimination. On perhaps the most important issue surrounding the *Ward's Cove* decision, both branches agreed to disagree and let the courts decide. This result may not have been decisive or effective policy, but it did allow a resolution of many other issues. Perhaps more important, it helped defuse volatile competition between race and gender discrimination. The political implications were evident in the 1992 election. Bush became more vulnerable to charges of race-baiting, and voters, particularly those from disadvantaged groups who benefit from civil rights laws, seemingly became more cynical about the president's intentions in civil rights. He did no better among blacks and actually fared much worse among women and Hispanics than he had in 1988 (*National Journal*, November 7, 1992, 2543).

Administrative Cases

Overview

The Pendleton nomination to the Civil Rights Commission was the first in a series of conservative appointments and later replacements for fired members who had criticized the Reagan administration for its handling of civil rights. Reagan clearly politicized the commission, and he and Congress later had to compromise on the number and terms of its members. The increased interbranch conflict brought criticism from civil rights supporters and Congress, both of which subsequently supported cutting the commission's funding. Reagan seems to have won; he got the policies he wanted as the commission retreated from scrutinizing civil rights activity. Near-stalemate over the Civil Rights Commission has persisted to the present. Even Bush's own nominee, Arthur Fletcher, criticized the president for inept handling of the 1991 Civil Rights Act (*New Orleans Times-Picayune*, December 15, 1991, A6).

The Lucas nomination to the Justice Department was the first sign that Bush was not really committed to civil rights. Initially the appointment seemed certain because the conservative black Republican was assumed to be more supportive of civil rights than his controversial predecessor, William Bradford Reynolds. Yet Lucas was very controversial for both personal and professional reasons. Eventually he was deemed unqualified to serve. His defeat was a failure for Bush, as Bush missed the chance to show minorities he cared about civil rights.

The administrative cases also have similarities and differences. Interest groups and Congress sent President Bush the message that they would accept no Reagan-style retreat on civil rights. Sending that message rejuvenated both actors. The nominations brought pro-civil rights activists together. The conflict over Lucas was not as long-lasting as Reagan's struggle with the Civil Rights Commission. Bush cut his losses; he did not rub salt in the wound by giving Lucas an interim appointment but placed him in a less controversial position in the Justice Department.

Impact

These two cases show the importance of appointments, personalities, and, at least in the first case, executive reorganization. How important is the Civil Rights Commission and what was the effect of Pendleton's selection and administrative changes? Opinions differ, but the agency certainly has symbolic importance to groups and individuals. It was established in 1957 under the Civil Rights Act of that year (PL 85-315). It began as a six-member, independent, bipartisan, fact-finding agency. It could issue subpoenas and investigate charges but lacked power to apply specific remedies to individual cases. Despite limited formal powers, the agency issued major reports during the 1960s. Two passed the commission unanimously but drew criticism from southern representatives (*Congress and the Nation,* 1:1965, 1609–14, 1634).[1] Undaunted, in 1966 the agency criticized the Department of Health, Education and Welfare for failing to monitor the implementation of school desegregation. Over the years the CRC's jurisdiction expanded to include discrimination against women, the aged, and the disabled.

Although the CRC has no enforcement powers, it makes findings of fact, has important monitoring responsibilities, and can make policy recommendations, many of which have subsequently become law. Still, its recommendations to Congress and the president are not binding. President Reagan's decision to politicize the agency more than previous presidents may have limited its potential response to presidential policy preferences in civil rights. As with the federal judiciary, both his and Bush's appointments moved the agency in a conservative direction. This case has shown that presidential appointments can influence even so-called independent agencies, and congressional criticism of the CRC continued under Bush.

The Lucas case is about a single nomination that never even cleared the committee stage in the Senate. It may seem insignificant compared to the successful appointment of Clarence Pendleton to the Civil Rights Commission, yet it had important implications for interbranch conflict. It occurred early in the Bush administration when many vacancies needed to be filled and demonstrates the need for stronger coordination within an administration for politically sensitive positions. To civil rights advocates, the head of the Civil Rights Division is a highly symbolic position, and with this nomination President Bush squandered generally favorable support among minority groups. The stalemate that occurred also impeded the president's legislative relations.

The case says much about the Senate's power of reviewing presidential nominations. Senate Democrats would reject even a black nominee if he were deemed unqualified. Like his early defeat on the nomination of John Tower for secretary of defense, Bush sought conciliatory relations with Congress. Yet vast policy and political differences remained and resurfaced with his nomination of Clarence Thomas to the Supreme Court. Bush seemed more anxious to reward loyal Republican politicians and contributors than had most of his predecessors. That alone made Congress leery of his later nominations. Subsequently he had even more trouble in the appointment process than Reagan had.

Policy Content: Do Subissues Matter?

Meaning and Importance of Civil Rights

Civil rights has expanded in scope as a public policy problem. What was seen until the 1950s as primarily the issue of racial discrimination against blacks has expanded over the past three decades to include Hispanics, Native Americans, women, the elderly, individuals with disabilities, institutionalized and incarcerated persons, gays, and other racial and special interest ethnic groups. President Carter's international human rights policy made civil rights a foreign policy concern.[2] While expansion to other target groups and issue areas broadened the public and congressional base of support, it may have diminished the focus and diluted sympathy from the rest of the public and among some members of Congress. Thus, greater party and philosophical polarization exists now than previously.

This expansion in scope and conflict has not necessarily enhanced our understanding of civil rights. There are still major disagreements and uncertainties about what equality means (Sniderman and Hagen 1985). Should we merely remove barriers, or should we seek equal results? If we accept the latter, then what are the appropriate remedies for achieving desired social ends? If guidelines and affirmative action are acceptable, are comparable worth and quotas going too far?[3] Disagreement continues over what constitutes legitimate government responses to perceived societal problems.

As illustrated in chapter 7, blacks and whites differ dramatically over the proper role for government. One poll found African Americans favoring by nearly 3:1 but whites evenly split on the question "Because of past discrimination, blacks who need it should get help from government that white people in similar circumstances don't get" (*Washington Post National Weekly Edition*, May 11–17, 1992, 11). Andrew Hacker (1992), in a controversial book, argues that whites say they oppose affirmative action because it is unfair to them but actually oppose it because it takes some of the "privilege out of being white." Hacker asserts that no matter how degraded their lives, whites have an advantage because they can believe in their "superiority" and at least know they are in no danger of becoming black.

Did Reagan and Bush make a difference in civil rights policy making? Budget figures for federal spending between 1981 and 1992, adjusted for inflation, show steep declines in almost all issue areas. Spending dropped 40 percent each for community development, community service, and social services block grant programs, 63 percent for job training, and 82 percent for subsidized housing (*Washington Post National Weekly Edition*, May 11–17, 1992, 11).

Some also blame the 1992 Los Angeles riot on this legacy. They argue that minorities are worse off than when the Watts riots occurred in the same city a quarter century ago. The verdict acquitting the four police officers of beating Rodney King particularly angered blacks. By huge margins, they felt blacks do not receive equal treatment from the criminal justice system. However, the verdict did bring increased understanding among whites about the black perspective on policy making. The resulting rioting was condemned but also better understood. It also was the catalyst forcing greater attention from President Bush and all Americans to the nation's widening economic and racial divisions. In a retrial at the federal level, two of the four officers were convicted of violating King's civil rights. These concerns reiterate the importance of civil rights in American politics.

The Importance of Issue Areas

The roles of actors and the results of government policy have varied by the type of policy. This book has assessed civil rights generally as well as specific issue areas, including education, employment, and housing. It has also focused on the groups targeted for such policies. I have shown throughout this book that target groups and subissues are closely intertwined.

Education, particularly school desegregation, was initially a racial issue but expanded to include second-generation discrimination and bilingual education, including disabled, institutionalized, and Hispanic groups. This subissue reveals the evolution of public policy (Kingdon 1984). School desegregation began in controversy and initially only the courts took a supportive (liberal) leadership role. As school desegregation became more acceptable, new issues such as second-generation discrimination emerged to stir new controversies (Meier, Stewart, and England 1989). Concerns regarding higher education also appeared in the late 1980s and into the 1990s.

Until recently, employment was the least controversial of the three issue areas. Budgets and personnel grew the most and presidential statements, actions, and results have been greatest here. Increasingly, employment became a gender as well as a racial issue. At first women were the least controversial target group. However, comparable worth was the civil rights issue of the 1980s (Gleason and Moser 1985, 600) and quotas, criticized by President Bush, were a focus in the early 1990s. Many of the remedies proposed for employment inequality are compensatory, and most Americans do not favor them.

Housing stirred the most controversy of the subissues. Because it generated the least presidential-congressional agreement, its budgets grew the least. The limited budgets of housing agencies precluded implementation. Congress's surprisingly high support for housing is an exception to its greater support for more general and symbolic policies (Edelman 1964).

Congress's preference for general and symbolic policies explains its outrage over President Reagan's efforts to politicize the Civil Rights Commission. The agency had a smaller staff and constituency, and a less clear mission than larger, more "substantive" agencies, and it was therefore an easier target. These features have led to widely different impacts of civil rights by subissues, the topic discussed next.

Consequences of Policies

Public policy may have several types of consequences. The governmental, let alone societal, impacts of public policies are difficult to establish and differ by subissue. While we can measure changes in levels of wealth or educational attainment, it is much more difficult to attribute such change directly to a government policy. Thus, about all that can be done is to infer whether societal changes may be due to government intervention. In this section I follow the familiar pattern of talking about overall (more general) policy changes before discussing the consequences of policy in the three issue areas.

Impact measures are often elusive; for recent years indicators are particularly difficult to obtain as the Reagan and Bush administrations reduced data dissemination of government documents.[4] Desegregation figures (in housing, for example) suggest governmental impact because policies are designed to increase opportunities for minorities, often through compensatory policies. Societal outcome measures are more general, having to do with attainment, well-being, or standard of living; hence the earlier distinction between equal opportunities and results. As examples, the proportion of students attending desegregated schools is a governmental impact measure, while years of education attained or attendance in college is societal. Although the distinction between governmental and societal is somewhat arbitrary, it is useful in this preliminary look.

Government Impact

General

Most data indicate that blacks are not experiencing income parity with whites (Farley 1984, 199). The gap in black incomes relative to whites, for example, while increasing from 52 percent in 1960 to 62 percent in 1976, dropped again to 55 percent by 1982 (United States, Bureau of the Census 1984, 463). One study found that by 1990, black median income was 58 percent of white median income (*Washington Post National Weekly Edition*, May 11–17, 1992, 9). Yet, by 1990, the percentage of blacks in the poorest group increased and decreased in the richest group from 1988 (see Table 8.1). Edsall and Edsall (1991, 160) argue that, although blacks are just 11 percent of the population, they constitute 36.4 percent of the bottom quintile in income. In another study median household income for blacks declined by 5 percent from 1989 to 1991 (*New York Times*, September 4, 1992, A12).

Interest group spokespersons charge that blacks are losing ground, reaching levels "that essentially guarantee the poverty of black children for the foreseeable future" (Children's Defense Fund, quoted in *New Orleans Times-Picayune/States-Item*, June 4, 1985, A2). The late Mickey LeLand, chair of the Congressional Black Caucus, similarly charged that the "progress made by blacks in the 1960s and 1970s is eroding." He pointed to the highest poverty rate (almost 36 percent for blacks) "since such recordings began" (*Washington Post National Weekly Edition*, February 18, 1985, 29). Both sources claim that this increased inequality is directly attributable to Reagan cuts, which reduced funding for the poor by about $10 billion per year. The black middle class has expanded, although here again the proportion of both black men and women making more than $25,000 per year in constant

Table 8.1

Income Distribution by Families, by Race, 1970–1990
(in %)

	1970	1980	1988	1990
All				
Under $5,000	3.2	3.4	4.0	5.2
Over $50,000	17.4	19.7	25.7	24.6
White				
Under $5,000	2.7	2.6	3.0	4.0
Over $50,000	18.6	21.0	27.4	26.1
Black				
Under $5,000	8.4	10.1	11.9	14.1
Over $50,000	6.7	8.0	12.6	11.0
Hispanic				
Under $5,000	—	6.3	8.4	7.5
Over $50,000	—	8.8	11.9	13.4

Source: United States, Bureau of the Census, *Statistical Abstract of the United States, 1991* (Washington, D.C.: GPO, 1991); 450; 1990 data from United States, Bureau of the Census, *Current Population Reports* (Washington, D.C.: GPO, 1992), 23.

Education

The impact of government policies on school desegregation appears clear and unequivocal. Southern public schools are much more desegregated than they used to be. The promise of the *Brown* decision has largely been achieved (Farley 1984, 199). Ironically, however, little progress toward desegregation has occurred in the North, where the proportion of blacks attending majority black schools has increased (Bullock 1984b, 87; Bullock and Rodgers 1975; Farley 1984, 23; see Table 8.2). Charles Bullock argues that school desegregation worked in the South because the policy was clear, standards were precise, agencies were committed and effective, administrative coordination existed, federal involvement was high, and a high benefit-to-cost ratio occurred (1984b, 87). He reminds us that other aspects of civil rights in the education realm have not been as successful, however, and that some of the effects of government policy may actually have been debilitating.

Second-generation discrimination is one such practice. It consists of various, often subtle, efforts to reduce contact between racial and ethnic groups. An example might be tracking less well-prepared minori-

dollars decreased after 1975 (*Washington Post National Weekly Edition*, April 15, 1985, 24).

Table 8.2

Racial Composition by Schools, by Percent Minority[a] Enrollment and Region, 1968–1980 (in %)

	1968	1972	1976	1980	% Change 1968–80
% Black students in schools with more than half minority students					
U.S. average	76.6	63.6	62.4	62.9	–13.7
South	80.9	55.3	54.9	57.1	–23.8
Border states	71.6	67.2	60.1	59.2	–12.4
Northwest	66.8	69.9	72.5	79.9	+13.1
Midwest	77.3	75.3	70.3	69.5	–7.8
West	72.2	68.1	67.4	66.8	–5.4
% Black students in schools with 90–100% minority students					
U.S. average	64.3	38.7	35.9	33.2	–31.1
South	77.8	24.7	22.4	23.0	–54.8
Border states	60.2	54.7	42.5	37.0	–23.2
Northwest	42.7	46.9	51.4	48.7	+6.0
Midwest	58.0	57.4	51.1	43.6	–14.4
West	50.8	42.7	36.3	33.7	–17.1

Source: Gary Orfield, *Public School Desegregation in the United States, 1968–1980* (Washington, D.C.: Joint Center for Political Studies, 1983), 4.

[a]*Minority* includes black, Hispanic, Asian, and all other non-Caucasian students.

ties into vocational programs while steering middle- and upper-class whites into college preparatory programs (Meier, Stewart, and England 1989). Thus, while desegregation has occurred at the highest rate in the South—indeed, it may be the most desegregated region in the country —the South also appears to have a higher degree of second-generation discrimination (Bullock 1984b, 86).

Employment

If the education picture is mixed, so is the employment situation for women and minorities. According to the Potomac Institute, the proportion of women, blacks, and other minorities in professional and management jobs more than doubled from 1970 to 1980. (See Table 8.3, where updated figures show even greater advances.) The increases are even more dramatic in federal employment, where the proportions of

Table 8.3

Employment in Professional/Management Jobs, by Sex and Race, 1970–1988
(in %)

	1970	1980	1988
Officials and managers			
Black	1.9	4.0	5.6
Hispanic	1.0	2.2	4.0
Women	10.2	18.5	39.3
Professionals			
Black	2.6	4.3	6.7
Hispanic	1.1	2.9	3.4
Women	24.6	37.2	49.8
Executive-level federal jobs			
Black	2.3[a]	7.0[a]	
Hispanic			
Women	1.5	6.2	

Source: Washington Post National Weekly Edition, April 15, 1985, 34; 1988 data from United States, Bureau of the Census, *Statistical Abstract of the United States, 1990* (Washington, D.C.: GPO, 1990), 389–91.

[a]Blacks and Hispanics combined.

women and minorities in executive-level positions more than tripled. The institute concluded that minority workers rose faster in private firms with government contracts than in those without them (*Washington Post National Weekly Edition*, April 15, 1985, 34). This is at least one indication that federal efforts were achieving their goals. Other statistics show, however, that despite progress among blacks and women, even in federal employment, they are overrepresented in lower-level positions but underrepresented in the upper ranks (Rodgers 1984, 103). Few women were appointed to top positions in the Reagan administration (*Washington Post National Weekly Edition*, February 24, 1986, 6–7). The Bush administration claimed that women accounted for 19 percent of full-time federal employees, but most were not in top staff positions (*National Journal*, October 19, 1991, 2563).5 In 1993, Bill Clinton named more minorities and women to his cabinet than any previous president.

Housing

Bullock and Lamb argue that "residential segregation is the rule rather than the exception" (1984, 2). Segregated living actually increased during the 1980s (*Washington Post National Weekly Edition*, January 14, 1985, 38; Edsall and Edsall 1991, 227). Blacks are moving to the suburbs at a slower pace than whites and even than other minorities, such as Asians or Hispanics (*New Orleans Times-Picayune/States-Item*, April 9, 1986, A26). In fact, the black-white segregation level in housing is twice that of whites compared with the above two minority groups (*New Orleans Times-Picayune/States-Item*, October 29, 1986, A6). Critics blamed the Reagan administration for many of these problems. They claimed that he reduced housing aid and funding levels, and they opposed his advocacy of vouchers (*Washington Post National Weekly Edition*, December 9, 1985, 10–11). Governmental policies have bitterly divided the minority community. The NAACP, for example, has opposed housing quotas because blacks may be passed over for whites to ensure fuller integration of public housing (*Washington Post National Weekly Edition*, December 2, 1985, 32).

Societal Impact

The government consequences surveyed above are further developed in the societal consequences that follow. Recall that the former refer to impact of *government* actions, often on individuals, while the latter refer more directly to broader *societal* impacts. Governmental consequences more often lead to societal ones rather than vice versa. However, the broader societal consequences of public policy are not always clear or easily ascertained. These data provide a beginning toward that end.

General

Blacks and Hispanics lag behind whites on every measure of economic and social well-being, and, on many measures, the gaps are widening rather than narrowing (Farley 1984, 13, 39). Racial disparities in income are magnified even more on net worth, where the figures for white families exceed those for blacks by twelve times and those for Hispanics by eight times (*New Orleans Times-Picayune/States-Item*, September 17, 1986, A1, 4). Relative to blacks, however, Hispanics may be worse off than previously. Their per capita income is lower than that for blacks, and, while Hispanics had a poverty rate of just two-thirds that of blacks in 1978–79, it was about the same in 1986 (*Washington Post National Weekly Edition*, September 15, 1986, 26).

Table 8.4

Poverty Rates by Race,[a] 1970-1991
(in %)

	1970	1984	1990	1991
All	10.1	11.6	10.7	14.2
White	8.0	9.1	8.1	11.3
Black	29.5	30.9	29.3	32.7
Hispanic	19.8[b]	25.2	25.0	28.7

Source: United States, Bureau of the Census, *Poverty in the United States, 1990* (Washington, D.C.: GPO, 1990), 16–17; 1991 figures from *New York Times,* September 4, 1992, A12.

[a]Data are for all families with and without children under 18 years of age.

[b]Data for Hispanics are for 1973.

Table 8.4 shows the poverty rate since 1970 and demonstrates greater increases for Hispanics than for other groups. Younger blacks are two and one-half times as likely to live in poverty than blacks ages twenty-four to thirty-four (*Washington Post National Weekly Edition,* May 11–17, 1992, 22). The poverty rate for all groups increased in 1991.

Education

We have seen that the goal of desegregating public schools in the South was largely achieved, but consequences do not end there, and the larger societal impact has apparently been continued segregation.[6] Far fewer minority than white children finish the eighth grade. The proportion of African Americans finishing high school is increasing, but the percentage going to college is decreasing, as was the number obtaining Ph.D. degrees (*Washington Post National Weekly Edition,* April 15, 1985, 24; and January 14, 1985, 38). For the first time in fifteen years, the number of blacks receiving Ph.D.'s increased significantly in 1991 (*Washington Post National Weekly Edition,* May 11–17, 1992, 37). Overall, the gap in the percent of those completing high school has increased considerably for blacks but not for Hispanics (see Table 8.5).

Employment

Perhaps the most severe statistic in the employment subissue is the unemployment rate. Table 8.6 reveals a widening gap between white and black unemployment in the 1980s. Many argue that the varied

Table 8.5

Educational Attainment by Race, 1980–1990
(in %)

	1980	1988	1990
% completing high school (18–24 years old)			
Whites	81	—	83
Blacks	60	—	77
Hispanics	—	63	55
% completing high school enrolled in college			
Whites	30	35	39
Blacks	25	25	33
Hispanics	29	29	29
Mean years of school completed			
Whites	12.1	12.5	12.7
Blacks	9.8	12.0	12.4
Hispanics	9.1	10.8	12.0
% of college professors			
Whites	91.0	—	89.0
Blacks	4.3	—	4.5
Hispanics	—	1.5	2.0
Asians	—	3.0	5.0

Source: Washington Post National Weekly Edition, February 10–16, 1992, 38, based on American Council of Education study.

employment gaps are a major cause of social unrest. The National Advisory Committee on Civil Disorders (1968) attributed much of the rioting in the 1960s to unemployment. Lower incomes also relate to inadequate education, teenage pregnancy, violent crimes, and dilapidated housing (*Newsweek*, January 28, 1985, 30), further revealing the interrelationship among issue areas. The Children's Defense Fund argues that one or more minority parents were more likely in 1983 to be unemployed (as are the children when they become teenagers) than in 1979 (*New Orleans Times-Picayune/States-Item*, June 4, 1985, A2). Unemployment overall increased in 1991–92 generally and disparities by race continue (see Table 8.6).

Contrary to the relative success in education, Rodgers (1984, 115) argues that several conditions hindered improvement in employment for blacks: unclear goals, weak enforcement, varied agency commitment, differential presidential support, and lack of coordinated efforts. With decreased hiring at the federal level during twelve years of the Reagan-Bush administrations, employment opportunities for minorities declined.

Table 8.6

Unemployment Status, by Race and Sex,[a] 1970–1991
(in %)

	1970	1975	1980	1988	1991
Race					
White	4.5	6.3	6.3	4.7	6.4
Black	9.4	11.4	14.3	11.7	12.4
Hispanic	—	—	10.1	8.2	6.9
Sex					
Male	4.4	6.8	6.9	5.5	7.1
Female	5.9	7.9	7.4	5.6	5.5
Total	4.9	7.3	7.1	5.5	6.9

Source: United States, Bureau of the Census, *Statistical Abstract of the United States, 1991* (Washington, D.C.: GPO, 1991), 380; updated with United States Department of Labor, Bureau of Labor Statistics, *Employment and Earnings,* January 1992 (Washington, D.C.: GPO, 1992), 27–34.

[a]Percent of labor force 20 years and over, in May of designated year.

Employment by gender shows some different patterns. Some contend that comparable worth would help alleviate some disparities, but the journalist Robert Samuelson asserts that is neither desirable nor attainable. He argues that discrimination does not greatly affect wages and about half of the pay gap can be explained by the fact that women have less experience, seniority, and unionization; that they balance home and work demands; and that they therefore accept (and desire) lower-level jobs with shorter hours and pleasant working conditions *(Newsweek,* April 22, 1985, 57). Some argue that women never catch up but Samuelson contends that raising women's wages would not raise output but would merely increase prices.

Housing

Another area where federal programs seem to have made a difference is housing. By the mid-1960s the proportion of blacks living in ghettos (substandard housing) declined but was still nearly four times the rate for whites (Bardolph 1970, 315–16). However, the limited data suggest an increase in substandard housing for blacks. Public housing is a $4 billion (annually) federal assistance program that many charge is riddled with crime, vandalism, illness, and other problems frequently associated with poverty *(Washington Post National Weekly Edition,* May 27, 1985, 26). The former Civil Rights Commission chair, Arthur

Table 8.7

Satisfaction Levels, by Race, 1963 and 1984
(in %)

	Family Income	Housing	Employment
1963			
White	68	76	90
Black	38	43	54
Difference	−30 points	−33 points	−36 points
1984			
White	65	83	71
Black	45	70	55
Difference	−20 points	−17 points	−16 points

Source: Washington Post National Weekly Edition, March 4, 1984, 38.

Flemming, charges that housing has been the least successfully implemented of civil rights issues (*National Journal*, January 12, 1985, 115). At the same time many residents who have lived in public housing all their lives remain there by choice (Farley 1984, 201).

Although African Americans continue to be less satisfied with their personal lives than whites, by 1984 housing and employment show a greater narrowing of satisfaction levels than does family income (see Table 8.7). Probably a main reason for the latter is that black family income levels are approaching those of whites *only* because a larger proportion of black families have two wage earners, frequently with each in not very satisfactory jobs (Rodgers 1984, 105). Perhaps another reason for relative satisfaction with housing is because in at least a few cities (e.g., Boston, Washington, D.C., New Orleans, Louisville, and St. Louis), residents are actually managing public housing projects. This kind of participation has seemed to improve both conditions and attitudes (*Washington Post National Weekly Edition*, May 27, 1985, 26). The success of implementation, then, has varied considerably by subissues of civil rights.

Reviewing the Results

We can briefly summarize governmental and societal impacts. Clearly the decreased income gaps have not reduced the poverty rate (Farley 1984, 94–95; United States, Bureau of the Census 1985, 455; *Newsweek*, March 7, 1988, 20). At the same time, the gap in net worth has widened. The bifurcation of minority incomes no doubt contributed to the 1992 Los Angeles riot.

While school integration outside the cities has increased, there has been no success in integrating public schools in large metropolitan areas; white enrollment in central cities has dropped dramatically (Farley 1984, 50–51, 199). Segregated education is growing for Hispanics but at least not getting worse for blacks (*National Journal*, January 18, 1992, 167). However, Reynolds Farley (1984, 17, 50–51, 199) says (and data suggest) that at least some minorities are narrowing the gap in educational attainment. Yet the gap in college attendance actually widened in the 1980s.

Racial and gender differences in professional employment have declined; higher proportions of both blacks and women are in white-collar and managerial jobs (Rodgers 1984, 102). Successful legislation in 1988 and in 1991 over the objections of Presidents Reagan and Bush attempted to deal with such discrimination in hiring. Although rules on hiring and promotion may have helped achieve this governmental goal, the societal impact is a continuing wide unemployment gap between white and minority males (*Newsweek*, March 7, 1988, 20, 24). Unemployment is particularly rampant (around 45 percent in September 1992) among younger minority males (*Monthly Labor Review*, November 1992, 68).

Discriminatory housing practices keep the races segregated and isolated (Farley 1984, 20; Lamb 1984). It is possible that it is now easier for blacks to move to formerly white neighborhoods (Farley 1984, 201). However, the quality of public housing is also declining (*Washington Post National Weekly Edition*, December 9, 1985, 10–11). Probably the relationship between governmental and societal impact is less in the housing subissue than in the other two. Recent programs to promote management of public housing projects by residents may bring societal benefits by the end of the century.

These impact data clearly are interrelated. As might be expected, progress toward greater equality has been made by minorities—even African Americans—but much of it by the still small but emerging middle class. For less fortunate minorities, both governmental and societal results have been minimal, and sometimes greater inequality has resulted. Employment is probably the key to family stability and may be the factor most related to others. With such a large proportion of minorities unemployed, particularly young people, it is no wonder that characteristics of family instability such as illegitimacy, delinquency, and infant mortality are greatest among the least fortunate members of U.S. society (*Washington Post National Weekly Edition*, January 11–17, 1988, 36; *Newsweek*, March 7, 1988, 20, 24). This discussion of impact suggests the utility of examining the nature of issues throughout the policy process, from the establishment of priorities to the assessment of societal outcomes.

Summary

The case studies presented here provide some basis for generalization. Interbranch cooperation in civil rights was threatened by growing partisanship in combination with divided government from the 1970s to the early 1990s.[7] Consensus was elusive in civil rights, perhaps because congressional leadership challenged recalcitrant presidents. Under more unified government beginning in 1993, actors should cooperate more. Civil rights is a policy area of considerable discretion and, thus, potential leadership. Congress, the president, the courts, the bureaucracy, and others deal with the highly emotional issues of civil rights, usually without political gridlock.

Interesting differences and similarities are revealed in agency budgets, programs, and results (policy consequences) across subissues. These impacts have varied considerably, showing the importance of policy content in studying civil rights. The three issue areas revealed different patterns, but, of course, commonalities appeared as well. They have each remained significant in civil rights throughout the modern era.

Education has experienced only moderate budget growth and programmatic actions. Some might say that is because it has been the most successfully implemented of the subissues, but even that is not a reality everywhere. Because school segregation in the North was largely ignored, it became both inevitable and ironic that the South would become more integrated than the supposedly more "enlightened" North (Rodgers and Bullock 1972). School segregation in the North often resulted from housing patters, and executive agencies were lax in enforcing fair housing standards. These subissues are clearly interrelated. The Office for Civil Rights pushed aggressive desegregation efforts that Richard Nixon tried to curtail (Panetta and Gall 1971). The OCR is now more diffused, and despite some opposition from agency lawyers, it largely fell in line with Reagan and Bush policies (Bullock and Stewart 1984).

Employment has revealed the greatest change in budgets and in enforcement. Yet, the proportions of women and minorities in government, professions, management, and elective positions are still far below their proportions of the population. The Reagan administration emphasized employment the most, and it continues to get most of the money, personnel, and, perhaps, tangible results. Bush generally took a more conciliatory tone in employment policy. He reluctantly signed legislation Reagan had opposed, and women at least were certainly more in evidence in the Bush White House than they had been in the Reagan administration. These two presidents bickered frequently with Congress, and lack of agreement between these branches reduced policy implementation and impact in the employment issue area.

As Bullock speculates (1984a, 188), housing seems the least successfully implemented (least change in budgets and programs) of these subissues. Generally fair housing expenditures and program changes by presidents and parties were small. Bush had a much more visible and assertive secretary of housing and urban development in former representative Jack Kemp than Reagan had in "Silent" Sam Pierce. After the Los Angeles riot in 1992, Kemp got his chance to advance his ideas, although under reelection pressures the president and others in Bush's administration quickly lost interest. Housing agencies have had a difficult time in implementation. Often the roles and responsibilities of relevant agencies have been unclear. Housing remains the single most segregated component of American life (*Newsweek*, March 7, 1988, 20).

The government interventions discussed in this book have generally tried to guarantee equality of opportunity. Equality of result is a different question, and this chapter has delved briefly into such results. Obviously some issue areas (apart from and within civil rights) are more amenable to government intervention than others, and a major assumption is that government has had an impact. Presumably the implementing actions of the bureaucracy discussed in chapter 6 have been among the greatest influences of all, and presidents have at least some influence over what agencies do. Still, it is debatable whether government intervention can effect societal change, let alone governmental or even program change.

During the past generation, civil rights policy has rapidly evolved.

Desegregation is widespread if not complete, particularly in elementary education, public accommodations, and voting. Segregation persists in housing, employment, and higher education, and the Reagan and Bush administrations were successful in exploiting and intensifying partisan differences over quotas. Busing and affirmative action are backlash issues for middle- and lower-class whites. Parents of both races now question the benefits of busing (*Newsweek*, March 7, 1988, 39). The strategies of the Reagan and Bush administration had some success in breaking off conservative voters from the Democratic coalition to win presidential elections (Edsall and Edsall 1991). Presidents Reagan and Bush clearly benefited politically from their conservative civil rights statements, actions, and results. Yet those same policies may have helped unify the Democrats in 1992.

Notes

1. The reports were issued in 1959, 1961, 1963, and 1965. Those in 1961 and 1963 were fairly comprehensive; the 1965 report focused exclusively on farm programs (*Congress and the Nation*, 1:1965, 1609–14).

2. Recall from chapter 1 that the definition of civil rights in this book is relatively narrow, excluding civil liberties and international human rights.

3. For forceful critiques of comparable worth, see *Newsweek*, August 11, 1986, 40, and April 22, 1985, 57; England 1992.

4. Numerous sources cite this reduction in information made available since 1981 to the public and scholars through depository libraries. One study documents a reduction in government publications by at least one-fourth (American Library Association 1991, 93).

5. During the Bush administration, one of twenty deputy assistants and thirteen of forty-five special assistants were women. Of the top aides, however, only two of seventeen were women, and neither was in the inner circle (*National Journal*, October 19, 1991, 2563).

6. There is, of course, huge variation in the quality of public education. Poorer urban children, disproportionately minority, go to the least well funded schools, while middle- and upper-class white children are more likely to attend higher-quality public schools. In addition, private school enrollment has increased significantly during the past decade.

7. The phenomenon of divided government has produced scholarly works by Mayhew (1991) and Fiorina (1992) and edited volumes by Thurber (1991) and Cox and Kernell (1991) as well as works published in the journal *PS*.

9

Conclusion

Themes of the Book

I now review the theme of *presidential leadership* throughout the policy-making process and analyze its contribution to *policy change*. Actors inside and outside of government are interested in the impact of policies, but they also contribute to that impact. Their interventions make a difference in the final shape policies take. Issue content is also important in differentiating policy impact. How have the issues and roles of actors changed over the years? How closely do civil rights policy outcomes correspond with earlier goals and other stages in the policy-making process? Evaluation is the examination of these varied results but is the least well understood stage. A stimulus-response model and case analysis help in this assessment.

Stimulus-Response Model

The chapter organization of this book follows the policy-making process, which is roughly analogous to the stimulus-response model, adapted as statements, actions, and results (Ripley and Franklin 1975). *Statements* usually can be equated with agenda setting and the initiation of public policy. Often, statements may be vague and symbolic, but they do contain specific policy preferences and recommendations. The data suggest the presidential role is preeminent here. Statements do vary by presidents and are related to subsequent actions and results.

Policy *actions* are, of course, more tangible than statements, and virtually every actor can do something to influence civil rights policy making. Although they may occur at any stage of the process, policy actions commonly are thought of as influencing the formal decisions of policy, particularly its modification and adoption. Often such actions are responses to presidents who usually set the stage or are the conduit for others to act.

Results are what happen after policies are enacted. They include responses, particularly of interpretation from bureaucrats and courts, who seemingly have the greatest say in the way policies are carried out. Ultimately, results refer to the impact of policies, the final stage of the policy process. The movement from statements to actions to results suggests a dynamic process. It is also circuitous. If a policy's impact is to reward or deprive particular groups sufficiently, they will probably seek to maintain or reverse the policy, thereby continuing the policy-making process.[1]

Policy Impact

Impact is the least well developed stage of the policy-making process. There have been many policy evaluation studies, but most have been impressionistic and idiosyncratic and have suffered from weak theoretical and/or methodological development (Nachmias 1980; Schick 1971). Thus many discrete studies of *programs* exist, but there are few broad-based evaluations of *policies*, let alone studies of broader societal impacts. Political reality often colors policy evaluation, and the conclusions drawn likely will be a function of who is doing the evaluating and what or whom is being evaluated.

The presidential role is my primary focus. Studies allude to the administrative presidency, but the notion has yet to be verified empirically; there has been little systematic evidence of whether presidents matter in policy implementation or impact. The presidential role in civil rights policy implementation is revealed here to be substantial, particularly under Presidents Reagan and Bush. Agencies may constrain presidents, but the president and his administration also establish the boundaries for bureaucratic enforcement of existing laws. This has been particularly true since the late 1960s, when the emphasis shifted to enforcement. The Reagan and Bush administrations are the most vivid examples because their enforcement policies were so explicit. These administrations were activist, but in reducing the role of government. To that end, they were innovative, unveiling the various policy tools available to a president. Assessing presidential impact on societal outcomes is very difficult, however. Future research should explore these societal (as well as presidential) impacts, as was attempted in chapter 8.

Congress evaluates through its oversight and investigative functions. Often this process is merely a cursory look at budget time. Presidents or cabinet officers may authorize a review of a particular program, although this is usually done only after considerable publicity necessitates action. Temporary advisory bodies also assess particular programs and make recommendations to the president. Agencies administering programs seldom initiate evaluation efforts on their own since they fear assessment and perhaps budget reductions (Schick 1971). Laws now mandate some evaluations of programs and agencies. Such techniques as zero-base budgeting (ZBB), PPBS (Planning-Programming-Budgeting-System), MBO (Management by Objective), and sunset laws are designed to strengthen weak but promising programs and single out the "inefficient" ones for elimination. Presidents have introduced such devices with only limited success.

The broadest (if not always the most scientific) evaluation of public policy is done by actors outside government: public opinion, the media, political parties, interest groups, and academics. These bodies make their views known through a wide variety of sources, including polls, election returns, political financial support, and written and spoken communications of various types. Although evaluations may be embarrassing and even carry a degree of political risk (in the event Congress and outside groups support negative conclusions), they may also give the president leverage over the bureaucracy.

This final chapter compares actor roles as rival explanations to the president in the policy process. It is hard to establish who has the greatest influence in civil rights policy making. Actor influence and policy impact vary widely across target groups and subissues. Presidential influence, whether leadership or followership, exists but varies greatly according to the stage of the policy-making process. Change of all types appears easier to measure than presidential leadership, but it, too, depends greatly upon the types of policy and actor relationships. Thus, these ideas are highly interrelated but often in ways not amenable to direct empirical inquiry. Such an assessment is necessary, however, because evaluation of impact is the most crucial (if most elusive) stage of the policy-making process.

Case Studies

How can the use of case studies facilitate the study of policy making? Although case analyses are often criticized, they can be an important pedagogical tool. This book examined four cases in some detail, two legislative and two executive ones. I covered all aspects of policy statements, actions, and results, thereby more fully explicating the entire process of policy making. The cases are related and contribute to cumulative knowledge. While just four cases do not constitute definitive tests, they help develop the theoretical framework of this book. In particular, they revealed patterns of interaction among those inside and outside government. It is hoped that more cases will be added in future research to understand better the role of presidents and others in civil rights policy making.

Presidential Statements and Actions

This book finds a significant role for presidents in civil rights policy. The presidential policy arena is a component (or subsystem) of the larger political system (see chapter 1). The president is central in the policy-making arena but nevertheless must interact with every other component in order to accomplish his preferred policy outcomes. In this section, I summarize presidential statements and actions by presidents individually, by political party, and across policy stages.

Many authors have written about the importance of cycles in determining presidential influence on public policy (Light 1982; Shull 1983; Rockman 1984; Kessel 1984). Normally cycles are thought of as regularized trends, but I use the term more loosely here. The grouping used in this book allows a general examination across the years for which data are available but also according to cycles in the presidency. The party in the White House is normally the longest cycle, frequently spanning two presidencies (but not more in the modern era). Individual presidential administrations are the short-range cycle, covering anywhere from two and one-half years (for Ford) to eight years (for Eisenhower and Reagan). These cycles were considered sources of presidential leadership.

Individual Presidents

Presidents have exercised varied but sometimes considerable influence in civil rights. Although generally a low priority for presidents, their leadership is critical in determining the direction and magnitude for civil rights policy. I acknowledge that the president often is not the driving force behind civil rights policy, but the power of the presidency usually is essential to change policy. It may range from strong legislative leadership, such as Johnson exerted with the Civil Rights Act, to a decision not to veto, as Ford decided with the Education for All Handicapped Children Act, to a movement away from government (or at least legislative) involvement, as Reagan initiated and Bush continued. These two presidents forced a reconsideration of the notion that an activist president pursues expansionist civil rights policies.

The experiences of the Reagan and Bush administrations reveal considerable differences from other presidents. One civil rights advocate argues that differing commitments by presidents since the 1960s have slowed the progress toward equality made by the courts and HEW (Middleton 1979). Johnson was civil rights' strongest advocate, while Reagan and Bush were powerful opponents. They were also among the most active while Ford and Eisenhower were the least active of modern presidents.

Table 9.1 rank-orders presidents on their statements and actions. The data show some support for the expectation relating ideological commitment to presidential assertiveness. Overall, Johnson and Carter rank highest while Eisenhower and Ford rank lowest on presidential statements and actions. One can interpret Reagan's "low" score (but rank of third in assertiveness) in different ways. He reflects extremes; he made conservative and symbolic statements, took few legislative positions, issued the most executive orders, and requested the least increases in civil rights budgets among contemporary presidents.

The findings for Bush are mixed. He was very assertive in statements and some actions but displayed low assertiveness in others (e.g., calls for judicial actions). The Bush data may seem inconsistent because so few data points are available. Thus, one must exercise care when interpreting his aggregate ranking because the types of statements and actions as well as variations among them are important. Also, we must examine the direction and level of presidential statements and actions.

Political Party

This study has revealed that Democratic presidents are generally much more supportive of civil rights in their statements and actions than are

Table 9.1

Rank Order of Presidents' Statements and Actions

	Statements			Legislative Actions			Executive Actions			Overall	
	No./Yr.	%L	No. Lines	No. Requests	No. Positions	No. Calls	EO	Budget Requests	Judicial Calls	Mean	Rank
Eisenhower	7.5	3	8	3	6	8	7	—	5.5	48/8 = 6.0	8
Kennedy	4	1.5	5	2	7	7	4	—	3	36/8 = 4.5	4
Johnson	2	1.5	6.5	1	1	3	5	1	2	23/9 = 2.6	1
Nixon	6	7	4	5	3	6	6	2	7	46/9 = 5.1	5.5
Ford	7.5	8	6.5	4	8	5	8	3	1	50/9 = 5.5	7
Carter	3	4	2	—	5	1	1	5	5.5	26.5/8 = 3.2	2
Reagan	5	5	3	—	4	2	2	4	4	29/8 = 3.6	3
Bush	1	6	1	—	2	4	3	6	8	41/8 = 5.1	5.5

Note: Values represent rank of each president on indicators of assertiveness. For % liberal (%L), the most liberal position is ranked highest, and for budget requests the greatest average increase is ranked the highest; the greatest requested cut is ranked lowest (see chapter 4). The other values reflect average number per year, or assertiveness. No. lines refers to the average length of policy statements; legislative and judicial calls are average number of times presidents requested action by these institutions in their policy statements (see chapter 3). EO refers to number of executive orders.

Republican presidents. Beginning first with statements, Democratic presidents give greater attention and support to civil rights than do Republican presidents, whose fewer statements are more symbolic. Democratic presidents view civil rights from a broader perspective than do their Republican counterparts. Democrats are also much more assertive on legislative actions, but Republicans are more assertive on executive actions, perhaps because Republicans more frequently face hostile Congresses. Republicans, then, seek administrative solutions more often than do Democrats (see chapter 5; Nathan 1983; but see Waterman 1989).

Responses also vary by party, with Democrats doing better legislatively than Republican presidents. That was not always the case with administrative, budget, judicial, and bureaucratic responses, however. These other responses vary more by presidential party. The findings fit the Republican strategy of appealing to lower-class whites (Edsall and Edsall 1991). The correspondence of such responses with presidential statements and actions is examined later in this chapter.

Presidents and Policy Stages

The relative importance of presidential leadership varies across the policy-making stages. I expected individual presidents to be more important than their party in agenda setting. That expectation generally was observed since variations by individual president were considerable on every measure. Party differences were substantial on most indicators of agenda setting but not for length of policy statement or calls for judicial action.

The expectations changed in policy formulation, where political party did differentiate presidential activism but not presidents' legislative symbolism or their propensity to issue executive orders. Individual presidents continued to reveal substantial differences in legislative activism (both budget and program requests) and in executive order issuance. Despite the lesser influence of political parties in presidential formulation than in their agenda setting, individual presidents are still the predominant leadership source.

These leadership sources continue to differentiate in the modification and adoption of civil rights policy. The expectations generally are accurate, since party differences are substantial only for support of presidents' vote positions, not for success of requests or congressional appropriations. Party of the president, then, loses some of its discriminatory value as the policy process unfolds. Perhaps party becomes less controllable for presidents as other political actors come on stage. Presidents individually continue to distinguish among the relevant variables (support, success, and appropriations).

In policy implementation, individual presidents again show much greater ranges than does party, particularly on program actions (cases resolved) and to a lesser extent on expenditures. Examination of policy impact in chapter 8 also revealed individual president and political party variations. The impact of the Reagan-Bush statements and actions was considerable. Thus, these sources of presidential leadership (individual president and political party) differ considerably across the entire policy-making process.

Does the Political Environment Matter?

Policy Actors

Those outside government have an impact on the very fragmented civil rights policy process. Interest groups have been particularly strong in getting civil rights policies enacted and in keeping decision makers aware of continued inequities. The general impact of political parties, while seemingly less than that of interest groups, is more important earlier in the policy process (e.g., agenda setting rather than implementation). Public opinion has shifted toward greater acceptance of civil rights generally. Governmental organizations have also varied greatly at different eras of and stages in the civil rights policy-making process. Government probably has been more important in civil rights than outside agents. All the national institutions—Congress, judiciary, bureaucrats, and presidents—have played important roles in shaping civil rights policy outcomes.

The interrelationship among relevant actors in the political system is important in the final makeup of programs. Presidents seek certain results from the political system. Actors do not merely respond; they can also push the president and, thus, modify his own statements and actions. Identifying major resources and constraints under which presidents operate and assessing relationships with other major actors show—at least partly—the extent to which their goals (desired outcomes) are met. Obviously, the president cannot be looked at in isolation if the process of policy making is to be fully understood. The policy approach provides a useful framework for an analysis of this process.

Public Opinion

This discussion considers the current impact of public opinion generally and on three subissues of civil rights. Mass opinions appear contradictory: "segregation is illegal but desegregation is not mandatory" (*Washington Post National Weekly Edition*, January 14, 1985, 38). Despite increasing support for the concept of desegregation, an NORC poll revealed that the "white majority feels that government would be overstepping its boundaries by pushing desegregation, and that many whites see desegregation as 'trying to protect one group by damaging another' " (*Washington Post National Weekly Edition*, January 14, 1985, 38). Many blamed President Reagan for lack of black progress (*Washington Post National Weekly Edition*, January 14, 1985, 24; *New Orleans Times-Picayune/States-Item*, January 24, 1984, sec. 1, p. 7; Yarbrough 1985). Yet this blame is itself a contradiction because, while the public opposed Reagan's *policies* in civil rights and in some other policy areas, it supported him *personally* at higher levels. Some say there has been a "softening of white attitudes toward blacks and the virtual disappearance of the once prevalent belief in white supremacy" (*Washington Post National Weekly Edition*, January 14, 1985, 38). Andrew Hacker (1992) disagrees, arguing that perceptions of superiority persist among whites.

School desegregation perhaps is the civil rights subissue with the most extensive public opinion data. While in the past whites adamantly opposed busing (see chapter 7), they do not appear to mind it much after it is implemented (Bullock 1984a, 182–83). Thus, as school desegregation and even busing have become common, so has public acceptance of them, especially among young people (*Washington Post National Weekly Edition*, March 10, 1986, 37). However, as in most policy areas, public opinion has followed rather than guided government action. Data on busing opinions by race are presented in Table 9.2. Whites expect school desegregation to continue and are more comfortable than previously that many of their children's schoolmates are black. At the same time, Department of Justice policies under Reagan increased white resistance to desegregated public education

Table 9.2

Reaction of Parents Whose Children Have Been Bused for Racial Reasons, 1978–1983
(in %)

Question: How did the busing of children in your family to go to school with children of other races work out?[a]

	1978	1981	1983
Blacks			
Very satisfactory	63	74	66
Partly satisfactory	25	21	28
Not satisfactory	8	5	6
Whites			
Very satisfactory	56	48	64
Partly satisfactory	23	37	24
Not satisfactory	16	13	11

Source: Louis Harris and Associates, Inc., A Study of Attitudes Toward Racial and Religious Minorities and Toward Women (New York: Louis Harris and Associates, Inc., 1978), 38–40; Louis Harris, "Majority of Parents Report School Busing Has Been Satisfactory Experience," The Harris Survey, no. 25, March 26, 1981; Louis Harris, "Black Voting the Key to Outcome in 1984," The Harris Survey, No. 58, July 21, 1983.

[a]Respondents were first asked, "Have any of the children in your family been picked up by bus to go to a school with children of other races, or hasn't that happened?" In 1978, 35 percent of blacks and 10 percent of whites answered affirmatively. In 1982, 43 percent of blacks and 19 percent of whites with schoolchildren answered yes; in 1983, the figures were 36 percent of blacks and 25 percent of whites with children in school. The question about busing experience was asked only of these respondents.

(Bullock 1984a, 180–81). An example was Reagan administration support of the Norfolk, Virginia, case that released school districts from school busing plans.

Trends in public attitudes toward equal employment are harder to assess, and as issues have moved from affirmative action and quotas to comparable worth, they have often become more gender than race related. One poll showed that 61 percent of men and 78 percent of women agreed that women are paid less fairly. Men of higher social status are more likely to state this position and to think that women could do their job (Washington Post National Weekly Edition, April 15, 1985, 37). Ninety percent of the population support equal pay for equal (the same) work, but there are disparities by gender in support for affirmative action goals. Women reveal somewhat greater support and much less opposition (by 15 percentage points) than men (Washington Post National Weekly Edition, March 17, 1986, 38). Studies in the 1990s suggested women never catch up to men in pay differential.

Relatively little public opinion data exist on the fair housing question. The political scientist Gary Orfield is quoted in the *Washington Post National Weekly Edition* (January 14, 1985, 38) as stating: "Whites are willing to have blacks live next door but opposed to government moves toward that end. What we have in public opinion polls is a rhetorical change that does not have any practical policy relevance whatsoever." Polls reveal more apathy toward civil rights than previously (Halpern 1985, 153). With the exception of compensatory actions like quotas, apathy characterizes the role of public opinion in civil rights policy. Such inconsistency and lack of salience does little to enhance one's faith in the ability of the general public to guide public policy.

Table 9.3 presents survey data revealing differences in perceptions by race on the subissues analyzed here. Blacks are much more likely than whites to think the government is doing too little to help African Americans and to support preferential treatment for blacks due to past discrimination. Racial differences are less over whether black children do better if they go to racially segregated schools and whether respondents prefer to live in an integrated neighborhood. The fact that there was no question on voting further confirms its acceptance as a more basic right.

These specific attitudes in public opinion polls may be related to more diffuse levels of support for civil rights. Race affects the mass public deeply and relates to the cultural order. Thus, there is a need to look at both political culture and public policy to understand racial attitudes (Sniderman and Hagen 1985, 20). We have seen that the perceptions of men and women differ somewhat, but blacks and whites reveal vast differences in their perceptions of the causes and consequences of inequality. These differences may even have led to "symbolic" racism, where whites think blacks are not willing to live by the same value system (Sniderman and Hagen 1985, 22). Racial attitudes have increasingly contributed to structures of political beliefs. In fact, Carmines and Stimson argue that ideology is largely a racial dimension (1980, 17).

Interest Groups

Among actors outside government, interest groups have played the most significant role in civil rights policy making. From Thurgood

Table 9.3

Differences by Race in Perceptions, by Issue Area
(in %)

		Whites	Blacks
Overall	Is the federal government doing too much, too little, or about the right amount to help American blacks?		
	Too much	18	5
	Too little	29	71
	About right	36	13
Education	Do black children do better if they go to racially mixed schools?		
	Better	39	48
	Worse	4	6
	No difference	38	41
Employment	Because of past discrimination should qualified blacks receive preference over equally qualified whites in such matters as getting into college or getting jobs or not?		
	Should	14	40
	Should not	80	50
Housing	Would you prefer to live in a neighborhood with mostly whites, with mostly blacks or in a neighborhood mixed half and half?		
	Mostly blacks	0	8
	Mostly whites	33	2
	Half and half	46	68

Source: Adapted from *Newsweek*, March 7, 1988, 23.

Marshall and the NAACP in 1954 to the Leadership Conference on Civil Rights today, interest groups exert pressure on many phases of the process. Their influence probably is greater later in the process, and Bullock and Stewart show how interest groups can affect policy implementation (1984, 409). Civil rights organizations have mobilized black voters (Tercheck 1980; Cohen, Cotter, and Coulter 1983) and have educated the public about discrimination. Additionally, they claim credit for pushing programs that have improved economic and social conditions and expanded the black middle class.

However, civil rights interest groups seem to be having a diminishing impact on policy making. Critics charge them with preaching a "litany of despair [that only] racial integration and preferential government programs will ultimately bring blacks into the economic mainstream" (*Washington Post National Weekly Edition*, May 27, 1985, 25). Such critics as Robert L. Woodson, director of the National Urban League, argue that many government programs in the past have not always worked and that the black community must disentangle itself from overreliance both on government programs and on established interest groups. He argues that often "'indigenous organizations and grass roots leaders' have better solutions" (*Washington Post National Weekly Edition*, May 27, 1985, 25). Interest group advocates today do seem to have diminished in importance, as evidenced by their inability to crystallize opposition, even against the policies of the Reagan and Bush administrations. They continue to be a force in the civil rights policy process, however, and their influence could increase in the Clinton administration. Unfortunately, interest group data are very difficult to acquire.

Political Parties and Others

Political parties have played lesser roles than interest groups in later civil rights policy stages, but their platforms and pronouncements over the years probably have influenced agenda setting. The parties have differed over time, with Democrats early on being less supportive but then becoming more pro–civil rights than Republicans. The columnist George Will explains how the modern parties differ: "Republicans define justice more in terms of equality of opportunity than of result. . . . [They] have accepted the federal responsibility for . . . civil rights, but have resisted 'race conscious' policies such as group entitlements" (*New Orleans Times-Picayune*, February 20, 1984, 1, 11). Civil rights was more partisan under Reagan and Bush than it was earlier (Edsall and Edsall 1991).

Democrats brought civil rights to the agenda as a net gain but may show less support as the value of their black coalition diminishes (Stern 1992). Generally, the media and elections seem to have little direct impact on civil rights, but no doubt they have been an indirect influence over time. The media have been an independent agenda setter and social critic. Political party differences among voters and members of Congress on civil rights have been much less than party difference among presidents. Data from the National Election Studies do suggest variation over time in the salience of civil rights to the electorate. Seemingly, the 1992 election was less influenced by civil rights than most presidential elections due to Clinton's moderate positions.

Presidents

I now discuss actors within government. We have seen that the president's influence in policy making varies considerably according to the particular policy stage. The policy cycle normally takes much time—often longer than presidents have. Certainly their influence is greater earlier in the process than later. Presidents have greatest control over the policy agenda. Seldom is any incumbent president able to see the full implementation of his programs, and almost never is there an objective evaluation of them before he leaves office. One might presume that since the Constitution requires the president to "take care that the laws be faithfully executed," he would have substantial influence over policy implementation. Although execution (or implementation) of public policy is the traditional function of the executive branch, the president may find himself as constrained at that stage as at any other.

Presidential influence usually has been important in civil rights policy making, if not always the most important element. The substantial civil rights bureaucracy may not allow diminution of its power; "bureaucratic politics" may prevail. Yet presidents, particularly Lyndon Johnson and Ronald Reagan, made a difference in civil rights, not only in setting the agenda but throughout the policy process. Less consistent presidents, like Richard Nixon and George Bush, also seem able to influence policy change. Bill Clinton likely will be more consistent.

The two major influences on the civil rights policy-making process are political environment, which can lead to *presidential leadership,* and nature of the issues, which often is reflected in *policy change.* The president's influence (like that of all actors) is limited at any particular time and across any particular subissue of civil rights policy. Other actors influence presidents apart from simply responding to their stimuli. However, the president may be the only actor involved in *each* stage of policy making. Those inside government variably influence civil rights policy making, as was posited in chapter 2, Table 2.3.

Congress

In the twentieth century, Congress did not take an early leadership role in civil rights. Although legislation was late in coming, it has had profound effects. Often Congress did not pay much attention to implementation, and, since it rarely set the agenda or initiated policy on its own, it confined its role largely to modification and adoption. Even though Congress modified few presidential positions on votes, it was assertive by enacting few of presidents' legislative requests. Thus, Congress adopted few civil rights policies preferred by presidents. Through the mid-1980s, Congress was the most conservative of the three branches in civil rights. It often blocked civil rights legislation and often exempted its members from the laws it passed. Congress has supported presidential initiatives in civil rights less than in most other policy areas, approving only one-third of proposals (Shull 1983, 131).

Of course, many important bills eventually passed, but Congress's conservative image remained until the late 1980s. Only when confronted by conservative Presidents Reagan and Bush did Congress take a leadership role.[2] From studies of representation, we know that on civil rights issues members of Congress act most like delegates, their votes correlating with attitudes in their districts (Clausen 1973; Miller and Stokes 1963). As attitudes change, congressional behavior should also change. Support in Congress for equal treatment under the law is greater now than ever before, due to increased representation of women and minorities after the 1992 election.

In the early period, Congress was at its most assertive during the 1960s, particularly in fair housing. It reasserted itself under Reagan, giving him fewer cuts in civil rights than he requested. Yet the shift away from legislative solutions continued, despite the extension of the Voting Rights Act in 1982 and the large majority of members of Congress initially supporting a 1984 civil rights bill. Conservatives in Congress and in the administration succeeded in bottling up the bill.

It was not until March 1988 that Congress passed the Civil Rights Restoration Act over Reagan's veto. Some members considered it the most important civil rights legislation in twenty years. Despite this action, civil rights seems less a mainstream congressional concern. According to the columnist David Broder, "The idea of using government legislation to aid victims is out of fashion" (*Washington Post*, October 8, 1984, A19). Even some civil rights supporters who recognize that past legislation was important assert that "the old strategies have run their course. New efforts must focus on ending dependence on government and encouraging the growing movement among blacks to rely on themselves for an improved life" (*Washington Post National Weekly Edition*, May 27, 1985, 26).

Legislation in 1990–91 was very controversial (see case in chapter 4). President Bush was forced by external events to pull back from strong opposition to what he had previously called a quota bill. Charges of race-baiting against the president led him to endorse the legislation, thereby ensuring continued leadership by Congress on civil rights. The Los Angeles riot in May 1992 kept congressional attention focused on civil rights. Conservative Presidents Reagan and Bush ultimately could not prevail, at least through legislative means. Accordingly, they used the courts and bureaucracy more extensively than their predecessors. Unified government beginning in 1993 should increase presidential-congressional cooperation in civil rights.

Judiciary

The courts took an early lead and have remained important in civil rights. They took the initiative in school desegregation and continued the liberal course set in 1954. Resistance from the public, Congress, and some presidents moderated the Supreme Court's civil rights positions by the late 1970s. Both the public and the Supreme Court became more deeply divided over employment, where sentiment leans toward compensatory action (e.g., limited affirmative action) but not preferential treatment (e.g., permanent quotas). The Court took little action on fair housing. The Court's growing conservatism (74.8 percent liberal in 1981–84 vs. 98.5 percent liberal in 1961–64; Baum and Weisberg 1980) is probably for different reasons than the same trend that occurred in Congress. Although one of those reasons is member replacement, judicial appointees have only moderately supported the views of their appointing president (e.g., Johnson = high, Ford = low, Eisenhower = moderate).

Reagan and Bush appointees began moving the courts at all federal levels back in a conservative direction (Detlefsen 1991). Reagan's appointees were the most conservative among all modern presidents. Clinton's appointees likely will be both representative and responsive to civil rights advocates. Despite obvious influence by the public, Congress, and presidents, the *Bakke* and *Weber* cases are instances where final determination of acceptable civil rights enforcement remains the purview of the Court. Its impact on civil rights policy in the United States is undeniable and continuing, despite Congress's overturning of some of their decisions in the late 1980s and early 1990s.

Bureaucracy

Executive actions during the 1970s, 1980s, and 1990s frequently supplanted the legislative actions of the 1960s. Thus, these two types of policy actions reveal an inverse relationship.[3] Bureaucratic agencies play the pivotal role in policy implementation and have surprising discretion over budgetary, organizational, and programmatic aspects of civil rights enforcement. Expenditures can be manipulated by agencies, certainly more so than requests or appropriations. Expenditures (in all subissues combined) grew most under Johnson and least under Ford. While the trend is toward decreasing outlays, Reagan did not cut civil rights as much as his critics charge. Budgets were cut more drastically under Bush. While agencies can also influence their organization and programs, obtaining comparable measures of such implementing activities across issue area, let alone by agency, is very difficult.

The seeming discretion agencies have over civil rights enforcement diminished under Reagan and Bush through their successful manipulation of all executive actions (e.g., appointments, executive orders, budgets, reorganizations, and programs). Agencies became more diffused, politicized, and overburdened in the Reagan administration, thereby decreasing agency discretion in civil rights enforcement. Presumably this politicization was a conscious effort on the administration's part. Bush seemingly used administrative actions less often or effectively than Reagan.

Responding to Presidents

Why do some presidents succeed with their civil rights policy preferences while others, apparently, fail? Table 9.4 examines responses of various actors to presidential statements and actions, ranking presidents as in Table 9.1. In both tables I added each rank and divided by the total number to attain an overall score. The findings in Table 9.4 show that Johnson and Nixon obtained the greatest responses while Eisenhower and Bush were least successful in this regard. Johnson did poorly only with support from the Supreme Court as a whole, where Nixon was deficient in legislative support and appropriations. Nixon did well in implementation so his seeming paranoia about the bureaucracy was unjustified (Aberbach and Rockman 1976; Cole and Caputo 1979).

Table 9.4

Rank Order of Responses to Presidential Statements and Actions

| | Legislative[a] | | Budget[b] | | Executive[c] | Judicial[d] | Overall | |
	Success	Support	Appropriations	Expenditures	Implementation	Supreme Court	Mean	Rank
Eisenhower	4	7	—	—	—	5	16/3 = 5.3	7
Kennedy	5	4	—	—	5	1	15/4 = 3.8	5.5
Johnson	2	1	2	4	1	6	17/6 = 2.8	1
Nixon	1	5	5	2	2	3	18/6 = 3.0	2
Ford	3	—	1	5	6	4	19/5 = 3.8	5.5
Carter	—	2	4	3	3	7	19/5 = 3.8	5.5
Reagan	—	6	3	1	4	2	16/5 = 3.2	3
Bush	—	3	6	6	7	—	22/4 = 5.5	8

[a]Highest figure equals least success and support; figures from Table 6.1.

[b]Means for four agencies; highest number is least correspondence to president's budget requests; figures from Tables 4.4, 6.4, and 6.5.

[c]Average number of civil rights cases terminated for Department of Justice; larger number is least success (greatest differences) between liberalism of preferences (chapter 3) and implementation (chapter 6).

[d]Based on differences in presidential liberalism score and aggregated liberalism of Supreme Court as a whole; closest correspondence equals highest rank; data from Table 7.1.

Why were Eisenhower and Bush so ineffective (i.e., lowest rankings in Table 9.4)? Part of the reason may have been some inconsistency on their part compared to Johnson and Nixon. Several presidents fall in the middle: Kennedy, Ford, and Carter were very different in ideology, but all were only moderately assertive. Kennedy did well with the Supreme Court but not with other institutions; Ford succeeded only in appropriations from Congress (perhaps because of his great interest in budgeting); Carter did well with Congress but not the Court.

Reagan received moderately close correspondence with his policy preferences (ranking third overall), particularly on agency spending and Supreme Court voting. Yet his first two appointees to the Supreme Court were somewhat distant from his positions, particularly on the issue of affirmative action (see chapter 7). Bush was least highly supported among all presidents (ranking eighth in responses). Although data are scant, he was the least successful president in obtaining correspondence with his budget requests from Congress, on expenditures from the bureaucracy, and on agency implementation (see Table 9.4). Bush's many judicial appointments could have longer-term effects.

Comparing Tables 9.1 and 9.4 permits some conclusions about assertiveness in presidential stimuli and subsequent responses. Johnson and Reagan obtained exactly the same (high) rank in both tables; thus, they must be considered presidents successful in civil rights. Eisenhower and Kennedy too are not far off in differences in their rankings. The remaining presidents probably reflect the notion that if presidents ask for little, they are more likely to get a greater portion of it. This was not true of assertive Reagan and Bush: the former was quite successful and the latter very unsuccessful in obtaining responses from other actors in accordance with their statements and actions.

Civil rights was a burning national issue from the mid-1950s to the late 1960s, and Lyndon Johnson played upon both fears and sympathies in his passionate advocacy. Although he was a pragmatic politician, operating with mixed motives, a favorable biography of the Johnson years states the case well: "Given the pressures for change, strong civil rights bills were all but inevitable. Yet no president less gifted than Johnson would have achieved as much and as quickly. In this case, his facilitative role was crucial" (Conkin 1986, 219). As is the case with the poverty program and several others, Johnson was better at formulation than at implementation. Certainly he faced more intense interest preferences than most other presidents.

The political climate Ronald Reagan faced in the 1980s was quite different. Civil rights issues were less intense. President Reagan not only had a more complicated bureaucracy in place, but public attitudes were more broadly supportive of equality. This changed climate had several effects. On the one hand, it prevented Reagan from backing too far off principles of equality. It ruled out avowedly racist statements and actions but resulted in apathy and the conclusion that discrimination no longer posed a problem, thus civil rights laws no longer needed strict enforcement. The Reagan administration reflected the latter course, perhaps motivated largely by a resentment to what the administration considered heavy-handed social regulation. It seemed fully aware of the ideological and political consequences of its statements and actions. Despite the bold leadership by President Reagan to alter civil rights policy, forces in the policy-making arena were strong enough to prevent much policy retrenchment.

George Bush also was an assertive president, more active in civil rights than many would have predicted. His statements and actions surprised many in being both numerous and also strongly conservative. Policy implementation (in the Department of Justice) was greater under President Bush than under any of his predecessors; that was not what he desired. Budgets were also much higher than he had requested; his very large cuts were not accepted by Congress and agencies. Bush was not able to get the kind of responses from other government institutions that other assertive presidents had obtained.

Do Presidents Really Matter?

Civil rights policy in the 1980s and early 1990s was markedly different than it was a generation before. The Reagan and Bush administrations limited government action designed to prevent discrimination and to undo the consequences of past discrimination. Reagan, particularly, revealed a unique aspect in the range of possibilities for presidential leadership. More rhetoric and action prevailed under President Bush, but he was not able to influence civil rights policy making as much as his predecessors did.

Civil rights provides a good basis for examining whether presidents matter and how much policy change occurs. This analysis has been wide ranging, from case studies of the Reagan and Bush administrations to quantitative assessments of actor statements, actions, and results. Despite limitations of individual measures, it suggests some insights into presidential leadership in civil rights and of changes in the policies themselves.

Presidential Leadership

Although Ronald Reagan took few legislative actions, his executive actions were unparalleled. He and Bush also used strong rhetoric to rekindle and recast civil rights policy. More than any presidents, they show the importance of public statements in shaping the governmental agenda on civil rights. They also shrewdly used other tools of the presidency such as the budget. Both paid a price for their opposition to civil rights, however, because it seems that at least rhetorical support is now a requisite that constrains the actions of the president.[4] Although the president influences civil rights, civil rights, conversely, influences the president. Presidents must often and convincingly voice support at least for equality of opportunity. The expansion of civil rights to include a variety of groups and large numbers of people makes it mandatory for the president to make overtures and gestures to them; the civil rights constituency has grown. Although Reagan's and Bush's statements and actions did not result in negative electoral consequences, their actions did not go unnoticed by civil rights advocates.

The Reagan and Bush administrations returned civil rights to the forefront of the domestic policy agenda. If this policy represented an attack on civil rights, it was done in the guise of a broader ideological purpose. Although the evidence is limited, their administrations had significant effects on enforcement. A newspaper column showed that the top legal official in the Bush EEOC repeatedly overruled staff recommendations and ordered action favorable to employers. This revelation is consistent with the charges others have leveled (*Newsweek*, March 7, 1988, 20, 24; Amaker 1988; Stewart 1993; Yarbrough 1985).

Did these presidents succeed? Did the Reagan and Bush administrations usher in a new era of presidential policy making in civil rights? Did they make the late 1980s and the early 1990s the "presidential decade" in civil rights? But their preferences were policy contraction rather than expansion, reversing the direction that civil rights policy had taken during the past generation. Although their success varied, their decisions, compared to those of Lyndon Johnson, provide the parameters within which future presidents will have to act in the realm of civil rights.

Why do some presidents succeed with their civil rights policy preferences while others, apparently, fail? Attentiveness, ideological commitment, and consistency in statements and actions appear to pay off. All these characteristics require follow-through on the part of the president to obtain the desired responses from the public policy arena. Presidents like Johnson and Reagan exhibited these characteristics, while others like Eisenhower, Ford, and Bush did not. All these presidents *were* ideologically distinct, but assertive and consistent (e.g., rational follow-through from statements and actions); such presidents obtain their way more often. Thus, presidents can influence the process if less so the nature of issues and the political environment of civil rights policy.

Policy Change

Implementation success and policy impact have varied by subissues. They are also interrelated; poverty, crime, poor quality education, unsanitary health and housing conditions, and job dissatisfaction often go together. Some government programs seem to be working (e.g., school desegregation, affirmative action in federal contracts, greater local control of public housing), but more subtle forms of discrimination occur, particularly in the private sector, and seem to defy easy solution by government (e.g., second-generation discrimination, the seeming unworkability of comparable worth, redlining and racial steering of housing in neighborhoods). These are examples of the unintended consequences that public policies often have.

Minorities have made progress, perhaps more in an absolute than a relative sense. Still, higher proportions of minorities than whites are living in poverty in the 1990s than did in the 1960s. Robert Woodson concludes that while the black middle class has gotten larger, governmental aid programs "often have little impact on the plight of the underclass. . . . Many promote dependency and destroy individual initiative" (*Washington Post National Weekly Edition*, May 27, 1985, 25). Woodson sees the only solution as self-help and private economic development. The columnist William Raspberry argues that inadequate effort is part of the problem. "The underclass needs to learn what the middle class takes for granted, that their fate is mostly in their own hands" (*Washington Post*, March 4, 1988, A25).

Some (including Presidents Reagan and Bush) argued that numerous well-intentioned programs of the 1960s did not work. Thus, it is fair to ask whether government is sometimes as much the problem as the solution. Unfortunately, this question is one of the most difficult to answer for scholars seeking to evaluate the impact of public policy. Jennifer Hochschild (1984) argues that incremental policies have not worked, at least in the school desegregation realm. But that is a sub-issue of relative success, and, if she is correct, then only nonincremental comprehensive statements, actions, and results are likely to bring about greater governmental and societal change. While such commitment seems unlikely in the foreseeable future, presidents can and do make a difference throughout the civil rights policy-making process.

Is There a Reagan-Bush Civil Rights Legacy?

Civil rights has been an evolving policy, passing through identifiable stages and eras. One can identify the 1950s as the judicial decade, in which impetus and the direct actions came primarily from the courts. The 1960s can be seen as the legislative era, when much (although obviously not all) of the activity emanated from Congress. The Johnson period was a historical anomaly, as the president took the lead in civil rights. For convenience, the next stage can be said to begin at the decade: the 1970s ushered in the administrative era. During this period executive enforcement of statutory law, presidential directives, and court decisions were the central thrusts. Presidents since LBJ have not been as active legislatively, but Ronald Reagan and George Bush were assertive in different ways in the late 1980s and early 1990s, suggesting that they were the major influence on civil rights, and making this period the presidential decade.

The late 1980s and early 1990s offered the potential, if not always the actuality, of presidential leadership in civil rights. The policy area provides the opportunities for presidential discretion and policy potential. For example, the after-tax income of the poorest 10 percent of the population decreased by over 10 percent from 1980 to 1990 while that of the richest 1 percent grew by over 87 percent (Edsall and Edsall 1991, 220). Because income and race are related, the Reagan administration produced substantial policy change. Reagan and Bush took advantage of a renewed agenda and created a substantial civil rights legacy. That legacy seems likely to be furthered by the courts but will also be muted by a resurgent Congress and bureaucracy.

George Bush issued strong statements and actions in civil rights. The fact that they were more conservative than those of Ronald Reagan surprised most observers. During his four years in office, Bush tried to maintain the conservative Reagan civil rights legacy. In some ways he even expanded on it. Bush blamed the 1992 Los Angeles riot in part on social programs of the 1960s and 1970s.[5] His more modest proposals reveal diminishing support for civil rights in the political environment. By playing on the fear and frustration of lower-class whites, particularly, both Presidents Reagan and Bush left a substantial civil rights legacy, but it was not a kinder, gentler one.

Notes

1. The civil rights policy process, as is true in any policy area, is often messy. Sometimes we observe an inverse relationship among statements, actions, and results. There was no policy making on civil rights during most of U.S. history. Dramatic changes occurred during the 1960s and 1970s, but legislation, if not administration, slowed subsequently until the late 1980s and early 1990s. Government effort diminished thereafter (e.g., expenditures as a proportion of the total federal budget have declined).

2. Evidence may be the overwhelming bipartisan support for overriding Reagan's veto of the Civil Rights Restoration Act (73–24 in the Senate and 292–133 in the House). Congress proved particularly assertive under Presidents Reagan and Bush.

3. For example, a correlation of $r = -0.293$ exists between legislative requests and executive orders.

4. For example, Reagan was forced to shelve rescinding Johnson's executive order on affirmative action. At the same time, general public support for the president's handling of his job is unrelated to his civil rights statements ($r = -0.08$) and actions ($r = 0.193$ with legislative position-taking).

5. In a national poll taken shortly after the riot, 55 percent blamed the Reagan-Bush administrations versus just 42 percent blaming the 1960s social policies as the cause of "urban distress" (*Washington Post National Weekly Edition*, May 18–24, 1992, 37).

References

Aberbach, J.P., and B.A. Rockman. 1976. "Clashing Beliefs within the Executive Branch: The Nixon Administration Bureaucracy." *American Political Science Review* 70 (June): 456–68.

Abraham, H.J. 1985. *Justices and Presidents: A Political History of Appointments to the Supreme Court.* 2d ed. New York: Oxford University Press.

Amaker, N.C. 1988. *Civil Rights and the Reagan Administration.* Washington, D.C.: Urban Institute Press.

Ambrose, S.E. 1984. *Eisenhower.* New York: Simon & Schuster.

American Library Association. 1991. "Less Access to Less Information by and about the U.S. Government," *DTTP* 20, no. 1: 93.

Anderson, J.E., ed. 1979. *Public Policy-making.* 2d ed. New York: Holt, Rinehart and Winston.

———. 1990. *Public Policymaking: An Introduction.* Boston: Houghton Mifflin.

Anderson, J.E., D. Brady, C. Bullock, and J. Stewart. 1984. *Public Politics and Policy in America.* 2d ed. Monterey, Calif: Brooks/Cole.

Asher, H.B. 1988. *Presidential Elections and American Politics.* 4th ed. Chicago: Dorsey Press.

Ball, H., and K. Green. 1985. "The Reagan Justice Department." In Yarbrough 1985, pp. 1–28.

Barber, J.D. 1992. *Presidential Character.* 4th ed. Englewood Cliffs, N.J.: Prentice-Hall.

Bardolph, R., ed. 1970. *Civil Rights Record.* New York: Thomas Y. Crowell.

Baum, L.A., and H.F. Weisberg. 1980. "The Sources of Change in Legislative and Judicial Politics: Civil Rights from 1949–1976." Paper presented at the annual meeting of the American Political Science Association, Washington, D.C., August.

Beck, N. 1982. "Parties, Administrations, and American Macroeconomic Outcomes." *American Political Science Review* 76 (March): 83–93.

Binion, G. 1979. "The Implementation of Section 5 of the 1965 Voting Rights Act." *Western Political Quarterly* 32 (June): 154–73.

Black, H.C. 1990. *Black's Law Dictionary.* 6th ed. St. Paul, Minn.: West Publishing.

Boles, J.K. 1985. "Women's Rights and the Gender Gap." In Yarbrough 1985, pp. 55–81.

231

Brady, D.W., and B. Sinclair. 1984. "Building Majorities for Policy Changes in the House of Representatives." *Journal of Politics* 46 (November): 1033–60.

Brauer, C.M. 1977. *John Kennedy and the Second Reconstruction.* New York: Columbia University Press.

Bullock, C.S. III. 1981. "Congressional Voting and Mobilization of a Black Electorate in the South." *Journal of Politics* 43 (August): 662–82.

———. 1984a. "Conditions Associated with Policy Implementation." In Bullock and Lamb 1984, pp. 184–207.

———. 1984b. "Equal Education Opportunity." In Bullock and Lamb 1984, pp. 55–92.

Bullock, C.S. III, and C.M. Lamb, eds. 1984. *Implementation of Civil Rights Policy.* Monterey, Calif.: Brooks/Cole.

Bullock, C.S. III, and H. Rodgers, Jr. 1975. *Racial Equality in America: In Search of an Unfulfilled Goal.* Pacific Palasades, Calif.: Goodyear.

Bullock, C.S. III, and J. Stewart, Jr. 1984. "New Programs in 'Old' Agencies: Lessons in Organizational Change from the Office for Civil Rights." *Administration and Society* 15 (February): 387–412.

Burk, R.F. 1984. *Eisenhower Administration and Black Civil Rights.* Knoxville: University of Tennessee Press.

Burke, J.P. 1985. "Presidential Influence in the Budget Process." In *The Presidency and Public Policy Making,* ed. G.C. Edwards, S.A. Shull, and N.C. Thomas, pp. 71–94. Pittsburgh: University of Pittsburgh Press.

Burns, J.M. 1978. *Leadership.* New York: Harper and Row.

Campbell, C. 1986. *Managing the Presidency.* Pittsburgh: University of Pittsburgh Press.

Campbell, C., and B. Rockman, eds. 1991. *The Bush Presidency: First Appraisals.* Chatham, N.J.: Chatham House.

Carmines, E.G., and J.A. Stimson. 1980. "The Faces of Issue Voting." *American Political Science Review* 74 (March): 78–91.

———. 1989. *Issue Evolution.* Princeton: Princeton University Press.

Carp, R., and C.K. Rowland. 1983. *Policy Making and Politics on the Federal District Courts.* Knoxville: University of Tennessee Press.

Carter, H. III. 1986. "South Africa at Home: Reagan and the Revival of Racism." *Playboy,* January, 107–8, 214, 218, 220.

Chamberlain, L.H. 1946. "President, Congress, and Legislation." *Political Science Quarterly* 61 (March): 42–60.

Christenson, R.M. 1982. "Presidential Leadership of Congress." In *Rethinking the Presidency,* ed. T.E. Cronin, pp. 255–70. Boston: Little, Brown.

Clausen, A.R. 1973. *How Congressmen Decide: A Policy Focus.* New York: St. Martin's Press.

Cohen, J.E. 1982. "A Historical Reassessment of Wildavsky's 'Two Presidencies' Thesis." *Social Science Quarterly* 63 (September): 549–55.

Cohen, J.E., and P.R. Coulter. 1983. "The Changing Structure of Southern Participation." *Social Science Quarterly* 64 (September): 536–49.

Cole, R., and D. Caputo. 1979. "Presidential Control of the Senior Civil Service." *American Political Science Review* 73 (June): 399–413.

Congress and the Nation. Vols. 1–7. 1:1965; 2:1969; 3:1973; 4:1977; 5:1981; 6:1985; 7:1990. Washington, D.C.: Congressional Quarterly.

Congressional Quarterly Almanac. Annual. Washington, D.C.: Congressional Quarterly.

Congressional Quarterly Weekly Reports. Washington, D.C.: Congressional Quarterly.

Conkin, Paul K. 1986. *Big Daddy from the Pedernales: Lyndon Baines Johnson.* Boston: Twayne Publishers.

Converse, P.E. 1964. "Nature of Belief Systems in Mass Publics." In *Ideology and Discontent,* ed. D. Apter, pp. 213–55. New York: Free Press.

Cox, G.W., and S. Kernell, eds. 1991. *Divided Government.* Boulder, Colo.: Westview Press.

Cronin, T.E. 1980. *State of the Presidency.* 2d ed. Boston: Little, Brown.

Davidson, C., ed. 1984. *Minority Vote Dilution.* Washington, D.C.: Howard University Press.

Davis, E. 1983. "Congressional Liaison." In *Both Ends of the Avenue,* ed. A. King, pp. 59–95. Washington, D.C.: American Enterprise Institute.

Day, D.S. 1980. "Racial Politics: The Depriest Incident." *Journal of Negro History* 65 (Winter): 6–17.

Denton, R.E., Jr. 1982. *Symbolic Dimensions of the American Presidency.* Prospect Heights, Ill.: Waveland Press.

Detlefsen, R.R. 1991. *Civil Rights under Reagan.* San Francisco: Institute for Contemporary Studies.

Downs, A. 1967. *Inside Bureaucracy.* Boston: Little, Brown.

———. 1972. "Up and Down with Ecology: The Issue-Attention Cycle." *Public Interest* 28 (Summer): 38–50.

Drew, E. 1983. "A Political Journal." *New Yorker,* May 9, p. 83.

DuRivage, V. 1985. "The OFCCP under the Reagan Administration." *Labor Law Journal* 36 (June): 366.

Easton, D. 1965. *A Framework for Political Analysis.* Englewood Cliffs, N.J.: Prentice-Hall.

Edelman, M. 1964. *Symbolic Uses of Politics.* Urbana: University of Illinois Press.

Edsall, T.B., and M.P. Edsall. 1991. *Chain Reaction.* New York: W.W. Norton.

Edwards, G.C. III. 1980a. *Implementing Public Policy.* Washington, D.C. Congressional Quarterly Press.

———. 1980b. *Presidential Influence in Congress.* San Francisco: W.H. Freeman.

———. 1981. "Quantitative Study of the Presidency." *Presidential Studies Quarterly* 11 (Spring): 146–50.

———. 1985. "Measuring Presidential Success in Congress." *Journal of Politics* 47 (May): 667–85.

———. 1989. *At the Margins.* New Haven: Yale University Press.

———. 1991. "George Bush and the Public Presidency." In Campbell and Rockman 1991, pp. 129–54.

Elder, C.D., and R.G. Cobb. 1983. *Political Use of Symbols.* New York: Longman.

England, P. 1992. *Comparable Worth: Theories and Evidence.* Hawthorne, N.Y.: Aldine de Gruyter.

Engstrom, R.L. 1986. "Repairing the Crack in New Orleans' Black Vote." *Publius* 16 (Fall): 109–21.

Eskridge, W.N., Jr. 1991. "Reneging on History? Playing the Court/Congress/President Civil Rights Game." *California Law Review* 79 (May): 613–84.

Eyestone, R. 1978. *From Social Issues to Public Policy*. New York: John Wiley and Sons.

Farley, R. 1984. *Blacks and Whites: Narrowing the Gap?* Cambridge: Harvard University Press.

Feagin, J.R., et al. 1991. *A Case for the Case Study*. Chapel Hill: University of North Carolina Press.

Fiorina, M.P. 1992. *Divided Government*. New York: Macmillan.

Fishel, J. 1985. *Presidents and Promises*. Washington, D.C.: Congressional Quarterly Press.

Fisher, L. 1974. *President and Congress*. New York: Free Press.

———. 1975. *Presidential Spending Power*. Princeton: Princeton University Press.

Flaxbeard, J.M. 1983. "Presidential Policy Making: The Use of Executive Orders and Presidential Support on Civil Rights Issues." Paper presented at the annual meeting of the Southern Political Association, Birmingham, Ala., November.

Formisano, R.P. 1991. *Boston against Busing*. Chapel Hill: University of North Carolina Press.

Gallagher, H.G. 1974. "Presidents, Congress, and Legislation." In *The Presidency Reappraised*, ed. T. Cronin and R. Tugwell, pp. 267–82. 2d ed. New York: Praeger.

Gallup, G.H. 1972. *The Gallup Poll: Public Opinion, 1935–1971*. 3 vols. New York: Random House.

Gallup Opinion Index and Gallup Report. Various.

Garrow, D.J. 1978. *Protest at Selma*. New Haven: Yale University Press.

Gates, J.B., J.E. Cohen, and S.A. Shull. 1988. "Presidential Policy Preferences and Supreme Court Appointment Success, 1954–1984." Paper presented at the annual meeting of the Western Political Science Association, San Francisco, March.

Gleason, S., and C. Moser. 1985. "Some Neglected Implications of Comparable Worth." *Policy Studies Review* 4 (May):595–600.

Gleiber, D.W., and S.A. Shull. 1992. "Presidential Influence in Policy Making." *Western Political Quarterly* 45 (June):441–67.

Goldman, E. 1969. *The Tragedy of Lyndon Johnson*. New York: Alfred A. Knopf.

Goldman, S. 1985. "Reorganizing the Judiciary: The First Term Appointments." *Judicature* 68 (April/May):313–29.

———. 1991. "The Bush Imprint on the Judiciary." *Judicature* 74 (April/May): 294–306.

Gordon, K. 1969. "The Budget Director." In *The Presidential Advisory System*, ed. T. Cronin and S. Greenberg, pp. 58–67. New York: Harper and Row.

Greenstein, F.I. 1982. *Hidden-Hand Presidency*. New York: Basic Books.

Hacker, A. 1992. *Two Nations: Black and White, Separate, Hostile, Unequal*. New York: Charles Scribner's Sons.

Halpern, S.C. 1985. "Title VI Enforcement." In Yarbrough 1985, pp. 137–56.

Hammond, T.H., and J.M. Fraser. 1980. "Faction Size, the Conservative Coalition, and the Determinants of Presidential Success in Congress." Paper presented at the annual meeting of the American Political Science Association, Washington, D.C., August.

———. 1984. "Studying Presidential Performance in Congress." *Political Methodology* 10, no. 1: 211–44.

Handberg, R., and H.F. Hill, Jr. 1984. "Predicting the Judicial Performance of Presidential Appointments to the United States Supreme Court." *Presidential Studies Quarterly* 14 (Fall): 538–47.

Heck, E.V., and S.A. Shull. 1982. "Policy Preferences of Justices and Presidents: The Case of Civil Rights." *Law and Policy Quarterly* 4 (July): 327–38.

———. 1983. "Civil Rights Policy Making: An Overview." In *Political Ideas and Institutions*, ed. E.V. Heck and A.T. Leonhard, pp. 146–49. Dubuque, Iowa: Kendall Hunt.

Heclo, H. 1975. "OMB and the Presidency. The Problem of Neutral Competency." *Public Interest* 38 (Winter): 80–99.

Hochschild, J.L. 1984. *New American Dilemma: Liberal Democracy and School Desegregation.* New Haven: Yale University Press.

Howard, J.W. 1968. "On the Fluidity of Judicial Choice." *American Political Science Review* 62 (March): 43–57.

Janis, I. 1982. *Groupthink.* 2d ed. Boston: Houghton Mifflin.

Jones, B.D., ed. 1989. *Leadership and Politics.* Lawrence: University Press of Kansas.

Jones, C.O. 1984. *An Introduction to the Study of Public Policy.* 3d ed. Monterey, Calif.: Brooks/Cole.

———, ed 1988a "Ronald Reagan and the U.S. Congress." In Jones 1988, pp. 30–59.

———, ed 1988b. *The Reagan Legacy.* Chatham, N.J.: Chatham House.

Kellerman, B. 1984. *Leadership: Multidisciplinary Perspectives.* Englewood Cliffs, N.J.: Prentice-Hall.

Kernell, S. 1986. *Going Public.* Washington, D.C.: Congressional Quarterly Press.

Kessel, J.H. 1974. "Parameters of Presidential Politics." *Social Science Quarterly,* 55 (June): 8–24.

———. 1975. *Domestic Presidency.* North Scituate, Mass.: Duxbury Press.

———. 1984. *Presidential Parties.* Homewood, Ill.: Dorsey Press.

Kingdon, J.W. 1984. *Agendas, Alternatives and Public Policies.* Boston: Little, Brown.

Kluger, R. 1976. *Simple Justice: The History of Brown v. Board of Education and Black America's Struggle for Equality.* New York: Alfred A. Knopf.

Lamb, C.M. 1984. "Equal Housing Opportunity." In Bullock and Lamb 1984, pp. 148–83.

———. 1985. "Education and Housing." In Yarbrough 1985, pp. 82–105.

Lamb, C.M., and M.T. Lustig. 1979. "The Burger Court, Exclusionary Zoning, and the Activist-Restraint Debate." *University of Pittsburgh Law Review* 40 (Winter): 169–226.

Lambries, D. 1983. "The Presidents' Symbolic Agenda." Paper presented at the annual meeting of the Southern Political Science Association, Birmingham, Ala., November.

Lazin, F.A. 1973. "Failure of Federal Enforcement of Civil Rights Regulations in Public Housing." *Policy Sciences* 4 (September): 263–73.

LeLoup, L.T. 1979. "Fiscal Chief: Presidents and Their Budgets." In Shull and LeLoup 1979, pp. 195–219.

LeLoup, L.T., and S.A. Shull. 1979. "Congress versus the Executive: The 'Two Presidencies' Reconsidered." *Social Science Quarterly* 59 (March): 704–19; also in Shull 1991, pp. 36–52.

————. 1993. *Congress and the President: The Policy Connection.* Belmont, Calif.: Wadsworth.

Levine, E.L., and E.M. Wexler. 1981. *PL 94–142: An Act of Congress.* New York: Macmillan.

Light, P.C. 1982. *The President's Agenda: Domestic Policy Choice from Kennedy to Carter.* Baltimore: Johns Hopkins University Press.

Lindblom, C. 1980. *The Policy Making Process.* 2d ed. Englewood Cliffs, N.J.: Prentice-Hall.

Lipset, S.M. 1985. "The Elections, the Economy and Public Opinion: 1984." *Policy Studies* 18 (Winter): 28–38.

Lowi, T.J. 1972. "Four Systems of Policy, Politics, and Choice." *Public Administration Review* 32 (July/August): 298–310.

Loye, D. 1977. *Leadership Passion.* San Francisco: Jossey-Bass.

MacRae, D., and J. Wilde. 1979. *Policy Analysis for Public Decision.* North Scituate, Mass.: Duxbury Press.

Marshall, D.R. 1990. "The Continuing Significance of Race." *American Political Science Review* 84 (June): 611–16.

Mayhew, D.R. 1966. *Party Loyalty among Congressmen.* Cambridge: Harvard University Press.

————. 1991. *Divided We Govern.* New Haven: Yale University Press.

Mazmanian, D.A., and P.A. Sabatier. 1983. *Implementation and Public Policy.* Glenview, Ill.: Scott, Foresman.

Meier, K.J. 1975. "Representative Bureaucracy: An Empirical Analysis." *American Political Science Review* 69 (June): 526–42.

Meier, K.J., J. Stewart, Jr., and R. England. 1989. *Race, Class and Education.* Madison: University of Wisconsin Press.

Middleton, L. 1979. "The Executive Branch Stumbles." *Southern Exposure* 7, no. 2: 32–37.

Miller, J. 1984. "Ronald Reagan and the Techniques of Deception." *Atlantic Monthly,* February, pp. 62–68.

Miller, W.E., and D. Stokes. 1963. "Constituency Influence in Congress." *American Political Science Review* 57 (March): 45–56.

Miroff, B. 1976. *Pragmatic Illusions: The Presidential Politics of John F. Kennedy.* New York: McKay.

————. 1979. "The Presidency and Social Reform." In Shull and LeLoup 1979, pp. 174–94.

Moe, R.C., and S.C. Teel. 1970. "Congress as Policy Maker: A Necessary Reappraisal." *Political Science Quarterly* 85 (September): 443–70.

Monthly Labor Review, Department of Labor. Washington, D.C.: Government Printing Office.

Morgan, R.P. 1970. *The President and Civil Rights.* New York: St. Martin's Press.

Mowery, D.C., and M.S. Kamlet. 1984. "Budgeting Side Payments and Government Growth." *American Journal of Political Science* 27 (November): 636–64.

Nachmias, D., ed. 1980. *Practice of Policy Evaluation.* New York: St. Martin's Press.

Nathan, R.P. 1983. *The Administration Presidency.* 2d ed. New York: John Wiley and Sons.

National Journal. Selected issues.

National Opinion Research Center (NORC). *NORC Report.* 1984. Chicago: University of Chicago.

Neustadt, R.E. 1955. "Presidency and Legislation: Planning the President's Program." *American Political Science Review* 69 (December): 980–1020.

———. 1980. *Presidential Power.* 3d ed. New York: John Wiley and Sons.

New Orleans Times-Picayune/States-Item. Selected issues.

New York Times. Selected issues.

Newsweek. Selected issues.

O'Connor, K., and L. Epstein. 1983. "The Rise of Conservative Interest Group Litigation." *Journal of Politics* 45 (May): 479–89.

OMB. *See* United States, Office of Management and Budget.

Orfield, G. 1975. *Congressional Power: Congress and Social Change.* New York: Harcourt, Brace, Jovanovich.

———. 1980. "Research, Politics, and the Antibusing Debate." *Law and Contemporary Problems* 42 (Autumn): 141–73.

Orfield, G., and C. Ashkinaze. 1991. *The Closing Door: Conservative Policy and Black Opportunity.* Chicago: University of Chicago Press.

Ott, D.J., and A.F. Ott. 1972. *Federal Budget Policy.* 3d ed. Washington, D.C.: Brookings Institution.

Panetta, L.E., and P. Gall. 1971. *Bring Us Together: The Nixon Team and the Civil Rights Retreat.* Philadelphia: Lippincott.

Parker, F.L. 1990. *Black Vote Counts.* Chapel Hill: University of North Carolina Press.

Peterson, M.A. 1990. *Legislating Together.* Cambridge: Harvard University Press.

Polsby, N.W. 1969. "Policy Analysis and Congress." *Public Policy* 18 (Fall): 61–74.

———. 1984. *Political Innovation in America: Politics of Policy Initiation.* New Haven: Yale University Press.

Pomper, G.M., and S.S. Lederman. 1980. *Elections in America.* 2d ed. New York: Longman.

PS. Selected issues. Washington, D.C.: American Political Science Association.

Public Papers of the Presidents of the United States. Annual. Washington, D.C.: Government Printing Office.

Puro, S. 1971. "The United States as Amicus Curiae." In *Courts, Law, and Judicial Processes,* ed. S. Ulmer, pp. 220–29. New York: Free Press.

Ragsdale, L. 1984. "Politics of Presidential Speechmaking, 1949–80." *American Political Science Review* 78 (December): 971–85.

Ranney, A., ed. 1968a. *Political Science and Public Policy.* Chicago: Markham.

———. 1968b. "Study of Policy Content." In Ranney 1968a, pp. 3–21.

Report of the National Advisory Commission on Civil Disorders. 1968. New York: Bantam Books.

Redford, E.S. 1969. *Democracy in the Administrative State.* New York: Oxford University Press.

Richardson, J.D. 1899. *A Compilation of the Messages and Papers of the Presidents, 1789–1897.* 10 vols. Washington, D.C.: U.S. Congress.

Ripley, R.B. 1969. "Power in the Post–World War II Senate." *Journal of Politics* 31 (May): 465–92.

238   REFERENCES

———. 1972. *Kennedy and Congress.* Morristown, N.J.: General Learning Press.

———. 1985. *Policy Analysis in Political Science.* Chicago: Nelson Hall.

Ripley, R.B., and G.A. Franklin, eds. 1975. *Policy-Making in the Federal Executive Branch.* New York: Free Press.

———. 1986. *Bureaucracy and Policy Implementation.* 2d ed. Homewood, Ill.: Dorsey Press.

Rivers, D., and N.L. Rose. 1985. "Passing the President's Program: Public Opinion and Presidential Influence in Congress." *American Journal of Political Science* 29 (May): 183–96.

Rockman, B.A. 1984. *The Leadership Question.* New York: Praeger.

Rodgers, H.R., Jr. 1984. "Fair Employment Laws for Minorities." In Bullock and Lamb 1984, pp. 93–117.

Rodgers, H.R., Jr., and C.S. Bullock III. 1972. *Law and Social Change: Civil Rights Laws and Their Consequences.* New York: McGraw Hill.

Rohde, D.W., and H.J. Spaeth. 1976. *Supreme Court Decision Making.* San Francisco: W.H. Freeman.

Rowland, C.K., and R.A. Carp. 1983. "Relative Effects of Maturation, Period, and Appointing Presidents on District Judges' Policy Choices." *Political Behavior* 5, no. 1: 109–34.

Russett, B.M. 1970. "International Relations Research: Case Studies and Cumulation." In *Approaches to the Study of Political Science,* ed. M. Haas and H. Kariel, pp. 425–40. San Francisco: Chandler.

Sabatier, P., and H. Jenkins-Smith. 1993. *Policy Change and Learning.* Boulder, Colo.: Westview Press, forthcoming.

Schell, J. 1975. *The Time of Illusion.* New York: Vintage.

Scher, R., and J. Button. 1984. "Voting Rights Act: Implementation and Impact." In Bullock and Lamb 1984, pp. 20–54.

Schick, A. 1971. "From Analysis to Evaluation." *Annals [of the Academy of Political and Social Sciences]* 394 (March): 57–71.

Schwarz, J.E., and L.E. Shaw. 1976. *U.S. Congress in Comparative Perspective.* Hinsdale, Ill.: Dryden Press.

Scigliano, R., ed. 1962. *The Courts: A Reader in the Judicial Process.* Boston: Little, Brown.

———. 1971. *The Supreme Court and the Presidency.* New York: Free Press.

———. 1984. "The Presidency and the Judiciary." In *Presidency and the Political Systems,* ed. M. Nelson, pp. 392–418. Washington, D.C.: Congressional Quarterly Press.

Scotch, R. 1984. *From Goodwill to Civil Rights.* Philadelphia: Temple University Press.

Seidman, H., and R.S. Gilmour. 1986. *Politics, Position and Power.* 4th ed. New York: Oxford University Press.

Shank, A. 1980. *Presidential Policy Leadership.* Lanham, Md.: University Press of America.

Shattuck, J.H. 1978. "You Can't Depend on It: The Carter Administration and Civil Liberties." *Civil Liberties Review* 4, no. 5 (January/February): 10–27.

Shull, S.A. 1977. *Interrelated Concepts in Policy Research.* Beverly Hills, Calif.: Sage Publications.

———. 1979. "An Agency's Best Friend: The White House or Congress?" In

Shull and LeLoup 1979, pp. 219–38.

———. 1983. *Domestic Policy Formulation: Presidential-Congressional Partnership?* Westport, Conn.: Greenwood Press.

———. 1989a. *The President and Civil Rights Policy.* Westport, Conn.: Greenwood Press.

———. 1989b. "Presidential Influence versus Bureaucratic Discretion." *American Review of Public Administration* 19 (September): 197–215.

———, ed. 1991. *The Two Presidencies: A Quarter Century Assessment.* Chicago: Nelson-Hall.

Shull, S.A., and L.T. LeLoup, eds. 1979. *The Presidency: Studies in Public Policy.* Brunswick, Ohio: King's Court.

———. 1981. "Reassessing the Reassessment: Comment on Sigelman's Note on the 'Two Presidencies' Thesis." *Journal of Politics* 43 (May): 563–64; also in Shull 1991, pp. 73–74.

Shull, S.A., and J. Vanderleeuw. 1987. "What Do Key Votes Measure?" *Legislative Studies Quarterly* 12 (November): 573–82.

Sigel, J. 1988. "Amicus Curiae Briefs by the Solicitor General during the Warren and Burger Courts." *Western Political Quarterly* 41 (March): 135–43.

Sigelman, L. 1979. "A Reassessment of the Two Presidencies Thesis." *Journal of Politics* 41 (November): 1195–1205; also in Shull 1991, pp. 63–72.

Sinclair, B. 1985. "Agenda, Policy, and Alignment Change from Coolidge to Reagan." In *Congress Reconsidered,* ed. L.C. Dodd and B.I. Oppenheimer, pp. 291–314. 3d ed. Washington, D.C.: Congressional Quarterly Press.

———. 1991. "Governing Unheroically (and Sometimes Unappetizingly): Bush and the 101st Congress." In Campbell and Rockman 1991, pp. 155–84.

Sniderman, P.M., and M.G. Hagen. 1985. *Race and Inequality: Study in American Values.* Chatham, N.J.: Chatham House.

Songer, D. 1982. "Policy Consequences of Senate Involvement in the Selection of Judges in the United States Courts of Appeals." *Western Political Quarterly* 35 (March): 107–19.

Sorensen, T.C. 1965. *Kennedy.* New York: Harper and Row.

Sperlich, P.W. 1975. "Bargaining and Overload: An Essay on Power." In *Perspectives on the Presidency,* ed. A. Wildavsky, pp. 406–30. Boston: Little, Brown.

Spitzer, R.J. 1983. *The Presidency and Public Policy.* Birmingham: University of Alabama Press.

———. 1993. *The President and Congress.* New York: McGraw Hill.

Stern, M. 1991. "The Great Republican U-Turn: Civil Rights, Now and Then." Paper presented at the annual meeting of the Southern Political Science Association, Tampa, October–November.

———. 1992. *Calculating Vision: Kennedy, Johnson and Civil Rights.* New Brunswick, N.J.: Rutgers University Press.

Stewart, J., Jr. 1993. "Between 'Yet' and 'But': Presidents and the Politics of Civil Rights Policy Making." In *The Presidency Reconsidered,* ed. R.A. Waterman, pp. 327–46. Itasca, Ill.: F.E. Peacock.

Stewart, J., Jr., T.E. Anderson, and Z. Taylor. 1982. "Presidential and Congressional Support for Independent Regulatory Commissions: Implications of the Budgetary Process." *Western Political Quarterly* 35 (September): 318–26.

Stidham, R., and R.A. Carp. 1986. "Presidential Influences on Federal District Judges' Policy Preferences." Paper presented at the annual meeting of the Southwest Political Science Association, San Antonio, March.

Stone, W.J. 1980. "Dynamics of Constituency: Electoral Control in the House." *American Politics Quarterly* 8 (October):399–424.

Sundquist, J.L. 1981. *Decline and Resurgence of Congress.* Washington, D.C.: Brookings Institution.

Tate, C.N. 1981. "Personal Attribute Models of the Voting Behavior of U.S. Supreme Court Justices." *American Political Science Review* 75 (June):355–67.

Tercheck, R. 1980. "Political Participation and Political Structures." *Phylon* 41 (March):25–35.

Thernstrom, A.M. 1987. *Whose Votes Count?* Cambridge: Harvard University Press.

Thomas, N.C. 1983. "Case Studies." In *Studying the Presidency*, ed. G.C. Edwards III and S.J. Wayne, pp. 50–78. Knoxville: University of Tennessee Press.

Thompson, R.J. 1985. "The Commission on Civil Rights." In Yarbrough 1985, pp. 180–203.

Thurber, J.A., ed. 1991. *Divided Democracy.* Washington, D.C.: Congressional Quarterly Press.

Turner, J. 1970. *Party and Constituency: Pressures on Congress.* Rev. ed. by E.V. Schneier, Jr. Baltimore: Johns Hopkins University Press.

United States, Bureau of the Census. Annual. *Statistical Abstract of the United States.* Government Printing Office.

————. Civil Rights Commission. Selected reports.

————. Office of Management and Budget. Annual. *The Budget of the United States Government.* Including *Special Analyses.*

Vanderslik, J.R. 1968. "Constituency Characteristics and Roll Call Voting on Negro Rights in the 88th Congress." *Social Science Quarterly* 49 (December):720–31.

Vaughn, P.H. 1976. "The Truman Administration's Fair Deal for Black America." *Missouri Historical Review* 70 (March):291–305.

Walker, J.L. 1977. "Setting the Agenda in the U.S. Senate: A Theory of Problem Selection." *British Journal of Political Science* 7 (May):423–45.

Walker, T.G., and D.J. Barrow. 1985. "Diversification of the Federal Bench: Policy and Process Ramifications." *Journal of Politics* 47 (May):596–617.

Washington Post. Selected issues.

Washington Post National Weekly Edition. Selected issues.

Waterman, R.A. 1989. *Presidential Influence and the Administrative Presidency.* Knoxville: University of Tennessee Press.

Wayne, S.J. 1978. *The Legislative Presidency.* New York: Harper and Row.

Weekly Compilation of Presidential Documents. Selected issues.

Whicker, M., and R. Moore. 1988. *When Presidents Are Great.* Englewood Cliffs, N.J.: Prentice-Hall.

Wildavsky, A.B. 1984. *The Politics of the Budgetary Process.* 4th ed. Boston: Little, Brown.

Wilson, J.H. 1975. *Herbert Hoover: Forgotten Progressive.* Boston: Little, Brown.

Wines, M. 1982. "Administration Says It Merely Seeks a 'Better Way' to Enforce Civil Rights." *National Journal* (March 27):536–41.

Yarbrough, T., ed. 1985. *The Reagan Administration and Human Rights.* New York: Praeger.

Index

Steven A. Shull is research professor of political science at the University of New Orleans. He is the coauthor of *Congress and the President: The Policy Connection*; the author of *Interrelated Concepts in Policy Research*, *Presidential Policy Making: An Analysis*, *Domestic Policy Formation*, and *The President and Civil Rights Policy*; and editor or coeditor of five volumes, including *The Two Presidencies: A Quarter Century Assessment*. His articles have appeared in *Journal of Politics*, *Western Political Quarterly*, *American Politics Quarterly*, *Social Science Quarterly*, *Legislative Studies Quarterly*, *Policy Studies Journal*, and many other books and scholarly journals. Currently, Professor Shull is studying presidential influence in policy making and in the veto process. He serves on three journal editorial boards and has served on four national or regional association program committees. Shull was named a Fulbright senior scholar to Hong Kong and won his university's career achievement award for excellence in research in 1986. He received his Ph.D. from Ohio State University in 1974.